WEEKEND WARRIORS

$\mathscr{W}$EEKEND $\mathscr{W}$ARRIORS

by

Paul L. Cooper

Sunflower University Press®

P. O. Box 1009 • 1531 Yuma • Manhattan, Kansas 66505-1009 USA

© 1996 by Paul L. Cooper

Printed in the United States of America on acid-free paper.

ISBN 0-89745-202-X

Cover: Reserve Squadron VF-871's Lieutenant Commander William E. Harrison painting out "Weekend"
of "Weekend Warrior" sign on an F4U. Executive
Officer Lieutenant Thomas G. Cooper, Jr., holds the
paint. (U.S. Navy photo)

Layout by Lori L. Daniel

Contents

Acknowledgments

*D*URING THE *three-plus years involved in writing this chronicle of young Reservists unexpectedly thrust into war, I was assisted in small and large ways by many people. The text and opinions are mine; however, the entire effort involved the help and support of others. Gaps in time had to be bridged and factual details confirmed. Although my personal records were extensive, they were augmented by recollections of mementos of others when questions arose as to time or event. Their recall of specific occurrences helped me tie things together properly. Most assistance came from members of the* immediate VF-871 family, the Reserve fighter squadron in which I served, along with support and encouragement from others. All of these many contributions, during both the research and writing phases, were essential to the overall completeness and accuracy of the work.

Expressions of gratitude to former enlisted shipmates go to Jim Blyler for his suggestion long ago that my diary be used to write a book and for his helpful critique of the manuscript; to Ed Watson for his recollection of events and photos and for an invaluable historical report of VF-871, which I did not even know existed; to Frank Musso who provided a scrapbook photo and allowed access to his memory; to Del Fuller who provided copies of a long-sought squadron photo as well as useful newspaper clippings; and to Jerry Jacobsen for sharing some fond remembrances of our days together.

Among the pilots, who were and remain my heroes, special thanks to Don Frazier, Ed Reed, and John Underwood, who provided insights regarding the fliers on the firing line daily, and to Skipper Bill Harrison's wife Doris, who shared information concerning her late husband's post-squadron career.

Thanks to author friends Sylvia Scheuber, Ted Fuller, Bill Larkins, and Bruce Watson for many helpful publishing tips. My appreciation to my brother Dick, a former NAS Oakland active-duty USNR "station-keeper," for access to his collection of naval aviation magazines and personal photographs. Lastly, my gratitude to my wife Marie who became my spouse during the early months of the adventure and remains my loving partner in life and best friend since. My love and appreciation for her personal remembrances and for putting up with my self-imposed isolation while researching and writing about a long ago, almost forgotten war.

Introduction

WINSTON CHURCHILL *called them "twice a citizen." They are military Reservists, the individuals who pursue a civilian career, fuel the economic engine of state, and, at the same time, train and prepare to defend the nation during times of war or national emergency.*

The evolution of the Naval Reserve, specifically the Air Reserve from the end of World War II through the end of the Cold War, perhaps since 1970, could be called revolutionary. Naval aviation was a force in transition from 1945 until the early 1950s. After the war with Japan ended on

August 15, 1945 — V-J Day — America's mood demanded instantaneous and total demobilization. Downsizing after World War II was dramatic. In mid-1945, the U.S. Navy had 98 carriers on active status. One year later there were 23, and at the outbreak of the Korean War only 15.

The reduction in strength, however, provided trained air crews and maintenance personnel for the Reserve program. Reserve Air Stations had little difficulty finding naval aviators, who wanted to maintain flight proficiency; and enlisted men, trained in aircraft maintenance and logistics, enjoyed an association with buddies. Individual Reservists were assigned to squadrons that trained and flew Air Station aircraft on drill weekends. Active-duty Navy personnel were specifically assigned to the training and administration of Reservists. These TARS, as they were called, also provided maintenance for aircraft assigned to Air Stations. Formal schooling was not available, but local training was provided to improve job skills and qualify for promotion. Three Reserve recalls were conducted under this system of taking people back into the service, with mixed results. The largest of these was during the Korean War.

Navy planners were challenged to stay ahead of the increased "power curve" created by the recall of Reservists, but were to do so in an atmosphere of tighter budgets and reduced Regulars manpower. Naval aviation was confronted with a serious threat to its very existence, and the future was in doubt through much of the late 1940s. At the same time, there was rapid change in aircraft technology, and the jet engine and higher attainable speeds created doubts about the compatibility of this technology with the aircraft carrier. During the Korean War, accident rates aboard ships proved greater in jet aircraft squadrons than the combat casualty rate, partly because of the newness of the aircraft type. This rate dropped dramatically, however, with the development of the angled flight deck, which allowed a "bolter" — an aircraft that had missed the arresting wire — to take off without smashing into the aircraft parked on the bow.

In 1970 a major change occurred with the establishment of the Naval Air Reserve Force. The Force was comprised of two attack and two anti-submarine air groups, overseen by Regular Navy Air Group Commanders. Each squadron, commanded by a Reservist, had a nucleus of active-duty officers and enlisted personnel. Air groups were provided aircraft carrier "deck time" — operational training; squadron carrier deployments were conducted; and formal training and drills were authorized to ensure that all necessary qualifications could be achieved and maintained. Pilots were required to maintain at least day carrier qualification, which was less onerous than that for nighttime flying. For the first time, Reserve squadrons were combat ready and deployable, but their aircraft models were not yet the same as those being flown in the Fleet. The maintenance capability of a carrier could not keep flying more than one model of a particular aircraft without major modifications to test-bench equipment (engines and ancillary equipment). This was called "intermediate maintenance" because serious cases were simply pushed over the side.

A "total force" concept was inaugurated in 1973, which increased the responsibility of the National Guard and Reserve forces, as partners with the active-duty forces, for carrying out national security strategy. War planning in the Navy Department took on a whole new meaning. The Regular Navy took a serious interest in a trained Reserve and pushed for modern equipment for Reserve units. The term "horizontal integration" was introduced, and new aircraft were purchased in sufficient numbers to supply both Regulars and Reserves — both would have the same type of equipment so that any one could be substituted for another. Reserve squadrons received the first aircraft purchased, the F/A 18, before some Regular Navy squadrons.

After years of talk, the integration of Reserves with the Regular Navy became a reality. Today, the Naval Reserve represents 20 percent of the total force. Every Navy command has its Reserve component. Personnel travel to their "gaining command" — the one to which they are attached — on a quarterly basis and normally spend two weeks a year there. It is not unusual to see an organizational chart, at an Air Station or on a ship, with Reservist names in assigned slots next to their active-duty counterparts.

Volunteer spirit has always been at the very heart of the Naval Reserve, allowing it to grow into one of the truly elite elements of our armed services — a major change since the 1950s.

V. J. Anzilotti
Rear Admiral U.S. Naval Reserve (Ret.)

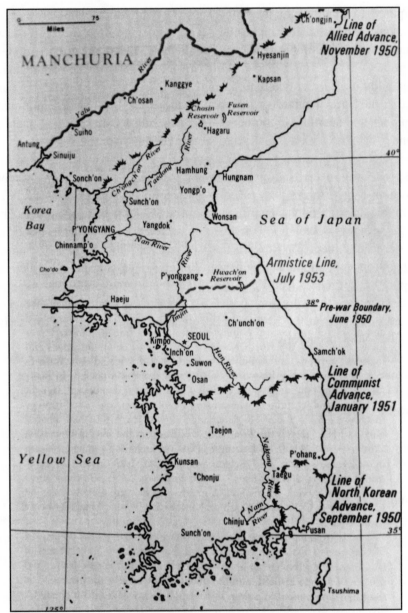

North and South Korea, showing prominent features and fighting fronts, 1950-1953. (From *The Naval Air War in Korea* (Baltimore, MD: Nautical & Aviation Publishing Co., 1986). Used by permission.

Prologue

O N A SUNDAY morning in 1950, the politically determined border separating North from South Korea was violated. A surprise invasion of South Korea by troops from the North ignited a three-year period of hostilities that took the lives of more than a million people. This tragic clash tested, for the first time, the resolve of the United Nations and heavily involved the United States. Despite this involvement, the hostilities were classified not as a war but as a lesser important "conflict," one that cost more than 54,000 American lives in those three years. The subsequent Vietnam War, by contrast, took 58,000 American lives over a span of 10 years.

This staggering toll of human life in such a short period suggests a need to examine more closely the semantics of military/political terminology. The designation of "conflict," perhaps, reflected a political attempt to reduce criticism of American involvement in the questionable UN effort. Whatever the motivation, the military operation was clearly and indisputably — to those involved — a war.

Although American military casualties are known, the total cost of the Korean War to military and civilians of both sides may never be known. Estimates have reached as high as 2.2 million military killed or wounded, and 4.4 million civilian casualties. An accurate assessment of the true cost is difficult, because North Korea and the People's Republic of China have not provided casualty figures.

The Korean War has also been referred to as the "forgotten war," despite the fact that more than five million American men and women served. The war, which involved so many and produced such staggering casualty figures, produced only a stalemate. It became the first war in this century involving the United States that resulted in an armistice but no treaty. And the geography of this historic region, divided after World War II, remains today politically separated, more than 40 years after the fighting ceased.

Although the war produced no victory, it introduced the proposition that the spread of Communism might be stemmed with U.S. military help. Further, a new policy of limited war was politically imposed. U.S. military strategies, such as full tactical use of new-generation aircraft in the first jet air battles, were restricted, as were ground strategies. This war without victory also launched political theories, which later influenced the American involvement in Vietnam.

Public acceptance of U.S. involvement in Korea, however, differed from both the prior World War II and the later Vietnam War. The emotional patriotism of World War II was clearly lacking as was the strident protest of Vietnam. Public reactions at the time could best be described as bordering on apathetic. Post-World War II economic recovery and pursuit of the American dream relegated what was sometimes called a "police action" to an incident of secondary importance. Concerns regarding our involvement in this first war in history where the military forces mustered by a world organization challenged an aggressor nation could be characterized as lackadaisical. Fear, anguish, and anger were largely confined to families of soldiers, sailors, Marines, and airmen drafted or recalled to active service from Reserve units.

The Korean War is remembered primarily as a land war, and yet the importance of the dedicated and valiant role performed by ground troops can never be fully appreciated or properly recognized. However, that war also marked the advent of air-to-air jet fighter combat.

The Korean War has generally faded from the national consciousness. Historical accounts, both in fiction and non-fiction, seem limited when compared to other wars of the century. Some reports of actions by certain military units have been written, but few have focused on the contributions of the part-time (one weekend a month) "weekend warriors" who were called to active service. Far too little has been written, spoken, and thought about the many who served in this tragic war.

This book will mostly cite Navy ships and Air Reserve squadrons called to duty on the West Coast early in the war. At the outbreak of hostilities, only 15 aircraft carriers were in service and only one was readily available for support in Korean waters. Carrier-based air support of Allied ground operations was recognized early as vital, but the ultimate degree of importance was unforeseen. In order to meet war-zone demands for additional carriers and air groups, reactivation from mothball fleets and Reserve units was necessary. And although other vessels and squadrons are referenced, the primary focus is on the reactivated *Essex*-class carrier, the USS *Princeton* (CV-37), and Reserve fighter squadron VF-871 from Naval Air Station (NAS) Oakland, California.

The events depicted herein are not necessarily dramatic or startling — not necessarily significant military events — but rather illustrate the typical experiences of some weekend Reservists called to war. Each effort, however, contributed to vital support of the troops on the ground. The state of our nation's readiness at the outset to carry on an evolving carrier-based air war is also explored. The events are generally noted chronologically and are principally taken from the author's personal diary and letters. Pertinent published accounts of background events during the cited periods were reviewed for descriptive augmentation.

The intent of this book is not to compare risks, efforts, or accomplishments with those who served in other wars, but to record certain events that should not be forgotten from a high-casualty war:

- to reflect on the unheralded, unspectacular, but important, contributions of Naval and Marine Air Reservists whose lives were disrupted by a call to duty in an undeclared war
- to reflect on what happened to the USS *Princeton*, NAS Oakland, and some of the officers and crew of VF-871 over the years
- and to comment on Korea, then and now, considering the conduct of further U.S. involvement should the unresolved war flare anew.

Although this account has been written from a citizen/sailor viewpoint, dates and times are referenced in standard military form. Many of the crew preferred to retain civilian terminology but the Navy dictated otherwise and required that its traditional system, including nautical references to walls, floors, and doors, be strictly followed. There was some resistance at first, but the Navy won out and the civilians ultimately became sailors. The text, therefore, conforms in most respects to the Navy way of doing things. Included are official Navy designations of ships and individual aircraft, where information was available and appropriate, for completeness of the work.

My observations, as a former Navy enlisted man, reflect a perspective from the ranks, but this does not in any way lessen my great respect for the commissioned men. Aboard ship, rank differences meant little — we were all one family.

Chapter 1

Outbreak of War
June-July 1950

*A**T 0400 LOCAL time on 25 June 1950 North Korean troops, supported by tanks and artillery, invaded South Korea across the 38th Parallel. The
Communist North attacked in a surprise attempt
to unify the country. The United Nations Charter, signed
only five years earlier, outlawed such aggression, and the
UN quickly acted to halt the hostilities. By a 9-0 vote, the
Security Council adopted a resolution sponsored by the
United States, calling for an immediate cessation of warfare and North Korean withdrawal to north of the 38th
Parallel.*

This precedent-setting action of the Security Council avoided a veto only because the USSR delegate had been boycotting meetings of the Security Council since January. Despite the resolution, the cease-fire order was ignored and North Korean troops advanced into Seoul, the capital city of the Republic of Korea. On 28 June, President Harry Truman ordered United States forces to come to the aid of South Korea under the banner of the United Nations.

The causes of the conflict were most complex and rooted in a history that had long denied Korea independence as a nation. Under Japanese control since the end of the Sino-Japanese war in 1895, Korea had been annexed by Japan from 1910 to 1945, until liberated by the forces of the Soviet Union and the United States at the conclusion of World War II. A line drawn at the 38th Parallel divided the Soviet-occupied North from the American-occupied South.

The United Nations General Assembly had determined in 1946 that elections should be held in all of Korea for the purpose of establishing a single national government. However, this effort failed, largely because of Soviet opposition to elections in areas under its control. Elections guided by the UN were held on 10 May 1948 in South Korea, establishing the Republic of Korea, which was formally recognized by the United Nations. A People's Democratic Republic of Korea was then proclaimed by the Communists north of the 38th Parallel.

Although there had been minor encounters between the North and the South for several months prior to the June 1950 attack, they were considered relatively inconsequential. In fact, real fighting was already taking place. Although the United States had maintained significant forces in Japan since World War II, it did not have a large contingent force of battle-ready troops to inject into a new and potentially major conflict. Despite this, the U.S. quickly responded to President Truman's order, and a battalion of the U.S. Army 24th Infantry Division was flown on 1 July from Japan to Pusan, Korea. On the following day, U.S. troops began moving to battle positions about 75 miles south of Seoul.

During the first few days of the war, North Korean tanks were virtually unopposed in their move through the South where they quickly captured Seoul. On 3 July, at Wonju, 50 miles southeast of Seoul, American troops made their first contact with North Korean forces. On 9 July President Truman named General Douglas MacArthur Supreme Commander for UN forces. On 13 July Lieutenant General Walton H. Walker was named Commander of the U.S. Eighth Army in Korea, and six days later units of the First Cavalry and the 25th U.S. Infantry Divisions entered Korea.

The U.S. carried out its UN-mandated role expeditiously, under the circumstances, with American infantry forces. The gathering of necessary support services, however, was far more time consuming. Air support available from the U.S. Air Force in the early stages would have to be provided primarily from Japan. During the early weeks of the war, piston-engine B-29 Superfortresses flew from Japan and Okinawa to bomb North Korean targets. F-80 Shooting Star jet fighters flew from bases in Japan and South Korea, in support of ground troops. And at the same time, North Korean ground strategy logically sought to capture South Korean airfields and compel U.S. Air Force aircraft to fly long distances to and from targets.

The versatile "airfields" of naval aircraft carriers were unfortunately limited in number and capability. This was primarily due to the downsizing of naval aviation since the end of World War II from 98 in mid-1945 to just 15 by 1950. The total number of combat aircraft available for duty also had dropped from 29,125 in 1945 to only 9,422 in mid-1950. The number of pilots — both officers and enlisted — in active service had declined from 60,095 to 12,578 during the same period. As late as 1949, rumors persisted of a planned reduction by half in Marine aviation, and a limitation of the Navy to just four carriers and six carrier air groups.

The sorry state of U.S. naval aviation readiness was primarily the result of its military services quarreling over roles and capabilities. Both Navy and Marine air forces were decreased under the premise that they were not relevant to projected combat demands. And although the aircraft carriers of World War II had replaced battleships as the primary destroyers of enemy fleets, the Korean War dictated a new operational role. It was soon recognized that the carrier could serve as an effective new force where continued operations off a hostile coast were required. These floating, mobile airfields permitted valuable interdiction and close air support (CAS) sorties where land-based air power was unavailable or impractical. Furthermore, such capability could be used to increase land-based air power needed to accomplish specific target objectives.

The introduction of carriers into the war, while the technology was switching from the piston-driven propeller to jet aircraft operation, posed a challenge. Many fighter and attack squadrons still operated propeller-driven aircraft. Phasing in the jet-propelled Grumman F9F-2 Panther and McDonnell F2H-2 Banshee was not yet complete. Most Navy fighter squadrons still operated the versatile Chance Vought F4U-4B Corsair, a rugged fighter-bomber. The Corsair was the post-World War II mainstay of Navy and Marine fighter squadrons. Attack squadrons were primarily made up of the Douglas AD-4 Skyraider, an aircraft having the characteristics of a World War II fighter plus the additional capability of delivering a heavy offensive payload. The Skyraider had been first introduced to Fleet squadrons in December 1946.

In the spring of 1950, the Navy had recovered from the furious defense clashes of the preceding three years. Mothballing of ships had been reduced and congressional approval obtained for a new supercarrier later to be designated CVA-59, the USS *Forrestal*. But despite the bright hope for the future, the sudden Korean hostilities found the Navy weakened in its ability to immediately move into a new role in a new war. Ships of the U.S. Seventh Fleet, under the command of Vice Admiral Arthur D. Struble, were separated among several Pacific ports. At war's outbreak, only one light cruiser, four destroyers, six minesweepers, and a small amphibious force patrolled Japanese waters. No carriers were readily available in the area of hostilities.

In the early days of the war, Carrier Division (CarDiv) 3, under the command of Rear Admiral J. M. Hoskins, left Subic Bay in the Philippines heading for Buckner Bay, Okinawa. CarDiv 3 included one *Essex*-class carrier, the *Valley Forge* (CV-45), and a heavy cruiser and eight destroyers. In Okinawa the Division was joined by a contingent of British

Royal Navy ships that included the carrier HMS *Triumph*, the heavy cruiser HMS *Belfast*, and two destroyers. Vice Admiral Struble assumed overall command of this developing squadron, which later became the Task Force 77 Fast Carrier Force (TF-77). The Task Force (TF) consisted of a Support Group, a Screening Group, and a Carrier Group. The latter, consisting of the *Valley Forge* and the *Triumph*, was the strike force of TF-77.

A conference of military Commanders, including General MacArthur, decided that TF-77 should join the war. Targets around the North Korean capital Pyongyang were selected, including its airfield, railroad yard, and bridges. On 1 July the Task Force left Buckner Bay bound for the Yellow Sea. The *Valley Forge*'s Carrier Air Group 5 (CAG-5) was made up of five squadrons flying a mix of propeller and jet aircraft. Two fighter squadrons, VF-51 and VF-52, flew F9F Panther jets, while two others, VF-53 and VF-54, flew propeller-driven F4U Corsairs. The still somewhat new AD-4 Skyraiders were flown by pilots of VA-55. The British carrier *Triumph* operated squadrons flying propeller-driven Fairey Fireflies and Supermarine Seafires.

As Task Force 77 approached the combat zone, certain unknowns dictated caution. Many enemy airfields existed around the Yellow Sea and could pose the threat of air attacks upon the carriers and support ships. The possible existence of enemy submarines also suggested that appropriate precautions be taken. With defensive strategies in place, TF-77 launched the first offensive naval air strikes of the war. Before dawn on 3 July, 9 Seafires and 12 Fireflies were launched by the *Triumph* in a strike against the airfield at Haeju, approximately 60 miles south of the North Korean capital of Pyongyang. At dawn, CAG-5 launched its own strike of 12 Skyraiders and 16 Corsairs against the capital. Following the departure of the propeller flights, VF-51 launched its faster Panthers, intending to reach the targeted airfield before the prop planes and to destroy any air opposition. Two Soviet-built YAK fighters were shot down and three other enemy aircraft destroyed on the ground. The attacking Skyraiders and Corsairs damaged or destroyed four hangars and a nearby railroad yard. All planes recovered safely aboard the *Valley Forge*.

In a later afternoon strike against Pyongyang's railroad network, 15 locomotives were destroyed and pilots from both carriers returned the next day to finish off a railroad bridge damaged earlier. Skyraiders, dropping 500-pound bombs, demolished one span.

The two raids were successfully completed without losses, except for a landing accident on the *Valley Forge*. A battle-damaged Skyraider bounced over flight deck crash barriers and plowed into aircraft "spotted" (parked) forward. The damaged Skyraider and two parked Corsairs were wrecked and five other tethered planes damaged. Straight-deck carriers, like the *Valley Forge*, seemed susceptible to landing accidents by damaged jets or misjudged approaches.

Following the Pyongyang strikes, the Task Force returned to Buckner Bay. A new assignment took them to the Sea of Japan where, on the morning of 18 July, seven Panthers from VF-51 were launched on a reconnaissance mission up the eastern coast of North Korea. The pilots noticed the vital, unmarked Wonsan Oil Refinery, and late that afternoon, 10 Corsairs from VF-53, and 11 Skyraiders from VA-55, all heavily armed and loaded, attacked the refinery. Rockets and bombs quickly set a fire that burned four days, with a loss of 12,000 tons of refined oil.

Later in the month, TF-77's attention turned from bombing attacks to close air support of weary ground troops. With USAF support missions forced to operate from bases in Japan, the possibility of air support from Navy carriers was proposed. Carriers could operate as mobile airfields utilizing heavily armed, slower propeller aircraft. Carrier aircraft could function at close range off the Korean peninsula with relative ease.

General MacArthur had directed that all air support requests from the Eighth Army in the Pusan pocket should be coordinated through the Fifth Air Force, but the ground situation soon became so critical that the Eighth Army requested close air support directly from TF-77. The emergency request process was endorsed by all commands including MacArthur, and on 22 July TF-77 flew its first mission in support of ground troops. After refueling and a quick return to Sasebo, Japan, for rearming, the Task Force returned to sea. On 25 July, from a position 30 miles southeast of Pohang, emergency close air support strikes were launched.

In the early weeks the evolving role of naval aviation had tentatively gained experience in both interdiction and close air support missions. Due to the nature of critical fighting on the ground, TF-77 quickly shifted to an emphasis on close air support. It was clear that as the war evolved, so would the role of the carrier. This ability to quickly adjust to the needs of a changing war illustrated the immense value of a flexible system such as carrier-based aviation. However, the immediate challenge was to reverse the effects of the manpower and matériel reductions of 1945-1950 and to restore quickly the necessary operating strength, in terms of both fighting ships and skilled personnel.

Although a reconfiguration of Fleet resources was planned, implementation would require valuable time. Deployment of additional carriers to TF-77 command was already scheduled, but the *Essex*-class carrier *Philippine Sea* (CV-47) would not arrive on line until 1 August. Two smaller escort carriers, the *Badoeng Strait* (CVE-116) and the *Sicily* (CVE-118) were expected shortly thereafter. Other reassignments including the *Essex*-class *Boxer* (CV-21) and *Leyte* (CV-32) were scheduled later in the year. It was clear that carrier resources would have to be further supplemented in succeeding months.

The *Essex*-class carrier *Princeton* (CV-37) lay moored in a back channel at Bremerton, Washington. The ship had been one of the last carriers of its class built in World War II and was completed too late to effectively get into the war. But on 25 July 1950, pursuant to a decision to activate needed ships, the USS *Princeton* was ordered out of mothballs, and a new crew hastily assembled, assigned to prepare this first large reactivated carrier for war. Over 80 percent of the initial 2,500-member crew were Reserves and, although many had served in World War II, most had never served on a carrier. Although not totally unfamiliar with this type of fighting ship, many were particularly indignant at being called back to serve in a war few understood. On 28 August 1950 the new commanding officer, Captain William O. Gallery, USN, read the orders to formally commission the ship again to active service.

The big aircraft carrier was the fifth ship to carry the name **Princeton**. *The first screw-propelled warship of the Navy had been launched as the USS* **Princeton** *on 10 December 1843. The second, a ten-gun steamship, had been in service from 1851 to 1866; and the third, a gunboat, had been commissioned in 1897 and sold in 1919. The fourth* **Princeton** *(CVL-23), a light carrier, had begun service in the Pacific in 1943. After nine major combat operations, the ship was severely damaged on 24 October 1944 by enemy dive bombers in the battle for Leyte*

Gulf and later sunk by friendly forces. Although while in con-
*struction the new carrier's hull was tentatively called the **Val-***
***ley Forge**, on 8 July 1945 she was named **Princeton** (the fifth)*
in honor of her sunken predecessor. She was commissioned at
the Philadelphia Navy Yard on 18 November 1945. After brief
postwar operations in the Atlantic and the Pacific, on 21 June
*1949 the **Princeton** was decommissioned and placed in the*
Pacific Reserve Fleet at Bremerton, Washington.

Because the *Princeton* was the first large carrier recommissioned from
mothballs, the time required to get her ready for action was uncertain. The
ship's full load displacement was 33,000 tons, length 856 feet, beam 110
feet, depth 83 feet, with a maximum speed of 31 knots. A complement of
nearly 3,000 officers and men, including the air group and about 90
planes, was required for normal operations. The length of time needed to
recondition the machinery of this complex vessel could be generally estimated. Less certain, however, was how long it would take the new crew,
who hardly knew each other, to learn to run it. In World War II, with a
nation geared to mobilization and mass production, most ships took six or
more months to get into action. But the requirements of the unpredictable
Korean police action had created a more urgent need. The existing plight
of American ground forces in South Korea was serious, and if the *Princeton* was to provide necessary support, the recommissioning process had to
be accelerated.

The new Captain called upon his officers and crew to do whatever was
necessary to get the ship ready. He scheduled working hours around the
clock, with a target for pulling out in two weeks for the first trial run. Most
did not believe this was realistic, thinking that two *months* would be more
like it. However, the crew — whose lives had already been disrupted —
readily accepted this businesslike approach in contrast to a more typical,
leisurely peacetime routine. The 2,500 gunner's mates, signalmen, electronic technicians, machinist's mates, cooks, and ordinary seamen accepted the difficult challenge to become a smooth-working, precision crew
virtually overnight.

After a brief yard period of refitting and loading stores in Bremerton, the ship sailed up the coast to a desolate ammunition dock near Bangor, Washington. Officers and crew quickly recognized the mission of their ship, as tons of bombs and shells were loaded across the hangar deck. Bombs, torpedoes, small arms, aircraft ammunition, anti-aircraft shells, and rockets were brought aboard from five loading points on all sides of the ship. A total of 1,497 tons of ammo was loaded in 39 hours by the inexperienced hands. The ship then quickly weighed anchor for San Diego for flight operations training and a shakedown cruise — the readiness test under sea duty conditions.

The trip to San Diego provided an opportunity not only for essential crew experience but also as a tryout for Officers of the Deck. Valuable experience in maintaining course, speed, formation, ship integrity, and familiarity with ship characteristics and work schedules was gained. The Captain also observed the adaptability and capability of each officer, who would stand second to him in guarding the safety of the ship and its tactical reputation, during the long months at sea.

The *Princeton* moored at Oboe Peter, NAS San Diego, for the first time on 30 September 1950. There were reminders of the difficult job ahead as Panther jet fighters were lifted aboard for flight operations. Only six weeks after its recommissioning, the *Princeton* was rushed through the many drills and exercises required on a shakedown cruise. The Navy's Underway Training Groups inspected each warship for battle and operating efficiency before deployment to an active overseas area. All functions of the ship were observed and graded, and critiques were held in the presence of all officers. The greatest single responsibility for a deck officer occurs during flight quarters (when flying operations are taking place), when holding a correct heading becomes of critical importance to pilots taking off and landing.

The first flight operations on the USS *Princeton* in more than a year were completed by the new crew, but despite their extraordinary efforts, inspection results were somewhat disappointing. Passing marks were reluctantly assigned, influenced perhaps by the critical state of conflict in Korea.

The *Princeton*, officially considered ready for assignment to Fleet operations, was expected to immediately relieve the strain on carriers already in service. Her recall of crew, commissioning, and training had been accomplished in record time, and efforts were underway to ensure continuous availability of qualified air groups for her and other carriers. One recalled Reserve squadron, VF-871, that would later serve aboard the *Princeton* on this, her first actual combat cruise, was at that very time training for the challenge.

Chapter 2

Call to Arms
July-September 1950

THE IMMEDIATE *need for additional active naval air personnel, in virtually all categories, was recognized shortly after the outbreak of hostilities. Organized Reserve units across the country were evaluated for recall to active duty as complete units. Individual Reservists were also assessed for recall and transfer to fill out authorized strengths of reactivated units.*

No formal Reserve recall policy had existed at the start of the Korean War and consequently early recalls provided little or no time for those affected to wind up personal affairs. Although many Reservists believed they would be granted at least 24 hours before having to report in a national emergency, this was not always the case. Within weeks of 25 June, many Reservists were suddenly ordered to active duty. Commencing 23 July 1950, recalls were in process at locations all over the country for what would become 28 Navy and Marine Air Reserve squadrons. After receiving orders, most of the 3,104 "Weekend Warriors" — 728 officers and 2,376 enlisted personnel — reported for duty within 24 hours. No specific time allowances existed between an induction physical exam and active-duty report date. Unfortunately, a formal policy, allowing more reasonable notice and time to report for duty in this undeclared war, was not released until December.

In late morning on Friday, 21 July 1950, the doorbell of my home in Berkeley, California, rang unexpectedly. My mother advised me that the postman had delivered an official communication addressed to me, return receipt requested, from the United States Navy. Navy mail was not unusual at this time of the year, but return receipt mail was. I thought this communication may have had something to do with my usual summer Reserve squadron duty, but was shocked to read orders to report immediately for active duty with another NAS Oakland squadron. This communication was startling, because no national emergency had been declared by the President and no notice had been provided. The orders were also puzzling, as I was directed to report to VF-871, a fighter squadron, rather than to Photo Squadron VPP-876, to which I had been mostly assigned since joining the Air Reserves at NAS Oakland two years earlier.

I had not yet been weaned from either my close family ties or home, and found this sudden change in my young life very distressing indeed. I had lived all of my 20 years in comfortable Berkeley, attended nearby Catholic schools, and hoped to soon complete my college education at the University of California. The first of my large family generation to attend college, I already had finished two years, commuting to the City College of San Francisco. I had long dreamed of being the second in my family to attend prestigious "Cal." Aunt Vi, who lived with us, was the first.

I didn't have a problem with postponing my remaining studies at the University, believing such things could certainly wait. I was, however, disturbed with fears and uncertainties regarding my more immediate military future. The news of my recall was particularly troubling to my mother, Quina (a contraction of the Italian Pasquina), who possessed a worrisome nature. My father, Larry, accepted the news stoically when he returned home from work. He put in long hours as a driver/salesman for Langendorf Baking Company and was busily serving grocery stores when the letter had arrived. All possible scenarios were thrashed out that evening during a somewhat dour family supper. Our entire household — my folks, Aunt Vi, grandfather Billy, brother Dick, and sister Anita — participated in the somber discussion.

With growing alarm, I quickly tried to contact my high school and college friends, Jim Haughian and Vince Anzilotti, also Reserve members of VPP-876. I was disheartened to learn that neither had received similar orders. This was very troubling because I had joined the Reserves at their urging. The three of us had been close friends and for two years had carpooled to City College. Serving together would have made active duty much less painful.

The day after I received my orders, on 22 July, I reported to NAS Oakland and was greeted by many other recalled Reservists as confused as I. Informed that I had been transferred from VPP-876 to VF-871, I could not determine the reasons for this dubious honor. My rank as Airman Apprentice would hardly indicate a skill level critical for active-duty needs. Furthermore, my Reserve experiences had been devoted principally to the unskilled tasks of fueling and cleaning aircraft, usually a twin-engined SNB Beechcraft photo plane. After an afternoon of pre-induction orientation and paperwork processing by staff of my new squadron, I was released along with the others until the following morning.

My first day of formal military life, on 23 July 1950, was accompanied by a sobering suspicion that the course of my future, and that of my new mates, would be significantly different. Although my college studies had reached the midpoint, an interruption would not be devastating. However, other squadron members, particularly those who had served in World War II, were well into important phases of career and family life. Several pilots had good jobs with companies like Metropolitan Life, Standard Oil, and General Motors. And enlisted personnel also had been engaged in varied civilian life activities. Several squadron members were college graduates, and others, like myself, were still in the process of obtaining degrees. One recalled Reservist, Airman George Anno from Redlands, California, was particularly upset because he had completed six months active duty only a few months earlier. To make matters worse, George, a strapping 200-pound swimmer, had just been awarded an athletic scholarship at the University of California, Berkeley.

During the weekend, some men were allowed to present arguments to an officer on why they should not be recalled, but I was unaware of this process.

All personnel were advised by our squadron Commander, 29-year-old Lieutenant Commander William E. Harrison, a much-decorated World War II pilot, that we would remain at NAS Oakland for 10 days, during which we would be allowed reasonable time off to wind up our civilian affairs. Our squadron would then report as a unit to NAS San Diego to become part of a new air group. The short transition period at NAS Oakland provided an opportunity to make the change from part-time to full-time Navy life, in familiar surroundings. Daily routines were carried out in hangars, offices, and station properties formerly utilized on our Weekend Warrior basis. Initial administrative needs were addressed, including medical clearances, issuance of uniforms, and familiarization with Navy regulations and routines. Some enlisted crew members, hoping for last-minute reprieves from active duty, were sadly disappointed. After learning how to line up — military style — in the corridors of the base dispensary, we watched a corpsman deliver our medical records to the office of the Medical Officer. After a long wait, the record folders were returned and we were advised that each had been noted "physically fit for active duty." How this conclusion could be reached, without even a look by a doctor, was beyond me. I had held out hope that since my high school classmates had designated me "4F" — the Draft Board's designation for physically unfit — three years in a row, there might be something to it! A last hope for a quick return to inactive duty was quickly dashed.

The squadron, although not a newly organized Reserve unit, lacked a long tradition, having been commissioned only a few months earlier at NAS Oakland. The Commanding Officer of the new unit, Lieutenant Commander Harrison of Oakland, was no newcomer to naval aviation. One of the most decorated Naval Reserve fliers in World War II, the handsome, freckle-faced aviator had flown many combat missions in the Pacific theater. The Skipper had served with Squadron VB-16 on the

*new USS **Lexington** (CV-16) and had earned the Navy Cross
for his contributions in the first battle of the Philippine Sea
against the Japanese fleet. He also earned a Purple Heart
for injuries received in a strafing run on small boats at Truk.
Additionally, he was awarded the Distinguished Flying Cross
and the Air Medal with gold star, in lieu of five silver stars.
There was no question that the CO had earned his command.*

Although the ten-day period at familiar NAS Oakland was a welcome
reprieve, it provided only a superficial transition to full-time military life.
A relaxed adherence to regulations and dress, accompanied by the freedom for most to go home at night, was not really a difficult adjustment;
and the lack of routine daily work assignments, other than obtaining and
preparing uniforms, presented no undue work stress. The real change
began when, on 1 August, all hands were advised that our squadron would
depart for NAS San Diego the following morning.

After a final breakfast in the NAS chow hall at 0630, squadron members mustered for roll call assembly along with those of another recalled
squadron, VF-874, led by Lieutenant Commander Donald L. Watts of
Campbell, California. The final uprooting from homes and occupations
via airlift to San Diego was shortly underway. My bride-to-be, Marie, and
my mother were on hand to see us off. At 0830 on Wednesday, 2 August,
31 officers and 76 men of VF-871, along with the officers and men of
VF-874, departed aboard nine R4D transport aircraft, the Navy version of
the C-47, and headed south to the 11th Naval District. The intrastate flight
was typical for military travel of the time — uncomfortable. Many squadron members attempted to sleep on the hard bench seats aligned along
each side of the aircraft, while others played cards on the floor or talked.
The Skipper, who was traveling on my plane, soon joined five enlisted
men in a card game. Many expressions of sorrow at leaving home were
heard during the flight. One officer confided to the Skipper that he had
almost gone to pieces as he had put his kids to bed the previous night; and
as for me, I felt awful. Reality had set in.

Shortly after landing at the Air Station around 1120, our planes taxied to Hangar 526, the home of our new air group. As we disembarked the aircraft we were greeted with a huge banner above the main hangar door: "Welcome Weekend Warriors." The second word, "Weekend," had been appropriately crossed out.

The image of this banner and its clear message was burned into our brains as we lined up on the hot tarmac facing the hangar. We stood in formation for a welcoming address by the Air Station Commanding Officer, Captain W. L. Erdmann, and comments by other officials. We were released to go to lunch at 1300 and free to spend the rest of the day as we pleased.

Many settled in first at the assigned enlisted barracks 251 or the Bachelor Officers Quarters (BOQ), before getting acquainted with station facilities, and visits to the Enlisted, Chief Petty Officer, or Commissioned Officers Clubs followed.

The differences between NAS San Diego and our former home in Oakland were readily apparent. The much larger station, actually on Coronado Island, just off San Diego, was patrolled by ominous security vehicles which also monitored Air Station vehicular traffic. Enlisted crew leaving the Station on liberty quickly found out what a proper uniform was all about. One airman was directed by a gate Master at Arms to retie his tie, straighten his hat, button his cuffs, and get a haircut — all during his first attempt to leave the premises!

It was clear that regulations would be strictly enforced on this base. Military etiquette was the norm because the Station was also headquarters of the Commander Air Forces Pacific Fleet (COMAIRPAC). Saluting of officers, a rarity in Oakland, was required and expected at San Diego. During these early days in August 1950, our band of unhappy, homesick, and confused young Reservists discovered that we were, in fact, in the "real" Navy.

August began with organizational efforts involving not only our squadron but also the new air group of which we were a part. The call-up of Naval Air Reserves in July provided additional squadrons available for combat training. Ours was but one of ten Reserve squadrons on the Station, commonly called North Island, because it was at the northern end of Coronado Island. Five squadrons each were assigned to Carrier Air Groups 101 and 102, and each group of five was housed in one of the two crowded hangars. Assigning all ten squadrons to two hangars did not present an immediate space problem, however, as few aircraft were then available. Each of the two new groups (CAG-101, -102), after training, were to be assigned to a carrier to relieve the few air groups being repeatedly used in the war zone. A five-squadron configuration, as typified by the *Valley Forge*'s air group (CAG-5), was the standard employed at the outset of the war.

CAG-101 was comprised of Reserve Squadrons VF-721 (Glenview, Illinois), VF-791 (Memphis, Tennessee,), VF-821 (New Orleans, Louisiana), VF-884 (Olathe, Kansas), and VA-702 (Dallas, Texas). Joining our Squadron VF-871 in CAG-102 were VF-781 and -783 (Los Alamitos, California), VF-874 (Oakland, California), and VA-923 (St. Louis, Missouri). VF-781, our F9F Panther jet squadron, was viewed with some questioning awe because its pilots had volunteered in their entirety for activation. The remaining three VF fighter squadrons flying F4U Corsairs, including our sister squadron from Oakland VF-874, or our Skyraider Squadron VA-923, could not claim that distinction.

Standard squadron operating procedures were promptly developed and put into place. Reveille came at 0600 followed by breakfast and muster in the hangar at 0800. Four duty sections, requiring only one stint of weekend duty per month, were established and initial watches assigned. Compulsory dispensary visits involved a mini-physical and a variety of uncomfortable inoculations. Missing pieces of uniform or other required clothing were obtained, and slowly we began to resemble a regulation military outfit. Basic work assignments were planned, but little productive output could be obtained until our complement of aircraft was received. Some enlisted staff were temporarily detached and assigned duty in the mess hall for one month. Truck drivers qualified for Air Station driving licenses and were assigned vehicles. But despite the absence of meaningful work to do, there was always another line to stand in or errands to run on the Station's bus. Both pilots and crew members anxiously looked forward to receipt of our planes so that some real work could begin.

While our fellow air group squadron, VF-781, would transition to F9F Panther aircraft, our squadron would continue to fly the venerable fleet workhorse, the F4U Corsair. Long ago, the original XF4U-1 was Chance Vought's successful submis-

VF-871 pilots before recall on summer Reserve training, at NAAS El Centro. (Courtesy, J. Edward Watson)

sion in the Navy's design competition for a high-speed, high-altitude fighter aircraft. The manufacturer was awarded an initial Navy contract on 11 June 1938 to develop prototypes. On 29 May 1940, the first XF4U-1 was successfully flown at Stratford, Connecticut. On 1 October of the same year the prototype was subjected to speed tests and clocked at a speed of 405 mph — then a world record — while flying between Stratford and Hartford.

After further design modification and testing, the Navy awarded a contract to Chance Vought on 30 June 1941 to build the F4U-1 — the second plane to carry the name Corsair. The initial order of 584 planes was so indicative of the Navy's confidence in the Corsair that two additional associate contractors, Brewster and Goodyear, were added to assist in production. The first F4U-1 flew on 25 June 1942 and was delivered to the Navy a month later. By 13 May 1944, the three manufacturers had built a total of 3,000 Corsairs.

*Development of fighter-bomber concepts for the versatile aircraft was accomplished by Marine VMF-222 and Navy VF-17 combat squadrons. Bomb racks and release mechanisms were developed in service and adapted rapidly to other squadrons. On 18 March 1944, VMF-111 flew the first Marine fighter-bomber mission with eight modified Corsairs. Although originally designed as a carrier fighter, the British had a nine-month lead flying the Corsair from their carriers. Clearance was finally obtained for U.S. Navy carrier operations and more experienced Marine pilots flew the first missions against Japanese targets off the USS **Essex** on 25 January 1945.*

The first production F4U-4, the model in which our pilots would soon commence training, was granted final acceptance by the Navy on 31 October 1944. Later models were powered by the Pratt and Whitney R-2800-42W engine and rated as a 451 mph fighter. The new model added a four-bladed prop, engine air scoop, and a redesigned cockpit. Arriving late in World War II, some were used by Marine and Navy aviators from May 1945 until war's end. A total of 2,357 were produced by Vought, with the final aircraft completed in August 1947. All available models of Corsairs were flown in over 64,000 World

A U.S. Navy Air Reserve F4U-4 Corsair taxiing to the run-up area, at NAS Oakland. (Courtesy, Richard J. Cooper)

A U.S. Navy Air Reserve blimp and F4U-4 Corsairs on the flight line, at NAS Oakland. (Courtesy, Richard J. Cooper)

A U.S. Navy Air Reserve F2H-2 Banshee taxiing for takeoff, at NAS Oakland. (Courtesy, Richard J. Cooper)

War II combat sorties and successfully destroyed 2,140 enemy aircraft. There was no question that our pilots would be flying a proven, although older, aircraft.

The absence of meaningful work during the first few weeks at our new duty station, due to lack of aircraft, proved to be frustrating. The idle time provided a continuous source of griping about the recall, and an opportunity for the rumor mill to start. Hearsay ranged from our squadron remaining in San Diego until January, followed by discharge, to a stay of six months followed by sea duty. Inside information, supposedly from a variety of highly reliable sources, seemed to increase in quantity and creativity with each passing day.

My personal adjustment to military life in this unfamiliar environment was particularly difficult during these early weeks. A number of collect calls home were made from HEnley 3-9831, the nearest pay phone in the barracks.

War news began to produce some optimism, as the U.S. 1st Provisional Marine Brigade entered combat in defense of Pusan. The Marines joined with Army infantry in a campaign that showed signs of stemming the North Korean advance. Both Navy and Marine Corsairs worked effectively with ground controllers in providing effective carrier-based close air support.

Crew behavior also became more reckless, perhaps due to idle minds during the day. One enlisted member went AWOL and ended up spending a night in the San Diego city jail. He wandered into a city police station while in a drunken state, looking for his liberty and identification cards, and was promptly booked for the night. He faced the Skipper in a Captain's Mast — a disciplinary hearing — on 14 August and was restricted to the base until 2 September. A group of four others, dubbed the "Tijuana kids," regularly "hit the beach" on liberty, returning noisily around 0300 to the protest of those sleeping in the south end of the barracks.

A number of crew members contented themselves with concocting comprehensive plots to gain discharges either for contrived medical or family hardship reasons. One petty officer went so far as to petition the Red Cross for help with his hardship claim. An article in a local newspaper indicated that an effort was underway to permit release of married men with three or more children. Other educational pleas were prompted by news that five or six younger crew members would be discharged because they had not yet completed high school. A rumor highlighting a VF-874 member, supposedly granted a 30-day leave pending release to return to school, was a source of great inspiration.

Others busily researched the possibility of release to inactive duty for the purpose of returning to college. One of our pilots, Lieutenant Junior Grade William (Bill) Porter, advised me of Navy procedures that might be appropriate for requesting an educational release to inactive duty. Some even considered attempting to join a Naval Reserve Officer Training Corps (ROTC) unit at a college with admissions available. All the college options, however, were dashed when word was passed that men in another squadron, some already possessing Master's and Doctorate degrees, could not get released. It seemed evident that there was no compelling need at the time to get people into college programs to meet future officer requirements or to grant direct commissions. The Navy was much too busy recalling people into service to meet critical needs of the war to consider developing officers for the future. I decided not to initiate any formal efforts in this regard.

A select few airmen, whose lowly rank would normally be assigned to walk a specified post on a four-hour security watch, became quite adept at sleeping on watch. Some, like me, developed skills to doze while standing erect. Others would find a remote location on their post and actually sleep undetected in a prone position. One airman would simply check out his post along a line of our few parked aircraft, crawl onto an out-of-sight wing, and go to sleep. These tactics would be employed generally on late watches — midnight to 0400 — when duty officers were less likely to inspect the security posts in the perimeter around the hangar.

The squadron finally began to receive aircraft during the week beginning Monday, 14 August. The tempo of work did not appreciably increase at first but, as more planes arrived, the idle days began gradually to disappear. It was found that because many aircraft had been in preservation, the required bureau maintenance had not been completed. Planes received from the Fleet Air Service Squadron (FASRON) had come directly from open-air preservation at NAF Litchfield Park, Arizona. A number of cockpit fires and hydraulic leaks were a direct result of deterioration of wires, hydraulic lines, and rubber seals. Conversely, depreserved aircraft received from Overhaul and Repair (O & R) were found to be in very good condition.

But to immediately install the recently required bureau maintenance changes, it was necessary to pull personnel from other important squadron functions. This reduced the number available for specialized training assignments. Fortunately, the former civil service specialists in the squadron were able to handle the work load while less experienced personnel were concurrently being trained on the job. Initial assignments also evolved, as new tasks emerged relating directly to aircraft being received. My assignment, for example, began to focus around aviation storekeeper tasks. As each new aircraft arrived and was inspected and flown, new or replacement parts were often required. I was assigned to research appropriate catalogs and prepare requisitions specifying aircraft and other general supply part numbers. I would then pick up the necessary items from station stores. Additionally, as pilots began to flight-test aircraft, I would enter the hours flown and type of flying activity in the pilot's personal flight-log book. Other non-rated enlisted personnel who did not have a dedicated rating path, *e.g.* were "non-strikers" — without a career specialty — would be assigned to whatever new tasks had to be accomplished. One airman was unhappy being assigned as a fuel truck driver for another squadron in our air group. Three others were assigned on 21 August to join a work crew unloading and loading supplies and equipment on the carrier *Boxer* (CV-21), which had arrived at the station. During the next two days, additional crew were assigned by Leading Chief Petty Officer Ray F. Derry to ammunition-loading work parties on the carrier.

As air group squadrons continued to receive aircraft during the month, the flight qualifications of all pilots were evaluated. On 28 August, it was announced that three of our pilots had been traded for three from VF-781, the F9F Panther outfit composed of volunteers. The swap had something to do with the inability of the 781 pilots to transition from Corsairs to the newer Panther jets. The three were in the process of being checked out in jets and apparently had some unspecified difficulty in qualifying. Our squadron crew members commented that they hoped the incoming three would fit in with the laid-back, relaxed style of our "non-volunteer" pilots. On the same date, we also welcomed three new enlisted men brought in to meet specific skill needs.

As the month of August closed, news from the war front continued to brighten. Army and Marine ground troops were beginning to stem the advance of the North Korean army. Increased U.S. Navy and Marine carrier close air support strikes contributed greatly to slowing the enemy offensive. Although our forces were exacting a terrible toll from enemy troops in mid-month, Communist attacks continued until the end of August. An all-out effort was launched on 1 September by two divisions of the North Korean army to break the Pusan perimeter. TF-77 moved from its position off the north coast to add air group support to attacks against enemy troops and supply lines. The enemy attack was under control by 5 September, and on the 11th the 8th Army launched a general counteroffensive. This was quickly followed on 13 September by the first phase of General MacArthur's bold Inchon invasion.

The clever plan, involving amphibious landings behind North Korean lines, began with the attack and capture of the small — but critically important — island Wolmi-do, which lies at the approach to Inchon harbor. The attack, by the joint Marine-Army-Republic of Korea (ROK) force, was aided by pre-invasion naval air and surface ship bombardment. Close air support by TF-77 planes enabled our troops to secure the beachhead within the first 24 hours and quickly move on to capture Kimpo Airfield on 17 September. The largest assemblage of naval air power since World War II, lead by TF-77, included

*Carrier Division 1, **Philippine Sea**; Carrier Division 3, **Valley Forge**; and Carrier Division 5, on the newly arrived **Boxer**. The 15 squadrons of Carrier Air Groups 11, 5, and 2, respectively, were aided by two squadrons from Task Group 90.5, flying from the smaller carriers **Badoeng Strait** and **Sicily**, and two squadrons from Task Force 91's HMS **Triumph**. A variety of search, reconnaissance, patrol, and escort support was also provided by Task Force 99. In all, the invasion force, under the command of Vice Admiral Struble, contained 230 ships. Once the landings were secured, carrier groups of TF-77 shifted to interdiction missions behind main battle lines and over North Korea. Only 12 days after the landings, on 27 September, Seoul was recaptured by U.S. Marine and Army units. By the next day, all objectives of the landing had been met and South Korea was free once again.*

Spurred on by the apparent stabilization of the war, high hopes for an early end to the conflict again began to surface among squadron personnel. Despite a steady supply of new rumors concerning release, it was clear that our assigned tasks must still be carried out. Life went on and squadron members continued to prepare arriving aircraft for essential pilot training. The tail of each aircraft received was marked with a large capital "D," the tail code for our air group. Routine maintenance work continued, including repairs to the arriving planes. Non-routine work occurred too, such as repair to a wing tip damaged by an airman pulling a plane into the hangar. Our Engineering Officer, Ensign Daniel D. Miller, was less than overjoyed with this event. Although many planes had arrived, we were still short of our full complement, but each one that came in provided new opportunities for pilot training. As pilots spent more time in the air, my work entering flight time in individual pilot log books increased significantly.

Daily routines included, of course, the handling of personnel matters. Two enlisted crew members requested leave to get married, and I was one of them. Such requests were processed by the immediate officer, but the Commanding Officer had the final approval; Ensign Miller was most supportive, indicating he would recommend approval to the Skipper.

On 6 September, I was advised that Mr. Harrison wanted me to report to the CO's office on the second deck of the hangar. Our discussion evolved into a father-son chat about the responsibilities of marriage, ability to financially support a wife, and emotional preparation for such. He very kindly and patiently walked me though many important marital considerations. We carefully discussed elements of a likely family budget, leading to the important question of my financial solvency. He suggested that because I was not a rated Petty Officer that I think it over and possibly defer marriage until I made 3rd Class. But after futile attempts to dissuade me, during a follow-up meeting he finally approved my leave. He shook my hand and wished me luck, commenting that "love will find a way."

I was elated that my restrictive new Navy life would not obstruct our wedding plans. The Skipper and his officers had been most accommodating, and I was grateful. Marie expressed the same feelings when I telephoned the good news to her. Later, the Skipper approved a virtually identical, five-day October leave request for Airman Gerald A. Jacobsen, despite the fact that our squadron would then be temporarily located at Naval Air Auxiliary Station (NAAS) El Centro. Miller, recognizing that I was planning to leave El Centro the day before my 7 October Bay Area wedding, offered to have one of our pilots get me on a Navy flight to North Island. I could then easily connect with a commercial flight home from San Diego.

During September, we continued our transition to traditional Navy practices and procedures. We were advised that security watches in and about our hangar would now be conducted with loaded carbines. On 11 September, all personnel were taken to the Station firing range for weapons indoctrination and firing practice. Each was instructed in safe handling of the weapon and assigned to fire 15 rounds at a target. It was evident that I was not destined to be a marksman, as my assigned target was unscathed while the one assigned to the man next to me had 27 holes in it. Yet this didn't seem so bad for 27 out of the 30 rounds fired by the two of us had hit a target. As I saw it, that was better than missing completely! It didn't seem to matter anyway. I was judged qualified.

The "Tijuana Kids" continued to disrupt dorm 7 of the barracks. The latest prank was switching mattresses and generally infringing on the little privacy available in barracks life. Some of the stunts narrowly stopped short of blows, as things often got tense.

On 20 September the tension was broken by an announcement that we had received adequate planes for bombing and gunnery training at NAAS El Centro. The squadron was scheduled to arrive there on 1 October and return to San Diego on 14 October. Routine work would continue until 1230 Saturday, 30 September.

On 28 September, more squadron personnel changes were announced, with four enlisted men scheduled to receive dependency discharges. More surprisingly, one pilot would also be leaving. My friend, Lieutenant (JG) Porter, had received orders to inactive duty but details were unclear. Unconfirmed reports indicated that this decision was also based on family hardship circumstances.

Rumors continued to abound and "experts" had it that only pilots would go to sea. We would either be active for 18 or 24 months or be out by June 1951. But, despite all the high hopes for an early end to the war and these new and innovative stories of early discharge, it was clear that we were destined to move on to our next phase, whatever that might be. Because our aircraft had finally arrived and personnel soon would be stabilized, our squadron was expected to begin intensive preparations to become an efficient fighting unit. Clearly, bombing and gunnery training was the first step in honing the fighting skills of both pilots and support crew. Our squadron's success or failure in this critical phase would, no doubt, determine the immediate, and perhaps long term, future for our unit.

A VF-871 Engineering crew during bombing and gunnery initial training, at NAAS El Centro, October 1950.

Chapter 3

Getting Ready
October 1950-March 1951

CTOBER SIGNIFIED a turning point for both our squadron and air group. Despite rumblings to the contrary, shaped no doubt by wishful thinking, we were about to commence training for a more important assignment. Most made the trek to NAAS El Centro by airlift from North Island, but many went by private car down U.S. Highway 99; I tagged along with George Anno and we drove down Sunday morning.

Enlisted men stowed personal belongings in a small dusty barracks and officers went to an equally unpretentious BOQ. We mustered shortly before noon on Sunday,

Frank Musso, Harvey McCumber (on wing), Reno Ventimiglia, and Paul Cooper during bombing and gunnery initial training, at NAAS El Centro, October 1950. (Courtesy, George (Frank) Musso)

1 October. Our assigned hangar was also very small and would only accommodate our squadron, but despite the less sophisticated working quarters, it was nice to have the entire facility for our use. We were advised to expect a lot of hard work for two weeks, possibly up to 14 hours seven days a week. Liberty might or might not be granted, depending on our performance of training assignments. It was obvious that the objective of the upcoming training was not to get us ready for *inactive* duty.

The environment at El Centro was far different from that in the San Diego area. This temporary base was situated in the middle of a desert in the Imperial Valley, not far from the Salton Sea, an inland salt water lake. The station itself was designed to be functional — nothing fancy — just a place to get business done. And the business, in our case, would be training in bombing and gunnery under non-routine conditions.

Temperatures were extreme and the bugs annoying. Crickets, mosquitoes, cockroaches, scorpions, and an occasional tarantula were constant distractions. We were cautioned not to leave our boots on the floor at night as we might find a scorpion inside in the morning. Although this was not the garden spot of California, there were some redeeming factors. We could wear civilian clothes on and off the station when not on duty. This didn't amount to much, however, as there really wasn't anywhere nearby to go. We did not have to stand security watches, only more relaxed fire watches. The food was plentiful, and of good quality — and a large indoor swimming pool was available on the Station. Being approximately six miles from El Centro and any civilian activities, the pool was a welcome attraction. Otherwise, the air base seemed isolated, and the many unused dusty barracks and classrooms conveyed impressions of a seldom-used prison camp. North Island, despite all the irritating regulations, soon began to be viewed as a paradise lost.

As expected, the Squadron immediately commenced 12-hour work days. Pilots and crew members quickly adjusted to reveille before 0500, with daily routines starting at 0600 and ending, we hoped, at 1800. The work day often began around a small stove in the hangar, as the desert nights were very cold. But jackets were soon shed, once the oppressive heat of day settled in. Morning's frozen puddles would disappear and sun-softened tarmac was common in the afternoon. Because bombing and gunnery were the purpose of the training, ordnance and maintenance activities were key to the overall mission. Mechanics and ordnance crewmen struggled daily with their tasks so that pilots could fly as many armed runs over target areas as possible. Ammunition was belted; bombs and rockets lifted and loaded; and 18 aircraft serviced, repaired, and fueled, many times each day — all in the blazing heat of the desert. The skills of those on the ground and in the air were being honed under conditions modeled as closely as possible to combat circumstances. Pilots Bill Harrison, Al Donnelly, and Gordon George, engineering officer Dan Miller, and parachute riggers Bill George and John Young, additionally made successful freefall parachute jumps into the Salton Sea under the supervision of the NAAS Parachute Experimental Unit. All agreed that this experience could later prove beneficial. My support duties, including parts-chasing and record-keeping activities, took on increased meaning — pilots' log-book entries would be of critical importance for evaluating their combat fitness.

Although long work days with no time off became routine, liberty was granted those not on watch who had enough energy to "hit the beach." As might be expected in a desert environment, leisure attractions were few and limited to the nearby towns of El Centro, Brawley, and Westmoreland. The latter could best be described as a bawdy, Wild West town remarkably similar to those depicted in Western novels and movies.

On 14 October the squadron's first two-week period of rocket and gunnery practice was successfully concluded, and we returned to North Island with great relief. Reflecting upon all the hard work and discomfort, the general feeling was that we had done well. The squadron also smoothly accommodated two vital leave requests during the tour, resulting in two newly married members. Both Gerald Jacobsen and I had taken brides on 7 October — in ceremonies at opposite ends of California. Squadron officers had done everything possible to ensure that our leaves commenced without a hitch, thereby relieving the anxieties of our brides, our families, and ourselves. In my case, Ensign Miller ensured that I got aboard a Navy flight to NAS San Diego in time to catch a Pacific Southwest Airlines flight home from Lindbergh Field. It was touch-and-go for awhile getting out of El Centro, but all connections were made and I arrived home the afternoon before the wedding to the relief of all.

I was pleased that recently released pilot Lieutenant Porter and his wife could attend our wedding in Oakland. Porter and I had become friendly during the hectic pre-nuptial planning days. On one weekend, when we were both heading home to the Bay Area, we managed to get aboard the first Navy flight departing the Air Station heading north. Unfortunately, the flight terminated at NAAS Monterey, and we were on our own from there. We walked to the nearest highway to hitch a ride, and after a long wait in the sun along the roadside, we finally got as far as Gilroy. No further offers of free transportation were forthcoming, so we had to settle for a Greyhound bus the rest of the way to Oakland. During the long trip, Navy traditions regarding fraternization between officers and enlisted men were ignored, not to mention regulations prohibiting hitchhiking in uniform!

The return to NAS San Diego, as expected, was accompanied by a flurry of the latest rumors. The hot word was that we would remain in San Diego until March for further training, including additional visits to El Centro and a shakedown cruise on an aircraft carrier. The consensus was that we would definitely go to sea and not be released short of at least a year's active service. The speculation seemed to have validity as the squadron continued to receive an influx of new personnel, including many who were Regular Navy. Obviously, we were not being prepared at great expense to just simply be another unit of record. We would, most certainly, be put to the ultimate test of combat. Hope flamed anew, however, as 24 October news reports indicated that Secretary of Defense George C. Marshall had ordered the release of Reserves as soon as training was completed and replacements found. Despite the hopeful sound, the majority view was that a tour of sea duty would be considered part of the training. It didn't seem to make sense for the government to spend a lot of money training Reserve air groups and then releasing them without obtaining the essential relief aboard carriers at sea. The news was heartening though, in that the government had not forgotten about the plight of the recalled Reservists.

Normal North Island life resumed with an inspection that highlighted deficiencies in either clothing or the person. One airman got marked down for dirty dungarees and an inadequate shave. Others squeaked by with minor shortcomings. Following the inspection, the CAG Commander informed the squadron that another major inspection would take place in about one month, a formal, day-long, very strict affair. He commented that he thought we would be returning to civilian life in the not-too-distant future and encouraged us to make the most of our comparatively short time in service. He expressed hope that our squadron would make a good showing in the formal inspection.

In the meantime, once the short inspection was behind us and everyone back in regulation form, for the moment, the squadron focused on lighter

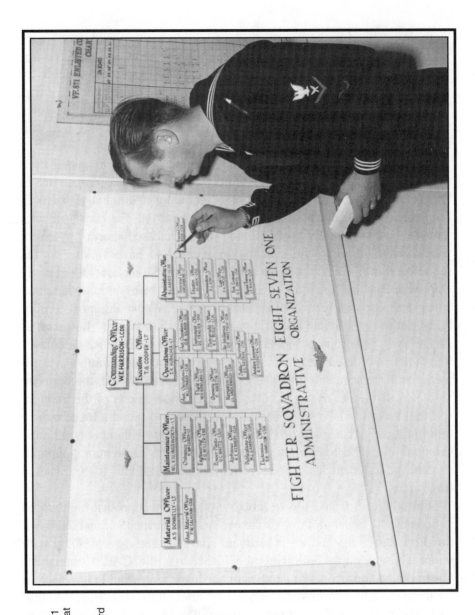

Yeoman 3rd Class Ralph C. Tarleton prepares the VF-871 organization chart, at NAS San Diego, 9 November 1950. (Courtesy, J. Edward Watson)

matters. On 25 October all hands were invited to a squadron picnic at Navy Field near Highway 101 in San Diego. The event was the Skipper's expression of appreciation for the effort we had put forth during the El Centro training. All usual work was secured for the afternoon, and beer, potato salad, hot dogs, and hamburgers were plentiful at the recreation facility. The day was capped off with a baseball game, after which crew members departed, along with much of the excess beer, to attend to their own pursuits.

George Anno drove me home to the apartment Marie and I had recently acquired near downtown San Diego, a small two-room on 7th Avenue, across the street from the El Cortez Hotel. Our modest new home included a small living room with a combined kitchen/bedroom and bath. The kitchen housed a wall bed which, when down, was about one foot from the stove and ice box. It was hardly luxurious, but we were happy with it.

On 28 October, the Skipper advised that our air group was scheduled to go aboard the USS *Philippine Sea* (CV-47) sometime in April. The impact of Secretary of Defense Marshall's earlier announcement concerning release of the Reservists was uncertain; if the schedule held, we would be gone for about six months. Life went on with the assumption that our training was for some predetermined purpose beyond our control. Squadron life reflected this assumption and settled into a routine. On occasion, problems arose to break that pattern of monotony. George Anno was the subject of one such circumstance. He was summoned by the Station's Legal Officer and advised that the San Diego Police Department had a warrant for his arrest. Needless to say, he was concerned, but was relieved to find that the warrant was for a neglected speeding ticket received in a nearby town, and that he needed only to report to the police station by 1800 that evening to take care of the matter.

Squadron routines continued to follow an almost predictable pattern, and although certain events were bound to occur at some point, those affected by them were often surprised anyway — November mess hall assignments, for example. The lucky three selected to replace those completing 30-day mess hall tours were George Anno, Jim Blyler, and me. We all knew this awful assignment was possible, but had hoped our names would never come up. Our personal belongings were quickly relocated to the mess hall barracks, a mini-physical completed, and we began the assignment without a whole lot of enthusiasm. Chow hall work hours began daily with muster at 0515 and ended at 1900, except every fourth day, when were allowed off at 1400. Only one weekend out of four would be free, but liberty was allowed at the end of each day, assuming one had any energy left. The hours were long and the work tiring, and the only benefit was that there was plenty to eat.

Our new duties included temporary assignment to Naval Air Station staff, which brought us into daily contact for the first time with Regular Navy personnel. Early conversations in the mess hall focused on the recently attempted assassination of President Harry S. Truman in Washington, D.C., and the ever-present rumor mill continued to grind within the largely Regular Navy environment. The Navy's announcement of the Reserve release plan prompted considerable discussion and speculation, even among the Regulars; it was thought that enlisted members were due out in July, with officers to follow in October.

News was regularly passed on to us mess hall "inmates" by our squadron members. We heard that four of five married men with dependents had received orders to report to the receiving station for hardship discharges. These actions were independent from the new Reserve release plan spelled out in detail in the 3 November issue of *U.S. News and World Report*. Needless to say, the published details prompted wild speculation among squadron members as to implementation in our air group.

⋘∞⋙

The news from the war front on 6 November was disconcerting as it conveyed ominous indications that the Republic of China might join the battle in support of North Korea. Should such occur, the recent positive gains by UN forces could be short-lived. Previously planned strengthening of U.S. carrier forces, however, continued to move ahead on schedule. The **Princeton***, having completed underway training activities in San Diego waters, quietly departed for the San Francisco Bay Area. NAS Alameda marked the final stop in the reactivation of this much-needed* **Essex***-class carrier. After boarding the Regular Navy air group, CAG-19, stores were loaded and final goodbyes said. On 9 November the* **Princeton** *departed San Francisco Bay. The remarkably fast reactivation, from mothball* to fighting-ship status, was complete as she headed for a stop in Pearl Harbor en route to Korea. Significantly, a number of troop transports loaded with Marine replacements had also departed San Diego Bay during the month for Japan and Korea.

After the **Princeton** was quickly sent steaming off to Pearl Harbor in early November, it reported to CINCPAC. The Allied Inchon amphibious landing by then had sent the Reds fleeing north and MacArthur issued his "home by Christmas" proclamation in late November 1950, giving us hope that perhaps we would not have to join the conflict after all. CINCPAC, however, dispatched the **Princeton** as planned to Japan but, while en route, things rapidly changed on the front, and a dispatch was received redirecting the ship to an early arrival in Korean waters. Crew members were not afforded an opportunity to gently settle in to new occupations, workplace, or geographical location because the war wouldn't wait for such luxuries. Almost before they knew it, these mostly recent civilians found themselves in the midst of the grim realities of a new, expanding war. Officers and crew of the still-adjusting ship immediately made their presence known.

Only ten days after its arrival with Task Force-77, the hastily recommissioned USS **Princeton** had volunteered to fly close air support missions around the clock instead of just during daylight hours. For the next week, missions were flown 24 hours a day in support of Marines being embarked at Hungnam. Ship's company and air group personnel provided essential support to departing Marines during this critical time.

For the next eight months the **Princeton**, flying the flag of the Commander Carrier Division Five, rotated with five other carriers to maintain three on line. During the remaining period of her deployment, she delivered one-third of the ordnance tonnage deposited by all of the six carriers that operated in the area. From the very beginning until the end of the long tour, the **Princeton** lead all ships in total missions flown and tonnage dropped on target. Her jets were the first to carry bomb loads into combat. **Princeton** planes, loaded with 30 percent more explosives than other ships, recorded fewer landing and takeoff crashes. These successes required close coordination and team-

Squadron VF-871 enlisted crewmembers march in front of CAG-102 F4U-4 Corsairs on the flight line, at NAS San Diego. (Courtesy, J. Edward Watson)

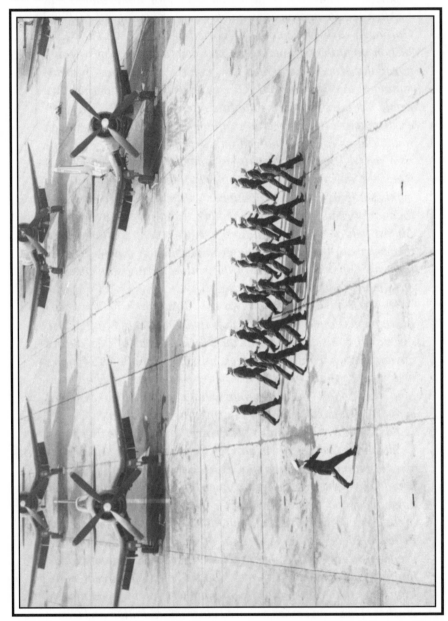

VF-871 F4U-4 Corsairs and VA-923 AD-3 Skyraiders (row 2) on the flight line, at NAS San Diego. (Courtesy, J. Edward Watson)

*work between ship's company and air group personnel. Under
the leadership of Captain Bill Gallery, the crew clearly set new
standards of carrier performance during this long tour of sea
duty.*

On the same date as the published *U.S. News and World Report* article,
VF-871 squadron members were informed that there was a strong possibility that our air group would be relocated — perhaps to NAS Miramar,
just north of San Diego; to NAS Moffett Field on San Francisco Bay; or
to NAS Alameda, outside San Francisco. We quickly voiced favor for
NAS Alameda, as did our sister Oakland squadron, VF-874. While the
news created excitement, there was also caution, because our hopes had
been dashed before. A "let's hope for the best" attitude prevailed.

Squadron training continued in a routine fashion throughout an
uneventful November. Unwanted mess cook assignments were handled,
with no serious mishaps — except when George Anno and I were alarmed
to see Jim Blyler being carried to the Station dispensary on a stretcher. He
had injured a finger washing dishes in the scullery!

My mess hall tour included two semi-promotions: I was first elevated
from chow-line server to chow-rusher (table attendant), and later to butcher shop helper. Each assignment afforded shorter work hours and better
liberty, more important to me since Marie's arrival. The job prerequisites
were welcomed, especially getting off early at 1400 on Thanksgiving
afternoon. An aberration in the work-hour improvement, however,
occurred on my duty day of 18 November, as my work day totaled 16.5
hours — hardly shorter. My exalted butcher-shop status also allowed me
to wear a cook's hat — a sign of great distinction.

The mess assignment fortunately allowed us to miss the big air group
inspection on 18 November. My new role as a cook, however, swept me
up in a "dress blue" inspection with Station personnel on the final weekend. In preparation, I stopped at a naval tailor in San Diego to have my
blue jumper cuff stripes repaired and the pants and jumper pressed. I
wanted no complications in my release from mess hall duty. My inspection went well, except for the Station captain's critical comment about the
quality of my haircut. He asked where I had gotten it and, not having the

courage to tell him my wife was the barber, I simply replied, "On the beach, Sir."

Our contacts back in the squadron advised us that following the squadron inspection, the Skipper had informed all hands that we would not be moving back north. The CAG Commander had visited both Alameda and Moffett Field, but could not find suitable hangar space at either for our air group. Another disappointment!

On Tuesday, 22 November my wife and I anxiously looked forward to receiving the first house guest in our small apartment, Aunt Vi from Berkeley. We were pleased that she could spend most of Thanksgiving week with us, and that we were able to show her around our favorite spot, Balboa Park.

As the month came to an end, the Skipper announced that his wife Doris had given birth to a 7-pound, 12-ounce baby girl, and morale was also picked up by the squadron's swimming team victory over Squadron VA-923 on 29 November. The team captured every event, with George Anno being the outstanding swimmer of the meet in three winning events. Lieutenant Junior Grade Jack Baum was victorious in two events, and Deke Taylor in one. A win in the freestyle relay wrapped up the team victory, in this first of a series of intersquadron swimming meets. While proud of the team's accomplishments, my morale independently blossomed upon my release from mess hall duty.

*The war situation in late November 1950 continued to worsen with the involvement of Chinese Communist troops. The 1st Marine Division engaged large Chinese forces and the 5th and 7th Marines were surrounded by enemy forces. On 1 December, the Division, trapped in rough terrain in the Chosin Reservoir area, initiated its breakout. Round-the-clock air support was provided by Marine air units and carrier air groups of TF-77. The carriers **Leyte**, **Philippine Sea**, and **Badoeng Strait** provided initial support. They were joined by the **Princeton** on 5 December, the **Sicily** on the 7th, the **Bataan** on the 16th, and the **Valley Forge** on the 23rd. The **Princeton's** first strike on the 5th occurred three months, seven days, and twenty hours after*

coming out of moth balls — a Navy record. Within a week, the **Princeton** *quickly became the Task Force workhorse. Many treetop-level close air support strikes were flown in extremely poor weather conditions.*

The Chosin breakout and evacuation by sea near Hungnan was finally over on 11 December, and a defensive perimeter established. The carriers **Philippine Sea** *and* **Leyte** *had been on the battle line for 52 consecutive days and shortly thereafter departed for Yokosuka, for rest and replenishment. Marine and Navy air support was assessed as vital to the ultimate success of the Chosin breakout.*

During this period, squadron members debated among themselves what the involvement of China might mean to the nation's commitment to the conflict. Fears were expressed that the entry of China could ultimately involve the Soviet Union and potentially evolve into World War III. U.S. casualties, according to early December news reports, had already exceeded 30,000, while losses of other UN nations could be counted only in the hundreds. The "police action" against "bandits" appeared to be developing into something far greater.

In preparation for our likely involvement in the conflict, six new men joined the squadron. We welcomed enlisted men Leonard Bizon, William Rettenmaier, and Albert DeLoach. And joining Don Frazier were new flying Ensigns John Moody, Wes Ralston, and Dick Lombard. Lieutenant Elmer Hubacher became the squadron's second pilot granted a release to inactive duty.

Signs of heightened war preparations were visible at NAS San Diego. On 4 December, daily assignments were modified and work parties formed to load the recently returned *Valley Forge* for a quick turnaround to Korea. I was assigned a 1600 to midnight shift on the first day. Other groups worked alternate shifts. On the same day, I was informed that I had been promoted to Airman (AN) effective 16 November. I could proudly wear three green stripes on my left sleeve. The *Valley Forge* disembarked the battle-weary CAG-5, replenished supplies (including a snow-plow), and loaded replacement air group CAG-2. The carrier, and relief air group consisting of Corsair Squadrons VF-24, -63, and -64, and Skyraider Squadron VA-65, departed on 6 December, after only six days at home. During a muster the Skipper informed us that our squadron was under consideration for transfer to a new air group being formed. We might be the only Reserve squadron in the group, which could be located at NAS Alameda, though we would not have to repeat all the training completed to date. The proposal action had to be approved in Washington, D.C., but a decision was expected shortly.

⋘∞⋙

Mid-December news reports focused on whether or not the Chinese would stop at the 38th Parallel and consider a peace treaty. Washington, D.C., speculation centered around whether or not President Truman would declare a national emergency and order full mobilization.

⋘∞⋙

Although all of this was unsettling, life went on. A recently formed squadron basketball team was playing often and winning some games against the other squadrons, including VF-874. Stores colleague Bill Norton suggested that I go out for the team. Games were usually played at Navy Field, and liberty was permitted after each. I could go home to our apartment afterwards, and this was a prime motivator in my decision to join. Unfortunately, we also had to endure another thorough inspection on 15 December, one that included various drills that only involved volunteers. I was not involved because I had learned early to be selective regarding volunteer assignments. There was also no haircut problem with this inspection because I got a regulation cut from a professional barber.

On 18 December, a normal work day, the squadron Christmas party was held in our hangar. Santa Claus taxied up to the hangar in a plane, and carols were sung by squadron children, who each received a present. After the party many crew members went to the Ship's Service store to buy family gifts. Marie and I rode to and from the base with Jake Jacobsen and his bride and joined them in a little shopping.

The year concluded uneventfully in San Diego, and routine work continued, interspersed with many Christmas leaves. Many enlisted members spent their spare time stenciling personal serial numbers on issued clothing in regulation format. Although I had the duty on Christmas, I managed to get someone to standby for me so that I could enjoy Christmas dinner with Marie at the El Cortez Hotel.

*On the Korean coast that December things were different. During the afternoon of Christmas Eve day, the last Marine was evacuated safely from the besieged Hamhung-Hungnam area. Carrier-based aircraft continued to attack Chinese forces around the perimeter. Later, a night-flying Corsair from the **Princeton**'s VC-3 detachment patrolled over Hungnam, observing the burning port, while the last ships pulled out to sea. TF-77's involvement with Hungnam was, at that point, essentially concluded. Since reporting on station in the early morning of 5 December, the **Princeton** had provided support from Chosin, through the fighting retreat in bitterly cold conditions to the Hamhung-Hungnam withdrawal beachhead. Flight operations had been extended to 20 hours per day. Flight-deck personnel often worked in sub-zero winds with a velocity averaging 55 knots per hour; the savage wind and frost gradually permeated winter clothing. A soup kitchen was installed inside the island superstructure to increase the caloric intake of those working outside. On Christmas Day, the **Princeton** became the flagship of TF-77 under the command of Rear Admiral Ralph Ofstie. The ship's company and air group personnel carried out their difficult tasks far from home under nearly intolerable conditions.*

Holiday celebrations and personal leaves completed, the squadron commenced the new year with accelerated training activities. On Friday, 5 January 1951, our pilots and a select group of enlisted men departed for NAAS Saufley Field, Pensacola, Florida, for a week of carrier qualifications. Pilot qualifications were scheduled to begin the following Monday aboard the de-mothballed carrier *Monterey* (CVL-26), deployed to Pensacola as a training vessel for Navy and Marine aviators. During their absence, all seabags were inspected to ensure that uniform garments were stenciled with names and serial numbers in regulation form. I passed with flying colors. The volume of work also dropped while the pilots were away for qualification tests, and thus any who had not previously attended were sent to first aid training. Meanwhile, the government announced that 450,000 18-year-old recruits would be drafted during the year, although neither a war nor a national emergency had yet been declared. So much for our hope for de-escalation of the conflict. And more good news . . . we were advised we had to go back to El Centro on 21 January!

After work on 11 January, a wet wintry day, Jake and I boarded a liberty boat from North Island to San Diego. Jake was in rare form as he stood in the bow of the boat with the wind in his face spouting nautical sayings to the entertainment of a boatload of sailors. Earlier that day, mail from home brought the news that during December, my two friends, Vince and Jim, had been accepted into NavCad — for naval cadets — and they were then en route to Pensacola, Florida, to begin training as Naval Aviators. On the following day, we learned that the proposed Alameda transfer to form a new air group was still possible, but that the Skipper was fighting it. He reportedly was attempting to convince the powers that be to let us remain in CAG-102 and ship out as part of the all-Reserve air group.

Our pilots and all hands were back by 16 January, with reports that they did very well in Pensacola. The squadron was slated to regroup for departure to El Centro as scheduled on Sunday, 21 January, for two more weeks of bombing and gunnery practice.

During the interim days, a flood of rumors began to circulate regarding our immediate future. The accelerated nature of recent training, plus the presence of a number of carriers in California, heightened crew concerns. Speculation focused on whether the newly arrived *Antietam* or the *Boxer*, both at NAS Alameda, would soon board air groups. Fears were expressed that we would board the *Antietam* upon our return from El Centro. CAG-101, the other all-Reserve air group, was still rumored to board the *Boxer* soon. Most squadron members continued to support detachment from CAG-102 to join the proposed new group to be formed in Alameda.

On 18 January it was reported that the Skipper had stopped fighting the detachment, and a formal decision was expected after our return from El Centro. It was in the midst of all this speculation that squadron gear was loaded on trucks and personnel transported once again to El Centro for reporting at 1600 Monday, 22 January.

The squadron's second tour at El Centro quickly showed signs of being significantly different than the first. Crew members arose at 0430 for muster and early operations at 0600. During routine operations on 23 January, one of our pilots experienced a distinctly non-routine situation. Lieutenant Lee "Killer" Killingsworth was flying a bombing exercise when a cockpit electrical fire started around his legs. He radioed his wingman of the problem and advised that he was going to bail out. He flipped his plane onto its back in order to fall free, but found himself heading into a mountain. He made corrections to avoid a hill looming dead ahead while simultaneously assessing the distance to the ground below. He quickly decided not to abandon the $600,000 airplane and attempted instead to bring it in. He righted the aircraft and, reaching under the forward panel, began tearing out wiring suspected of causing the smoke; shortly thereafter he made a nice emergency landing. Despite the frightening situation, his quick decision to attempt to extinguish the fire rather than abandon the aircraft over the desert proved to be sound.

Work days at El Centro were as long and difficult as before, and the wear and tear of flight operations began to take a toll on the aircraft. An SNB, Bureau number 39812, was assigned for our use in ferrying crew and supplies between El Centro and North Island. Jake Jacobsen was assigned to shuttle on the daily flight to and from North Island to obtain replacement parts necessary to maintain flight operations. My role picked up also because I prepared the requisitions needed for Jake to obtain essential parts from NAS San Diego stores. At the end of the first week we were granted the weekend off, and many crew members returned to San Diego or elsewhere. Jake and I drove back together to rejoin our brides.

Week two at El Centro began with Monday-morning flights canceled due to heavy rain. We also received news that not only had the crew left our temporary base over the weekend but so did the Skipper. It was reported that he flew up to NAS Alameda to review available space and found a hangar that would accommodate an air group. On Tuesday, 30

The VF-871 Supply staff: Reno Ventimiglia, Jim Blyler, Paul Cooper, Ken Colwell, Harvey McCumber, and Ensign Dan Miller, at NAS San Diego, February 1951.

January, a dispatch was received advising that we would join a new air group, location to be determined. It was also announced that CAG-101 would begin its shakedown cruise on the *Leyte* the following Monday and probably board the *Boxer* for sea duty when completed. Rumors once again swirled uncontrollably, but our final week concluded on Friday, 2 February, with an afternoon squadron party. The gathering was similar to the picnic held in San Diego after our first training tour, except for the addition of some entertainers imported from nearby towns. Party or no party, we all were happy to go back again to San Diego. Despite the Skipper's plane receiving a few bullet holes while towing a target, and Lieutenant Killingsworth's cockpit fire, the two weeks had been otherwise uneventful.

CAG-101 commenced shakedown training on Monday, 5 February, as scheduled. Our post-El Centro squadron duties on that date were curtailed, as only two of the four duty sections were aboard. Duty sections two and four had not been required to report back until the following day. Sections one and three were slated to be permitted three days off on the next weekend. Return to El Centro was confirmed, for not one but two more weeks, commencing 25 February. On 13 February, the Skipper announced that although we would not be transferred to Alameda, we would not remain in CAG-102. Despite his efforts to keep us in the air group, our pilots lacked approximately 1,500 flying hours and, therefore, we would join a newly formed group. Our sister Oakland squadron, VF-874, and remaining CAG-102 squadrons, were scheduled to go to sea in May.

Despite disappointment that we would not be moving to Alameda, most were pleased that we would be joining a new group, thereby delaying sea duty. The Skipper said it would only be a one-month delay, but it might be a Mediterranean *vs.* Pacific cruise. There was general relief that a decision was finally made regarding our status.

Friday, 16 February, was a dreary day — rainy and foggy — thus flying was canceled in the afternoon. An event occurred, however, that was uplifting to squadron crew. A dispatch was received ordering fellow bridegroom Airman Gerald "Jake" Jacobsen to be transferred to the Commandant of the 11th Naval District and be commissioned as a Naval Officer. Despite a general belief that enlisted applications for direct commissioning would not be accepted, Jake had apparently gotten under the wire. While still an inactive-duty Reservist, he had completed his final application — shortly before receiving orders to active duty, and he had been accepted. His transfer orders were contingent upon resolution of any pending disciplinary actions, and he was advised that he would have a week to complete ten extra hours previously assigned him, for being late for muster, before he'd be allowed to transfer. After completion of commissioning processes Jake would be assigned to General Line Officer training at the Naval Postgraduate School at Monterey, California, for approximately six weeks, and from there Fleet assignment would follow. I was designated to take his place as the squadron parts-chaser with Jim Blyler replacing me.

Our joy for Jake, however, was quickly tempered when, during weekend duty, we learned that three of six members of VF-783 of CAG-102 had been killed and two others injured in a transport plane crash.

On 21 February we were advised that plans were under consideration for our squadron to go out on a shakedown cruise during the next month with CAG-102. This news was troubling to some pilots who feared that we might be reassigned back to our former air group because of VF-783's lack of a full complement of pilots. That squadron's pilot shortage had been upped to six and their overall readiness considered somewhat tenuous for imminent sea duty. Our pilots' concerns were heightened by rumors that the CAG Commander was attempting to get our squadron transferred back to the group.

The *Boxer* arrived at the San Diego Air Station from Alameda on the 24th to take aboard CAG-101. On the 26th, uncertainties and all, we reported again to El Centro for two more weeks of bombing and gunnery practice. I began this third tour still at North Island — which suited me just fine — as Ensign Miller had decided that vital procurement of parts could be expedited if someone was readily available to NAS stores. In my new stock-chaser assignment I was assigned to remain behind.

Things were quiet the first day, as initial parts requirements were low. One of our staff officers, also remaining on Station, attended a meeting in VF-783's Ready Room, further heightening transfer speculation. Then parts demands picked up significantly in mid-week, when numerous orders began arriving from El Centro. During my frequent trips around the station picking up parts, I observed CAG-101's planes being loaded aboard the *Boxer*.

On Thursday, 1 March, Ensign Jacobsen dropped by the hangar before leaving the following day for Monterey. As an "officer and gentleman,"

Jake did not have to display an ID card; he received a salute at the gate and entered the Station without delay. This was quite different from his sailor days when his car was frequently searched for civilian clothing or cameras. He also related that when he first reported to the San Diego Naval Station, he was subjected to standard enlisted treatment by the gate Military Police and was advised that he could park for only half an hour. After being sworn in, he reported the next day in his officer's uniform, was saluted, and was told he could park anywhere he wanted — for as long as he wanted! When he went to obtain his new ID card, he was escorted past a long line of sailors and got his picture taken immediately. What a difference the uniform made!

During Jake's visit to North Island, he also dropped in on the Station Supply Officer, with whom he had frequently done squadron business. The officer was drilling some men and asked if Jake, in his new role, wanted the task. But he declined because he knew many personally and just a few days previously had *been* one of them. He later commented that he felt fortunate in being in the right place, at the right time, to gain his promotion. Upon completion of training he expected to be transferred somewhere within COMAIRPAC, perhaps even back to North Island. End-of-the-week activities were highlighted by the departure on Friday of the *Boxer*, with CAG-101 aboard, bound for Korea.

My second week of special duty at North Island began in the same manner as the first had ended — with carrier activity. As work started on Monday, 5 March, the *Essex*-class carrier *Bon Homme Richard* (CV-31) steamed into the bay en route to North Island. The "Bonnie Dick," as she was called, was rumored to be the next ship to go to sea, with our old air group CAG-102 aboard. However, some planes loaded aboard later in the day were not identified with 102's "D" tail designation.

Meanwhile, in El Centro, training exercises were going well, and the Skipper pronounced our squadron ready for sea duty. On Tuesday, parts requisitioning picked up sharply. The Skipper flew into the Air Station in the early afternoon, en route to a meeting, and brought a number of requests for me to fill. A few more were brought in by George Anno on the late afternoon SNB, what would be comparable to a carrier-on-board delivery, or COD at sea. Miller had granted George time off to attend an evening chemistry class at San Diego Junior College. The Skipper visited the *Bon Homme Richard* to plan for our expected 26 March shakedown cruise. The planes that I noticed being loaded aboard the previous day were from a detached former CAG-101 squadron. They belonged to VF-821, which would join CAG-102 on its ten-day shakedown. Proposals under discussion also included the possibility of elements of our squadron joining 102 on this cruise.

Word got around that some events had taken place while the squadron was in El Centro that were cause for alarm. A gross practical joke that involved tampering with an airman's bunk and pillow nearly resulted in an all-out barracks fracas. Another incident involved an airman who wrote two letters directly to President Harry S. Truman, allegedly commenting negatively about the Navy and requesting transfer to the Infantry. The letters were particularly disturbing to the Skipper as they had not been sent in accordance with the chain of command, for appropriate action. Many political and military command levels had seen them before the Commanding Officer had had a chance to read them. The Skipper did not take kindly to these events. He advised that Reservists from Oakland who had not previously gone through Regular Navy boot camp would be ordered to do so if they didn't shape up. This threat had a most sobering effect, as no one in his right mind wanted to go through that ordeal.

The demand for parts continued to be heavy as the second week concluded. Late Thursday afternoon, Miller flew down in the SNB and waited with the pilots while I obtained critical parts. After a couple of wasted hours at Stores, due primarily to stock-number confusion, the desired parts were obtained and loaded on the plane. Before leaving, Miller advised that 72-hour passes would probably no longer be granted past the upcoming weekend, and any leave requests should be submitted soon. Leave could not be requested for dates after April 1. He was fairly certain we would be going to sea soon, but did not know exactly when.

Friday, 9 March, began in a very dramatic way for me. Shortly after I had checked in topside at the squadron office on the second deck of the hangar, Yeoman Ed Watson showed me a dispatch that had just been received. The confidential message directed that VF-871 and three other detached squadrons — VF-23, VF-821, and VA-55 — be deployed to relieve the USS *Princeton*'s CAG-19 on 1 June. The *Princeton*, including our new air group designated CAG-19X, would subsequently be relieved by CAG-5 aboard the *Essex* on 1 September. The deployment date and method were to be set later. The dispatch containing the long-awaited news was shown to an administrative officer of VF-874, our sister Oakland

Squadron VF-871 bombing and gunnery final training, at NAAS El Centro, March 1951.

squadron. After reviewing it the officer commented, "My gosh, are you guys getting off with just four months? Why, you may be out before we even get back!" At first blush, this official news that we had been dreading for so long didn't seem so bad, after all. Four months of sea duty beats six any time!

The four squadrons had been selected from four air groups, including VF-871 from CAG-102. The group was charged to quickly organize, train, and provide relief for the USS *Princeton* during its extended deployment. The Oakland squadron was joined in this challenge by Reserve Squadron VF-821 (CAG-101) and Regular Squadrons VF-23 (CAG-2) and VA-55 (CAG-5). The prototype group, temporarily called CAG-19X, was not yet officially designated with an Air Task Group (ATG) number — such designations would come later — but it had the distinction of being the first.

The challenge of integrating four squadrons, two Regular and two Reserve, with detachments from other specialized squadrons and shaping them quickly into an effective fighting group would be no small task. It would become evident during the nearly four-month test of the ATG model, while the war was reaching one year in duration, that the four squadrons and detachments proved the concept worked. The replacement air group would successfully carry out its assigned role, thereby enabling the *Princeton* to complete her vital extended tour.

Our post-El Centro week got started at a crawling pace on Monday, 12 March. The San Diego public transit system had gone on strike, creating a major traffic problem in the city. Bus riders like myself, and others living off base, were delayed getting to the North Island and Coronado water taxis. I called Chief Derry to explain that I had missed my usual boat because of the situation. Normally, the Chief was a stickler for punctuality, but on this occasion he was understanding. Thankfully, work for the day was low-key and squadron members settled back into NAS routines. Flight operations were canceled because most officers were given the day off. Rumors of the Saturday dispatch floated around, but we had to wait until evening muster for anything official.

The Skipper finally announced that we were out of CAG-102, would form new air group 19X, and would board the *Princeton* in May, confirming all the information in the dispatch that Watson and I had read. It was uncertain what would happen upon our return from sea duty, but he mentioned the possibility of us going out again later on another carrier.

Thus, a mid-May departure was expected with return in September, world conditions permitting.

The Skipper also commented that we would be able to compete with our former air group CAG-102, which would be aboard the *Bon Homme Richard,* during part of our time in the war zone. Some of the original Oakland Reservist members later revealed, for the first time, that during their last summer cruise the Skipper had asked how they felt about active duty. After receiving a negative response, he was said to have commented that he had already volunteered the squadron. With so many months of training behind us and our future determined, the consensus was — "What does it matter?"

On Wednesday word was passed that the rumored shakedown for the squadron aboard the *Bon Homme Richard,* tentatively scheduled for the 26th, was off. But although the two-week assignment as a unit aboard this carrier was canceled, many related individual short-term assignments commenced immediately. Squadron members of varied ratings were assigned to the ship for two days of orientation training. Jim Blyler was one of ten or so crew members who went aboard. The rotating assignments created shortages of staff available to stand watches, and thus the frequency of watch assignments sharply increased. On Friday the 16th, it was announced that our squadron shakedown cruise had been rescheduled for five days, aboard a carrier not yet named, during the last week of April. To make things worse, the weather during most of the week remained very warm, and the bus strike dragged on.

March passed uneventfully with most duties gradually reverting to the norm. The *Essex* (CV-9) entered San Diego Bay on the 23rd after undergoing a year of overhaul and modernization at the Bremerton Navy Yard. Leave requests were submitted and approved time off taken, and the *Bon Homme Richard* departed for Pearl Harbor en route to Korea. On 27 March the Bob Hope radio show originated from NAS San Diego, and all 18 tickets allotted to the squadron were quickly taken. The show was staged in the base theater with the limited seating reserved for service personnel only — no family members.

On the 29th, a finalized schedule for our shakedown cruise aboard the *Essex* was announced — covering a span of 11 days between 4 April and 4 May — with all shipboard training to be completed by 5 May. That same day, pre-cruise swimming tests were conducted including swimming clothed, floating, jumping into water, inflating clothing, and treading water without touching for 15 consecutive minutes. There were no squadron qualification problems.

*Aboard the USS **Princeton**, the month of March marked a departure from close air support missions toward a new commitment to interdiction strikes designed to inhibit movement of enemy supplies. CAG-19 began launching a series of these strikes against rail bridges. Attack strikes by Skyraiders from VA-195 on 3 March destroyed one span, damaged a second, and ruined the alignment of two others between Kilchu and Songjin. Later, Communist attempts to repair this concrete and steel bridge were nullified when a sixth and final strike finished the bridge, once and for all. During this period, the nature of the TF-77 interdiction campaign began to evolve from a focus on bridges and highways to rail targets — a shift that reflected an effort to more effectively impede enemy logistical supply efforts.*

In little more than two months our squadron's pilots would be assuming CAG-19's role in carrying out TF-77's ever-evolving mission. As March closed out in California, I was personally saddened when word from home brought news that two of my high school classmates had become Marine casualties in Korea. One had been killed in action and the other was twice wounded, although he had made it safely home to the Bay Area. Our training was essentially over, and soon it would be our turn to join the battle, which up to then, had been fought by others, like my classmates.

VF-871's Ensign John P. Moody, Jr., was the first pilot to bring a plane aboard the USS *Essex* (CV-9) on 5 April 1951. Moody celebrates his "first landing" on the deck of the modernized ship by serving a piece of traditional cake to the ship's Executive Officer, Commander Ralph M. Pray. (Courtesy, J. Edward Watson)

Chapter 4

Anchors Aweigh
April-May 1951

APRIL MARKED THE *beginning of VF-871's active-duty adventure. A new era also began for the venerable carrier the USS **Essex**, our shakedown cruise ship. On 4 April, the first contingent of squadron members, 80 men and 9 officers, boarded the ship for essential sea-going exercises. The following day the carrier's flight deck was alive with activity in preparation for the landing of aircraft for the first time in five years. Fifteen pilots from our squadron were scheduled to fly aboard on this memorable day.*

The honor of bringing the first plane aboard on 5 April,

went to VF-871's Ensign John P. Moody, Jr., who smoothly landed his
F4U-4 on the 27,000-ton flattop. Immediately after landing his Corsair on
the modernized vessel's flight deck, he was congratulated by the Commanding Officer, Captain Austin W. Wheelock, and the Executive Officer,
Commander Ralph M. Pray. Ensign Moody had previously served four
years as an enlisted Marine before becoming a commissioned officer and
pilot. The events of the day were later commemorated by the cutting of a
giant cake prepared by the ship's bakers. The March arrival of the *Essex* at
San Diego followed a year of significant overhaul and modernization.
Among major improvements were a strengthened flight deck, a stream-
lined island, and installation of personal escalators. The $40,000,000
update essentially established the *Essex* as the state-of-the-art namesake of
the fast carrier class.

Many personal leaves were taken on staggered dates between 4 and 13
April, while various squadron contingents were at sea aboard the *Essex*.
Short squadron exercises, of two to five days' duration, involved all 15
pilots, 40 to 50 enlisted men, and less than 10 deck officers. As intended,
leaves during this period provided a final opportunity to spend time with
family and friends prior to shipping out. On 10 April, while on my ten-day
family leave, we listened to the pre-recorded Bob Hope radio show from
North Island.

Upon my reluctant return on 16 April, I learned that 19 members, many
of whom had been with us since Oakland, would be transferred out of the
squadron. The transfers were for various reasons, including physical. Each
transferee would be permitted three choices of preferred Pacific Coast
Naval Air Stations. Although the goal was to grant one of the choices,
COMAIRPAC could unilaterally assign an individual elsewhere, based on
skill needs. The overall process stimulated much chatter as to who was
better off, those going or those staying, and the general feeling was that
those being transferred were, because they would be able to remain in the
States, even though they might end up with a longer active-duty period.
Most of those affected seemed to be satisfied, including George Anno,
who hoped that he would get one of his three Southern California
choices.

News events early in the week centered around General Douglas
MacArthur's San Francisco return, after having been relieved of command
by President Truman. A report also generating much interest concerned
Navy plans to begin releasing involuntarily recalled Reservists in July,

starting with Air Reservists. Ensign Miller returned on Wednesday from his extended leave to discover that he had been promoted to Lieutenant, Junior Grade. He also proudly reported that he had bagged a bear while hunting!

Except for my name appearing on the shakedown list for the following week, things were generally uneventful. Unexpectedly, however, a separate matter affecting my off-duty status got my immediate attention. Approval of my request for a Wednesday, 18 April, standby replacement was denied by Chief Derry. He advised that I must make an immediate dent in the 12 punitive mid-watches I had been assigned for being late for muster. He very clearly said that I must, without delay, begin working off those penalty watches.

Many planes at that time were grounded awaiting parts, and the intensity of my tasks sharply increased. On Thursday, while hurrying around the base in the squadron pick-up truck obtaining vital parts I, unfortunately, also picked up a speeding ticket. Obviously, this was not my lucky week. The consequences of this infraction were uncertain but would most likely result in additional punishment — hopefully nothing to restrict my ability to go home at night. But that would remain to be seen. . . .

On Friday, all pilots participated in air group operations with two *Essex* landings each, and then a return to North Island. Friday was devoted to repairing planes, and Saturday to loading gear aboard the carrier for Monday's departure on the general squadron shakedown.

On Sunday afternoon at 1600, an expanded group of 117 men and 16 officers began boarding the *Essex*. Our squadron boarded a warship as a unit for the first time. The primary purpose of this exercise was to participate as a squadron in CAG-19X group air operations. All enlisted staff went aboard except for the four yeomen, who were to remain at the Air Station. I was assigned to be the yeoman — a signalman/clerk — while at sea. After boarding with our sea bags and getting settled, liberty was granted until 0200 the following morning. There was little incentive to leave, however, as it was rumored that reveille would be at 0300. The ship was scheduled to pull out on Monday morning for five consecutive days off the coast of San Diego.

Our assigned quarters aboard ship were surprisingly clean and fresh. Enlisted crew members were even able to utilize a modern head (toilet) facility. A modicum of privacy was afforded by screened toilets rather than the linear, open, trough-like standard shipboard fixture. This luxury was especially welcome. Each bunk was equipped with a flameproof cover that could simply be pulled over the bedding and tied, eliminating the need to make it up.

The crew spent a restless night — for many, the first aboard a ship of any type. Fortunately, Monday morning we were not awakened until 0530. Following breakfast and 0715 muster we went to our pre-assigned work stations while the ship pulled away from the NAS main dock. As we moved seaward, life quickly settled into a shipboard routine and most of us novices began to adjust to the unaccustomed feel of a moving deck under our feet.

Initially, my assignment was to procure parts or other materials for our squadron, which quickly helped orient me to the many nooks and crannies of the huge ship. Presumably, my interim yeoman duties would follow at some point. Battle-station drills occurred frequently during that first day and included numerous firings of the big ship's guns.

Our 15 pilots began to fly aboard for group exercises around 1300. I experienced, for the first time, the excitement of aircraft dropping out of the sky to abrupt stops on the pitching deck. I gained a real appreciation for the skills of our pilots accomplishing this routine but dangerous task. Despite cold weather conditions, I thoroughly enjoyed this first experience and found it difficult to leave my position on the island high above the flight deck and the bridge.

On our second day at sea we were roused from sleep at 0430 but, after reporting for work, some of us found little to do. Mechanics, ordnance-men, and others involved with flight operations had been up for some time and had plenty of chores. Battle stations sounded in late morning and, interspersed with flight operations, the shipboard tempo became very hectic. Initially, some of us had difficulty finding our battle stations, which, no doubt, was the reason for the repeated drills. I was never really certain exactly where mine was. Occasionally, meals offered during a prolonged call to battle stations took the form of field rations — called C rations — consisting of a small round tin of prepared food, which could be heated in the can. The food seemed nutritious, and it was tasty, but the small portions were inadequate for hungry young men. I often felt as if I hadn't eaten at all. When not in battle stations, I usually remained in my work-station office one deck below the flight deck. I could hear the loud thump of returning aircraft being recovered immediately above my head. Late in the day, it was announced that a group of our pilots were going to fly back to North Island for the night. I decided to send a letter to my wife via one of the men. Lieutenant Olof P. (Ed) Reed graciously provided air mail service for me by dropping my letter in a mail box ashore.

Normally the ship operated approximately 130 miles from the San Diego coastline, but occasionally it sailed close to Coronado Island. Daily operations had been routine until Wednesday afternoon, when we suddenly altered course and headed for a body of water referred to as the Coronado Crossroads. We anchored at this unmarked spot in the ocean, about 10 miles offshore. I could see the outlines of some San Diego buildings, including the El Cortez Hotel, but couldn't see my nearby apartment building. Fog hanging off the coastline contrasted with the clear, sunny weather we were experiencing at anchor. We were joined by some smaller ships, took aboard an inspection party, and departed the Crossroads around 1800, heading again out to sea. The inspection party had been brought aboard to evaluate the fitness of CAG-19X as part of the required Operational Readiness Inspection. On 26 April, the air group and each of its squadrons would be evaluated for operational readiness. The inspection was conducted by COMFAIRALAMEDA and Commander Carrier Air Group 5. Three strikes were flown during the day with our squadron participating in each. Although sometimes referred to as the "illegitimate air group," we were given a rating of "good." Considering our short time together, this was a score to be proud of.

We were always escorted by at least one destroyer. At one point we were accompanied by four destroyers, one cruiser, and one tanker. Accelerated battle exercises during the balance of the week often required flight operations personnel to report as early as 0200, and occasionally for some, at midnight. Shipboard life evolved into a rash of unexpected GQ's (General Quarters) — to man battle stations — accompanied by simulated attacks on the ship, and the launching and recovery of pilots for defensive or attack practice missions. On Thursday, our pilots flew missions from 0300 until securing at approximately 2200 hours. During battle periods, it seemed that all of the ship's guns, large and small at one time or the other, joined the action — shaking the ship with a deafening roar. On Friday, one GQ session lasted from 0800 until 1100. Lunch was followed by a meeting with the Skipper, where he expanded on his preceding day's announcement that we would be shipping out on 19 May.

The modernized *Essex* contrasted sharply with shipboard impressions garnered during earlier work parties on the *Valley Forge*. In addition to the improved restroom facilities and flight-crew escalators, the ship was clean and had intercom speakers in each compartment. We listened to radio programs such as "Dragnet" or, on one occasion, the New York Yankees *vs.* Boston Red Sox game. A newspaper containing the latest wire releases was distributed daily. Soda Fountain, library, and post-office services were available. A fair comparison between the "Happy Valley" and the *Essex* was not possible, however, as the former was making a quick combat turnaround and could hardly be like a newly refurbished ship.

Despite all the rumors floating about during the week that our cruise would be extended through the weekend or perhaps even another week, we headed home. About 15 members would be required to spend another day aboard the following week, however, for additional specialized training.

We were scheduled to arrive back at North Island around 1400, and our pilots departed the flight deck early. The rest of us were delayed by a need to complete shipboard gunnery exercises, but after all required ordnance had been expended, we headed home. Following some delicate maneuvering by channel tugboats, pushing the massive ship sideways up to the Air Station dock, we tied up around 1730. In retrospect, the cruise was not as bad as most of us had expected, and certain perquisites of "ship's stores," such as purchasing cigarettes for eight cents a pack, would be missed. The excitement of aircraft launch and recovery, clear skies, clean air, the ship's roiling white wake fanning out and blending with beautiful blue Pacific Ocean waters would be remembered.

Although the squadron as a unit had completed primary shakedown exercises aboard the *Essex*, we were not yet totally detached from the venerable warship. As planned, a small contingent of enlisted men remained aboard on Monday, 30 April, for the additional training; further training was also on tap for our pilots, as four flights of Corsairs were scheduled that evening for night flying operations aboard the carrier. The first of four flights took off from North Island around 2100 bound for night landing practice. Night flight operations secured around 2130 when the last flight returned to the NAS. Duty section crew tied down and refueled recovered aircraft before securing operations for the day at 2200.

During that same day, each member was required to fill out a form to be used in assessing future release of Reserves from active duty. The form requested responses to questions involving the desire to remain on active duty, World War II veteran status, organized Reserve pay status, and whether recalled voluntarily or involuntarily. Word was also received that not all of our transferred former mates had obtained their first choices of new duty stations. A few had been assigned to NAS Los Alamitos or NAS Miramar, and only one would be stationed at North Island. A number remained to be assigned by COMAIRPAC.

With our remaining days in the States numbered, special leave requests and 72-hour passes were liberally approved. I was granted Tuesday off to spend the day with Marie and to visit high school friends. My day off included a drive to Los Angeles and Hollywood, including typical tourist stops at Paramount and Columbia movie studios and two CBS radio shows. This fun day was unique for me and Marie because, not having a car, we had seen very little of Southern California during my Navy sojourn. A number of passes were also approved for the upcoming weekend, as many squadron members prepared to relocate their families. Electronics Petty Officer Ken Stanford had already spent the past weekend arranging for an apartment in the Bay Area for his wife and child.

My return to duty on Wednesday included a pre-deployment physical examination and two more shots. On the following day, 3 May, Squadron Executive Officer Lieutenant Cooper advised me that my speeding ticket on the station had resulted in a restriction from liberty for five days! However, the good news was that the five restriction days would be applied to time already spent aboard the *Essex*. While I was celebrating this decision, a number of transferees departed the squadron for new assignments. More significantly, a 12-member advance group led by the Skipper boarded flights for Japan to join the *Princeton* for early orientation to air group combat operations. On Friday, I met again with the Exec (Executive Officer) and he confirmed that he would officially inform the Air Station Security Office of my designated suspension days. He also properly cautioned me to drive more carefully. I was most grateful for the Exec's compassion. My remaining free time, in the dwindling days before deployment, could be spent with my wife rather than confined to the station.

Suddenly, realization that our remaining time in the States was growing short prompted crew members to seek any time off that could be obtained. Marie and I left for home on the 0845 flight Saturday morning, 5 May. A number of other squadron members had also boarded flights home for the 72-hour weekend.

After relaxing with family and friends and wrapping up personal business, Monday return flights carried many saddened Oaklanders back to San Diego, including Marie and me. All hands appeared to have returned on time for Tuesday morning muster; however, we later discovered that one of our flock was missing. We had "secured" — stopped — in the early afternoon from packing squadron gear and had returned to the barracks. At 1545, our missing member, Jim Blyler, appeared in the bunkroom — his space on a return Navy flight from the north had been canceled and he had scrambled to get a later one. Shortly after storing his gear, he turned himself in to the Duty Officer as "absent over leave" and was escorted to the Exec for appropriate action.

My work day concluded with a fifth successive mid-watch and advice that only two more remained to complete my sentence. During the watch I met an enlisted Reservist who had already spent 6½ months at sea on two carriers, and had recently returned with a *Valley Forge* squadron. His Regular Navy squadron and air group planned to move into our hangar after we departed, and he hoped to be released to inactive duty before his current squadron shipped out again.

With our future sealed, all squadron aircraft were turned in and flight operations suspended. Our pilots would next fly as a unit when the missions would be for real, rather than practice. Work assignments during remaining days of the week involved crating of packed gear for transfer to our troop transport, the USNS *General William Weigel* (TAP-119), shortly followed by a cleanup of our hangar spaces for use by squadrons of the incoming air group. My major tasks were to return all excess aircraft parts or other supplies to station stores. The circulating "word" was that we would ship out no later than Wednesday, 16 May. With no aircraft and most gear packed, there was little reason for us to remain any longer.

Our last weekend in the States commenced early Thursday, 10 May. Liberal approval of 72-hour passes was expected to result in an exodus of officers and crew heading for highway, airport, or railroad. After mustering at 0800 to complete a few remaining cleanup projects, we mustered again at 1000. Although some were required to report Saturday, most were released until Monday morning. I was one of those lucky to get the long weekend off, and Marie and I decided to spend it at home in the Bay Area. We obtained rail tickets and left aboard the "San Diegan." Our first rail trip together ended at 0645 the next morning at the Southern Pacific Station at Third and Townsend Streets in San Francisco. The night was long, and sleep uncomfortable, but as each click of the rail brought us closer to home, we didn't mind at all.

Our final weekend together was pleasant, but it was difficult for us not to focus on our upcoming separation. We did many family things, including Mother's Day activities and short visits with relatives. We also tried to settle arrangements for Marie after my departure. Early Friday afternoon, she was interviewed and selected for a typist job on the University of California, Berkeley, campus. She would start work the first of June, following her return from San Diego. We also visited the campus police department for her to sign the required oath, pledging loyalty to the U.S. government.

Our weekend in the Bay Area came to an early close on Sunday, 13 May. We were unable to get a flight later than 1715 and had to return to San Diego earlier than we wanted, but were thankful for this last visit home together.

Our final North Island days began Monday, 14 May, with muster at 0745. Because no work was assigned, the muster appeared to be largely for purposes of determining whether or not all hands had returned. We mostly sat around until 0930 when we were advised that we could leave for the day at 1000. While I was waiting for the station bus, Ensign Jacobsen — on his way to the barracks to see me — pulled up in his car. We drove around the station for awhile, reminiscing about old times, and then parked near the Security office. We chatted until 1030, until he had to leave, and I grabbed the 1040 "nickel-snatcher" (the slowest and cheapest ride) launch for home. It was enjoyable spending a few minutes with Jake who, despite his new officer rank, still remembered his old "white hat" friends. I spent the remainder of the day with Marie at Balboa Park, one of our favorite San Diego haunts.

After dinner we straightened up our apartment and took a cab to Lindbergh Field to meet my mother. The two most important women in my life had decided to share the painful goodbyes, pack up our remaining belongings, and return home together. Tuesday's muster was more of the same, except for confirmation that we would definitely depart the following day. After being paid, we were again released for the day at 1000. My final hours with my two beloved ladies were as pleasant as could be expected under the circumstances. We spent the afternoon at the park and the nearby San Diego Zoo. The day was capped off with a late evening dinner at the Brass Rail Restaurant. Despite the enjoyment, we dreaded the morrow.

The fateful deployment day, Wednesday, 16 May 1951, finally arrived.

The apartment goodbyes were very painful and, as a result, Marie and Mother decided to ride along with me in the taxi. They could go no further than the NAS Coronado gate, and I had to leave them there while the cabbie took me to my barracks. I directed him to deliver my two sad ladies to the Broadway Pier near Fleet Landing in San Diego, where we were expected to arrive within the next 90 minutes. We boarded buses to the Navy launch area, loaded our bags on the launch, and headed for Fleet Landing. The trip from Coronado Island was not a happy liberty boat ride, like the many times in the past. Upon arrival, we lined up and marched to the nearby dock where our troopship *Weigel* was moored.

Fortunately, my mother and Marie had made it back in time and were waiting. After dropping my bags in the designated area, I was able to spend a few more precious moments with them. It all came to a painful end at 0830 when we were mustered for roll call and pre-boarding. After final hugs, kisses, and more tears, I joined my mates, picked up my bags, and departed the pier area through the security gate. As I reached the top of the gangway, I looked back and noticed our young pilot Ensign John Moody lingering on the dock saying final goodbyes to his wife. He was one of the last members of our squadron to come aboard.

I quickly stored my gear in assigned compartment 5C and came back on deck to catch last glimpses of my loved ones. I finally located them on the more distant port side pier. We waved and, with a rudimentary sign language, communicated effectively until 1100 when they went to get something to eat. Around 1145 I saw them returning and motioned to them to move over to the other side of the ship, to the starboard side pier. After a few anxious moments of searching, while also trying to get a good rail position, I spotted them standing near a naval officer. My friend Ensign Gerald Jacobsen, had come to see us off, and had met them on the pier. The starboard pier was much closer, and thus we immediately had a pronounced improvement in our sign language system. Being directly opposite each other and close enough to see facial expressions, we quickly became adept at lip reading; and although we could not hear each others voices, we could effectively communicate what was in our hearts. It was a welcome but very painful experience.

The joy of our fleeting private communications was suddenly dampened by the clamor of a U.S. Marine Corps band and accompanying majorettes. The patriotic renderings, although inspiring, irreparably disrupted our remaining tender moments. As the band played on, remaining passengers and gear were boarded and the gangway silently removed. Before I realized it, the ship was inching away from the pier. Suddenly, at 1315 I could no longer read the lips or expressions of Marie and my mother, and the moment of truth was upon me. I was leaving — for only God knew how long. I also recognized that many of us would not come back. I waved my handkerchief, as if leaving on a cruise ship, in a vain attempt to brighten the spirits of my two ladies. As we pulled farther out into the bay, I continued to focus on the two diminishing figures I loved most. My eyes remained fixed on their tiny figures on the pier until I could no longer distinguish them from the crowd of others suffering through this awful moment. Vic Koss of our squadron later confided to me that his wife had been present to see him ship out once, and neither wanted to go through that emotional ordeal again. I continued to look at the pier in the foreground of a diminishing skyline until we left the bay around 1400. The last distinguishable objects I could identify were the El Cortez Hotel and, immediately in front of it, our apartment building. As we passed North Island and moved through the channel to the sea, I went below deck. My life had moved on to a new, uncertain phase.

Although it was rumored that the *Weigel* — often referred to as the "Wiggle-Waggle" — was a converted cruise ship, the accommodations were more akin to a cargo ship. We were the cargo. Our crew compartment was a large bay jammed with multi-tiered racks of bunks. Mine was at the bottom of a tier of four, which meant that occupants of the three above used it and succeeding ones, as steps. The bunks were very close together, with the one immediately above about 15 inches away. It was difficult to turn over during sleep, and larger men had to get out and reenter to change position. No lockers were provided, and we had to live out of our tightly packed sea bags.

We were issued a pink card captioned "MSTSP (Military Sea Transportation Service Personnel) Assignment Card and Meal Ticket," and "no meals will be served without this card," which was to be punched before each meal. The purpose of the card was unclear, because it didn't seem likely that there would be stowaways on a troopship wanting free meals! Menus published in the daily bulletin, the *Weigel Word*, sounded appetizing but somehow did not measure up to the billing. The enlisted crew ate their meals standing up at functional, shelf-like tables, provided to conserve limited space in the chow hall.

The ship, commanded by Captain N. P. Sorensen, provided a variety of services that included sick bay, library, musical instrument and game checkout, movies, lost and found, ship's store, twice-weekly Bingo games, and daily coffee time for officers and Chief Petty Officers. Chaplain Paul A. Lloyd, a Catholic priest, was in charge of daily religious services, and conducted the Rosary and Mass, as well as Protestant services. Despite the extremely crowded conditions, the Captain, officers, and crew attempted to make the voyage as comfortable as a trip aboard a troopship could be.

The *Weigel* carried approximately 20,000 barrels (840,000 gallons) of fuel oil, with an expected trip consumption of 8,000 barrels. Traveling at a normal speed of 19 knots, the ship consumed 1½ barrels (63 gallons) of fuel oil per mile. Water was consumed at a rate of 300 tons per day, with an onboard distilling plant producing 250 tons daily. Each propeller weighed 30,000 pounds and revolved 92 times per minute. During our voyage, Chief Engineer D. W. Deeds was in charge of the ship's physical plant.

Marines aboard ship represented the "9th Draft," a term designating a specific consignment of troops for deployment to a particular theater of operations. After a vigorous six- to eight-week training period, followed by individual training in scouting, patrolling, map reading, squad tactics, and night attacks, the Camp Pendleton Marines came in units to the draft. Although the majority would go into combat for the first time, most of the officers and non-commissioned officers had previous military service. After assignment to the draft, they underwent a four-day bivouac under combat conditions and handled aggressor attacks, infiltrations, and guerrilla warfare exercises. They were also taught combat in towns, tank-infantry coordination, and amphibious principles, and were lectured on cold weather operations.

In addition to the ground Marines, a draft of pilots, radar technicians, radiomen, and mechanics from the El Toro Marine air base also were aboard. Upon arrival at their assigned base at Korea's Pusan Air Field for duty with the 1st Marine Air Wing, many would be assigned to ground radar or maintenance activities. Pilots would be assigned to fly jets, night fighters, or serve on the ground with forward observers directing air support. Most of the men had never been together before. They formed eight platoons of 50 Marine officers, 1 Navy officer, 334 Marine enlisted men, and 18 Navy enlisted men in the aviation draft. About half of the officers were Reserves, and the majority of the enlisted were Regulars. Some would remain in Japan for assignment.

Later in the voyage, the first major medical operation was performed aboard ship, an appendectomy on 2nd Lieutenant L. C. Taft from the El Toro aviation detachment. The surgery took place Saturday evening, 19 May, and was successfully performed on a rolling sea by Dr. G. Cox assisted by two other physicians and two operating room technicians from the 9th replacement draft.

Our first full day at sea aboard the *Weigel* found us passing time on deck as, during the morning, we were ordered out of our compartment so that the cleaning could take place. There was no work for us to do, so most spent their time reading, playing cards, or writing letters. After dinner, a rumor started that outgoing mail would be taken off the ship and deposited at a "mail buoy" about 0015. Vic Koss was supposedly designated to collect the mail, and a flurry of letter writing immediately commenced. But this was apparently a prank, as there were no witnesses later to any mail transfer at sea or sighting of a buoy.

Around 2000 I observed another new activity underway in our compartment — haircutting. One of our squadron entrepreneurs, Raymond C. Wiley — a self-proclaimed tonsorial talent — had set up a busy private enterprise. He offered a specialty haircut, commonly referred to as a "mohawk," which essentially was a shaved head, except for a thick strip of hair down the middle. He found a particularly eager clientele among the Marine contingent, and was kept extremely busy. The novel haircut was not in vogue long, however, because within a few days, the haircuts were declared non-regulation, and a large number of bald heads suddenly appeared aboard ship.

Our shipboard days began with reveille at 0700, breakfast, then muster at 0900. Sleeping compartments were usually cleaned thereafter, requiring all hands to be on deck. Many attended religious services during the mornings, and the daily Rosary often drew 70 to 90 participants. Lifeboat training drills during the first week gave us something to do other than remembering to set our watches ahead one hour on designated days. Many of us who had never been to sea would stand on deck near the rails, to marvel at the clear, sunny skies and the smooth, beautiful sea. The sunshine glinting off the ship's wake in late afternoon was something to behold. If the accommodations on deck had been more spacious or more comfortable, one could possibly imagine — while reading or dozing in the sun — being aboard a cruise liner on an ocean crossing. Unfortunately, the hard steel decks ruined such visions.

On Saturday afternoon, a bunch of guys got together and played music on deck for our enjoyment. The weather was exceptional, and we grew to accept blue skies as the norm. We would soon find, however, that the sea was not always calm. Late Sunday morning, the ship began to roll heavily, and shaving with blade razors became difficult — if not dangerous. Many began to experience the first twinges of nausea caused by an increasingly turbulent sea.

After a few days in crowded conditions with little to do, many — including some of our own squadron members — began to get bored. The increasing need for something to occupy our time was apparently recognized on Tuesday, as 28 members of our squadron were assigned to mess duty. Our unit was one of the many Navy detachments ordered to provide men to relieve Marine personnel who had been performing these unpopular tasks since departure. I was one of those selected and was assigned to the butcher shop with airman Bob Perez. Bob, well tanned from sunning on the deck, was not particularly excited about chow-hall work, but was glad for some diversion. Once again, the butcher shop proved to be a more desirable mess assignment than duty in the serving line. We, at least, could move around in the performance of various meat-cutting or preparation tasks. This was preferable to standing in one place for up to three hours at a time, as Jim Blyler and Emil Cigliuti did, three times daily.

Despite the obvious unattractiveness of mess hall duty, no one complained very much. We were even grateful for the little blue tags which, when attached to our shirts, excused us from having to stand in long chow lines. Our status as mess cooks allowed us to go to the head of the line, get our food, and go right in to eat. The sea air seemed to enhance my appetite, making this a valued privilege. The downside of the assignment was that we had to report for work daily at 0600, for the balance of the voyage.

As the ship moved toward the International Dateline, we had advanced our watches a total of five hours; we would lose an entire day once the 180 degree meridian was crossed. As the ship churned through the waters toward our destination, the sea and the weather began to show signs of major change around noon, deteriorating as the day progressed and destabilizing the delicate stomach balance of most aboard. Seasickness afflicted many of us, and men could be seen vomiting over the side, in passageways, and in the heads. The turbulence also slowed our appetites, and the evening chow lines were noticeably shorter. Although many sailors and Marines got sick, and a number of others felt queasy, I felt fine and enjoyed a hearty dinner as usual. The rough weather was expected to continue throughout the night.

Wednesday, 23 May 1951, was my wife's birthday, but it never happened aboard the *Weigel*. We went to bed on the 22nd and, after a rough night during which we crossed the International Date Line, we awakened on Thursday, 24 May. Our crossing at sea automatically enrolled us as esteemed members of the Golden Dragon Society, a legendary chapter of the Seaman's Society. Traversing this invisible point in the ocean was significant only to mariners; those crossing by air were not eligible for membership. All aboard would receive a Golden Dragon certificate signed by our CO and by the Master and Transport Commander of the vessel. This instantaneous loss of 24 hours would be regained in the same manner upon our return. The ship was running away from the sun, and upon crossing the 180 degree meridian, we were halfway around the world from Greenwich, England, where worldwide time is set. Although I was pleased to be a member of the mythical organization, I was disappointed not sharing Marie's birthday with her and that the day had even ceased to exist for me. I felt as if I had undergone a compressed Rip Van Winkle experience.

Most of the men in the squadron believed we were on the downhill side of our military assignment. Our training was complete and its effectiveness would soon be put to the acid test. One of the guys in the butcher shop told me that his CO, the CAG Commander, had advised his unit that the air group would be operating a total of 90 days, and then be relieved, and sent home in September. This was consistent with the original deployment dispatch received by Ed Watson. Many squadron members believed we would be released a month or two after our return.

Rumors continued to be created and actively circulated, and life aboard became repetitious, as we steamed toward our new home, the USS *Princeton*. I became a creature of habit, both in the religious and recreational sense. I routinely went to daily Mass accompanied by "Cig" Cigliuti and/or Bob Perez. I played all 20 games in the two sessions of Bingo scheduled during each week. Despite all the practice, I failed to win a thing. So much for experience! Canasta in the compartment with Doug Miller, Jim Blyler, and Bob Perez consumed many of my off-duty hours, until I was pretty well burned out with games.

On Friday evening in the Officers Salon, the ship's orchestra blended seven variety acts to produce a "Show of Shows." On Saturday evening, our fellow shipmates presented a musical variety show in the mess hall for the enlisted men. Sunday was a busy day in the butcher shop, cutting up pork chops; but on Monday there was little to do. Perez and I spent most of the day playing several games of Hearts with our boss, the civilian Chief Butcher. My last night aboard the *Weigel* was unceremoniously spent packing up, and playing yet more cards. I was ready for a different routine.

We were awakened at 0500 Tuesday morning, 29 May, had breakfast, and cleaned up our compartments. Later, most of us went up on deck to view the many islands the ship was passing en route to Tokyo Bay. As daylight increased, I was awed by the majestic sight of Mt. Fuji soaring 12,388 feet into the sky, crowned by a snow-covered summit. The mountain, in addition to being exceptionally beautiful, is also considered sacred by many Japanese. It was truly an inspiring gateway to Japan, a country still under World War II military occupation by the United States. Six of every seven square miles in Japan are covered by mountains, we were told. Although they enhance the beauty of the country, so much land is taken up by them that cities are overcrowded, and there is less land to use for farming.

As we entered Tokyo Bay, I quickly found the exhilarating image created by the mountain displaced by strong, pungent odors. The smells were coming from the bay waters which were then reportedly used for disposal of raw sewage.

We tied up at the Yokosuka Naval Base, about 30 miles south of Tokyo and a former major Japanese Imperial Navy installation, and moored at a dock directly across from the ship that would become our home for the next few months. The battle-hardened *Princeton*, with her large black numerals "37" on the island structure, was waiting for her new air group. Both docks at the base had berthed warships of the mighty Japanese Imperial fleet just a few short years earlier during World War II. But since the end of the war, the piers routinely housed and supported 50 to 60 U.S. vessels — carriers, escort and supply ships, destroyers, cruisers, and battleships. Plans were underway to headquarter the major naval command of the Far East in Yokosuka, thereby establishing it as a large U.S. naval center.

After securing the *Weigel* to the pier, we were greeted by a military band, and shortly thereafter, the Skipper, Lieutenant Commander Harrison, and Lieutenant Junior Grade Miller came aboard. They welcomed us and provided a quick political and cultural overview of the country we would shortly be visiting. The realities of war were also quickly brought home as they informed us that one of our pilots, Personnel Officer Lieutenant Horace Hawkins, had been shot down and was presumed killed in action. Lieutenant Miller advised us that the Skipper also had crash-landed, but was fortunate to be rescued in Korea, by a Navy plane. The fact that we had already lost two planes and one pilot, and had not yet functioned as an operational unit, was distressing.

The voyage aboard the *Weigel* could not be rated as smooth, considering that many had felt pretty bad at times, but during our journey, friendships were made with people from all over the country. Some would remain together in combat units but most would not. Chaplain Lloyd was praised for his tireless prayers, consolation, and advice, and for listening to the troubles and concerns of all who sought him out, irrespective of religion. Captain Sorenson and his crew did their best to make the trip enjoyable, providing what many believed was well above average troopship food, and an active entertainment program.

*The war news during the trip had also inspired hope for those soon to enter action. The daily bulletin reported the battleship **New Jersey**'s return to action, the Communist abandonment of their spring offensive and subsequent retreat, a successful Allied offensive, which thrust across the 38th Parallel into North Korea, and the virtual collapse of Red resistance along the Korean battlefront. While our immediate concerns centered on the safety of our squadron's pilots and men, our thoughts and prayers also went with the many Marines aboard who would soon be in the thick of the ongoing action on the ground.*

We disembarked with our bags around 1000 and were driven by truck the short distance to the *Princeton*. A muster was held on the dock, to make certain all hands were present, and within 15 minutes we boarded. Our first task was to locate bunks and lockers in the various designated sleeping compartments below deck. Unfortunately, my choices were already assigned. Aviation storekeeper Kenneth Colwell was similarly affected and we had to make do with the Squadron materiel shack, located under the flight deck, where we would sleep on cots that night. Jim Blyler and Bob Perez helped me move my gear to the distant location.

The big event for all of us was receiving mail that had been forwarded while we were en route. I was elated to find 11 letters waiting for me. In one, my wife advised me that she and my mother had returned to the Bay Area the Wednesday evening we departed San Diego. On the spur of the moment, they had quickly packed up our remaining belongings and hurried to the airport.

After getting organized and enjoying a fresh-water shower, I changed into my white uniform. Blyler, Perez, and I went on liberty for the first time in Japan. I converted five dollars into 1,800 yen at a rate of 360 yen to the dollar at the Naval Station administration building, and felt rich with the handful of large paper currency. We strolled for a while around the adjacent town of Yokosuka, checking out various shops. We wanted to expand our exploration as time permitted and decided to take a train on the Yokohama. First, however, we felt a compelling need to quench our thirst for cold beer at the Enlisted Mens Club. I, unrealistically, had my taste buds set for Burgermeister, my favorite local beer from home, but none was available so I had to settle for Heineken!

Our 45-minute trip to Yokohama cost only 100 yen, and we were directed to the military car, restricted to occupation troops. The car was very comfortably outfitted with leather seats and large windows. As we traveled through the countryside, I was surprised at how the contours of the hills and green slopes reminded me of California. Along the way, I was able to get a good view of some of the farms and small towns of rural Japan. Our train traveled at speeds averaging between 50 to 60 mph, on a route that took us through nine tunnels. Upon arrival, a small Army bus ride took us from the station into town where we sought direction to the Post Exchange

(PX), but it had already closed at 1700. We were referred to a second destination, the "Sokura Port," commonly referred to as the "Service Club." After much walking, we finally found the American music dance club, approved by the Army for occupation personnel. We spent our time drinking excellent Japanese beer at 120 yen per bottle, eating hard-boiled eggs, and listening to familiar music played by Japanese musicians. Later, we were joined by squadron mates John Young, Kenneth Wolfe, and a group of U.S. Army Reservists. Our squadron group left at 2130, transported by rickshaws, for the train station and the return to Yokosuka. A number of others from the air group and the Chaplain's assistant from the *Weigel* also returned on our train. We reboarded the *Princeton* at 2340 after a too brief, but enjoyable, glimpse of Japan.

The plan of the day for Wednesday, 30 May, was to get organized and assume our duties as soon as possible. I spent the morning hours getting acquainted with the huge ship, and storing essential gear. I obtained basic office supplies so that Colwell and I could procure parts and equipment on demand and moved numerous parts catalogs and files to our office, located adjacent to a catwalk below the flight deck port catapult. One positive note, other than receiving four more letters from home, was the completion of my "sentence" of watches. Chief Derry advised that he would allow me to count my unscheduled 1600 to 2000 flight deck watch that evening as my seventh and final mid-watch. I was glad to finally get this monkey off my back.

Our first full day aboard the *Princeton* was essentially a day of quiet preparation. We were all mentally readying ourselves to go to sea, this time not for training or transport, but for war. Our tedious training exercises were complete, and the following day we would weigh anchor for the war zone, to carry out our role as safely and effectively as possible. We hoped to return to the Yokosuka base in about 40 days, for a five- or six-day stay of rest and replenishment. Our view of Japan was so brief that it almost didn't qualify as a visit. There was much yet to be seen of this beautiful and historic country.

Although the news from the frontlines had recently been encouraging, no one could predict the unknown risks for our fliers that might be present two days hence when we joined TF-77 off the coast of Korea. Although our squadron had been mobilized as an organized unit and we had initially lacked equipment, our personnel complement was below the strength required for Regular units. We also were rusty on current procedures and combat tactics. Fortunately, we did not have to learn about new planes, as did other recalled Reserve units. A key objective in achieving combat readiness had always been to ensure pilot safety, as completely as possible. We believed that our maintenance and other support crews were well versed in preparing the aircraft. The overall goal was to provide the best-prepared planes and pilots possible.

We were confident that our training had been intense and thorough, but in war even the best may not be enough. We had already lost one of our flight family, and we shortly would go to sea "for keeps." Our intense preparations would need to be more than adequate to do the job successfully, without further casualties. We had come a long way, and were confident that the transition, from weekend civilian outfit to full-fledged fighting unit, was complete.

Chapter 5

War Zone
May-July 1951

*L*AST-MINUTE *preparations for departure from Yokosuka were evident aboard the* **Princeton** *on the morning of Thursday, 31 May. The carrier's abbreviated visit was concluded and many crew members were hurriedly completing letters prior to pulling out. Mailing limitations, similar to those experienced aboard the* **Weigel**, *would soon be in effect. Mail deposited after 0800 in the ship's post office would be held until our first replenishment operation. At sea, mail routinely would be transferred every three or four days during replenish-*

ment, or other transfer operations. Letters deposited in port had to be stamped with proper postage, but at sea, mail was free.

One busy writer was Airman Charles Stein, a slender, sandy-haired young Reservist from Pennsylvania, called up in November and assigned to VF-871. Shortly after boarding the carrier the previous day, Stein had received a waiting telegram from his wife advising that he was the father of twin boys. Needless to say, his quiet personality quickly became animated. He promptly set out to find the Skipper, Lieutenant Commander Harrison, within the unsettled quarters assigned the squadron, and excitedly displayed the telegram. Only two hours after his arrival, he was requesting emergency leave to go home. As would have been expected, the Skipper's response was, "Hell no, you just got here!"

With the brief liberty behind us and settling in complete, most were up at 0600 for breakfast. Final supplies were brought aboard as the crew completed remaining pre-sailing tasks. Shortly after 0800, gangways and lines were removed and we pulled away from our pier.

As the *Princeton* steamed out of Tokyo Bay, a day earlier than expected, en route to the Sea of Japan — the operating area for Task Force 77 — we considered where we had been and where we expected to go. Our pilots, after many training takeoffs and landings, would now use for real the skills gained during the preceding months. Upon our arrival in Japan, Lieutenant (JG) Dan Miller had reported that some of our pilots had already been tested under fire. During the uneventful return trip to Korea, we learned the extent of the advance contingent's combat action. The six men flown to the war zone ahead of us had included four pilots who were immediately pressed into action with CAG-19 — Skipper Lieutenant Commander Harrison and Lieutenants F. W. Calhoun, H. M. Hawkins, and F. Martin III. They were accompanied by Lieutenant (JG) Miller and Chief Petty Officer Ed Lilian.

Shortly after arriving aboard the carrier, the Communists — the Reds — launched their second spring offensive, and thus all available pilots were needed to fly close air support missions. VF-871's four aviators were quickly assigned to augment the *Princeton*'s two Corsair squadrons. On 16 May, one squadron pilot was assigned to combat air patrol (CAP) and two to a highway strike in the Yonkung area. The CAP was uneventful, but the strike planes reported that four railway cars were blown from their tracks. An enemy airfield and three planes were also reported damaged. On the next day, a flight of our four pilots was again assigned to a strike.

They damaged a highway bridge and bypass, and destroyed three buildings. Later, one of our squadron pilots joined a close air support mission in the area south of Singosan.

On Friday, 18 May, while on his second mission — a napalm run — the F4U flown by Lieutenant Hawkins from Berkeley was hit by ground anti-aircraft fire in the Chanjon area, 55 miles northeast of Seoul. He safely parachuted out of badly damaged plane 314 (Bureau number 81709) at 3,000 feet, but was behind enemy lines. While descending to the ground, he was hit by enemy small arms fire. Navy planes flew protective cover over him for two hours and attempts were made to recover him with a helicopter, but they were unsuccessful because the helicopter was driven off by small arms fire from Chinese infantrymen. The covering pilots observed Lieutenant Hawkins immobile and bleeding heavily from one leg. He was listed as missing in action and presumed dead. The Skipper's plane, 312 (Bureau number 97053), was also hit on the same mission by groundfire and his Corsair badly damaged. He was, however, able to remain aloft and managed to reach an emergency air strip. The small field, designated as K-18, was a forward airstrip 60 miles south of the 38th Parallel, bordering the village of Kangyoung. As he attempted an emergency landing, he encountered Air Force planes preparing to take off and unexpectedly had to pull up. As a result, he was forced to retract his landing gear and execute a successful pancake landing. He got out safely, but the normally durable Corsair was wrecked. Lieutenant Commander Harrison was uninjured and was shortly picked up by a Navy plane. The quick pick-up was fortunate because the airstrip was recaptured by the Reds that night. For the day, the four squadron pilots had demolished four trucks and had left fifty others burning, but lost one pilot and two planes.

The advance contingent of our pilots flew a total of 15 missions until the end of the offensive and the return of the *Princeton* to Yokosuka. Details of these first combat missions understandably produced concerns among others of our well-trained but yet untested pilot cadre. Squadron members expressed hope that Lieutenant Hawkins somehow might have survived. Most believed that until the area was retaken, and he — or his body — was recovered, we should hope for the best.

Aboard the *Princeton*, on that first day out from Yokosuka, the ship reflected a "de-mothballing" freshness. Accommodations in the crew sleeping compartment were clean, and I was finally assigned a bunk and locker, after having spent the first night in the matériel office. The office was large enough for Colwell and me to work in, but reasonably could accommodate only one sleeper at a time, and visitors, requisitioning parts or just socializing, dropped in day and night.

Our first flight operations began on Friday afternoon, 1 June, and our pilots flew for more than two hours. My remote work location under the flight deck was adjacent to an unused deck-edge gun tub, and thus I soon satisfied my fascination with aircraft operations, watching air group planes take off and land. During flight operations there was usually little supply work to be done but, after recovery, we busily requisitioned and picked up parts. Although the *Princeton* was nearly identical to the *Essex*, the initial parts-chasing duties allowed me to get used to the ship's unique characteristics. I was assigned special shoes and a yellow sweater, permitting me access to the flight deck during air operations. Jim Blyler initially was scheduled for rotating two-hour shifts in the flight deck island structure where during flight operations he would track the availability of aircraft by squadron. Between shifts, he often would cross the flight deck and spend time with us at any hour of the day or evening. He and others soon discovered that our small, quiet, out-of-the-way compartment was an excellent location from which to write letters home.

Maintenance crew members worked late into the evening on the flight deck, getting planes ready for upcoming TF-77 operations, and as we moved closer to the combat zone, we commenced blackout conditions after dark. By this time our air group had been officially designated CAG-19, no longer 19X.

Early Saturday morning, 2 June, I was sent to retrieve a 90-pound coil of rope stored deep in a hold at the lowest level of the ship. With two helpers, I manually moved the coil upward one deck at a time, until we finally got it to the hangar deck. Delivery to the flight deck then was easy — we simply placed the coil on the deck edge elevator along with a plane and rode up with it.

Through the overcast early that morning we observed a destroyer that would accompany us until we joined Task Force 77 later in the day, at approximately 1100. In addition to two other *Essex*-class carriers, the Task Force consisted of many other U.S. warships, including a battleship, two cruisers, and 14 destroyers. The destroyers, affectionately referred to as "tin cans," principally provided protection from enemy submarines.

We would be operating with two familiar all-Reserve air groups, the *Boxer*'s CAG-101 and our former CAG-102, which included Oakland's

VF-874, aboard the *Bon Homme Richard*. We had trained with both groups at North Island, and occasionally we would see their familiar air group tail markings as their planes flew near our ship. The large white letter codes, "A" for CAG-101 and "D" for CAG-102, would be routine for us again — this time in a much different environment. In addition to our own large "B" tail designation for CAG-19, planes in our air group were also identified by unique color codes. The forward section of the engine cowling and the upper tip of the vertical tail were marked with distinctive colors for each squadron. VF-23 used red markings, VA-55 green, VF-821 white, and our VF-871 blue.

Ten of the twelve squadrons serving aboard the three carriers then deployed in TF-77 were Reserves, a most unusual array of combat fighting units. VF-821 and VF-871 comprised the Reserve Squadron contingent of CAG-19, and VA-55 and VF-23 represented Regular Navy squadrons.

Not long after joining us on 2 June, six of our pilots took off at 1345 to fly their first official squadron missions in Korea. It was a beautiful flying day, and planes from our air group joined those from the other two carriers in a coordinated attack. Four of our planes made a rail strike, while the other flight of two planes directed naval gunfire reported or "spotted" in the Tanchon-Sonjin area. All of our fliers returned unscathed at 1650, reporting a railroad bypass damaged, a main track knocked out, and other targets damaged. On the way back, our Exec, Lieutenant Cooper, observed an ox cart suspected of transporting enemy supplies and also reported this target destroyed.

During flight operations our Task Force operated 30 to 40 miles off the Korean coast. The flight deck at such times was both busy and dangerous and was no place for those untrained or lacking specific need to be there. Many highly skilled men scurried about performing precise duties. Plane pushers handled the difficult physical work, quickly respotting aircraft on the deck to make room for recovering aircraft. Helicopters continually circled the ship in case a water recovery was necessary. I quickly learned that the gun tub and catwalk adjacent to my work station were as close to the action as an untrained person needed to be!

Our first Sunday at sea with the Task Force, 3 June, began with intensified air operations from all three *Essex*-class carriers. Shortly after 0400, the *Princeton* launched its F4U-5N Corsair pre-dawn morning "heckler" flights. Major elements of the strike operations plan followed later, with

Squadron VF-871 parachute riggers John T. Young and Jerry D. Irwin at work on an F4U-4 Corsair aboard the USS *Princeton* (CV-37). (Courtesy, J. Edward Watson)

the catapulting of F9F Panther jets. The port catapult on the flight deck was immediately adjacent to my work station gun tub, and where I watched the jets being fired off from both steam catapults.

Initial jet missions included circling the Task Force as combat air patrol to intercept unidentified planes or carry out photo reconnaissance tasks. The F4U-4 fighter-bombers, including six from our squadron, roared down the deck after the jets. Our Skipper assumed the lead of a flight of planes launched at 0800. The Corsairs were followed in close order by the mission's final component of Skyraiders. Mission objectives included another attack on bridges deep in North Korea and close air support for Marine ground troops.

CAG-102, aboard the *Bon Homme Richard*, was observed losing a plane during launch; crew members from our ship saw a Corsair take off, and then suddenly crash into the sea. Although the area was immediately searched by helicopter and escorting destroyers, from our vantage point we were unable to determine if the pilot had been rescued. We hoped that he was not from Oakland squadron VF-874.

While our strike was in the air, the flight deck was quickly cleared. Remaining spare and standby planes were either spotted forward or taken to the hangar deck. Crew members then took advantage of an anticipated three-hour lull in air operations to clean up as many regular duties as possible. I completed a number of pending parts-chasing tasks and went to Mass at 1100, unaware that I could have attended an earlier service at 0700. Sunday services normally were conducted on the hangar deck, unless there was a conflict with flight operations. On this occasion, most planes were on the flight deck for morning operations and space was available on the hangar deck for a larger congregation. During heavy operating days, church facilities were usually restricted to the small library, where services were repeated to accommodate all those desiring to attend. On this Sunday, a large cloth background imprinted with a cross was hung against a bulkhead behind the altar and folding chairs set up. Efforts to establish a church-like atmosphere were most effective, especially when augmented by recorded organ music.

As the strike aircraft began returning, the *Princeton* headed into the wind at 31 knots. The jets approaching at 110 knots were guided to recovery by the Landing Signal Officer (LSO). After an arresting gear cable was caught by a returning plane's tail hook, the nylon Davis barriers stretching across the deck from the island — to catch "bolters" — were dropped. Pilots quickly taxied over them to the deck-edge elevator for transfer to the hangar deck below. The air group recovery process continued as the propeller planes returned, first the ADs, and then the F4Us. As each one securely caught an arresting wire, the steel cable barriers used for prop planes were lowered. Each plane was hurriedly taxied or pushed forward for deck spotting or removal to the hangar deck, depending on deck and aircraft conditions. Landing planes requiring repairs were taken below and spotted in hangar deck spaces aft. All returning pilots were promptly debriefed in squadron ready rooms, and vital data concerning damage and destruction of enemy facilities and troops were assembled to facilitate future strike planning.

Another series of strikes was launched in the afternoon, with all planes returning safely. The flight operations were secured for the day around 1500, and the ship immediately commenced replenishment. During the day, two flights of four squadron planes each had been assigned to combat air patrol, and two flights of two to close air support missions. One flight of four planes also had gone on a bridge strike in the Tanchon area.

My duties had been relatively light during the afternoon so I spent most of my time on the catwalk observing strike launch and recovery, and the deck activity between flights. The flight deck during operations was a very exciting, but dangerous, place, but because I might one day need to be up there on an assigned task, I felt a need to at least get a sense of what went on. I was also curious as to how the whole process worked. I watched refueling and replenishment operations from the island for about half and hour and found that fascinating, too. A tanker ship pulled up on one side of us, and a destroyer on the other. Hoses were connected and fuel transferred — tanker to carrier to destroyer — in about three hours. Ammunition loading continued on into the night, with some squadron members assigned to that detail until 0200. Despite the many materials transferred to our ship during these hours, there was no mail.

The 1800 evening newscast on the ship's intercom system had announced that a flight of two Skyraiders and two Corsairs had been led by our Skipper, Lieutenant Commander Harrison, and was praised by the Commander of the UN ground troops for some of the best close air support he had seen. South of Kumhwa, under the guidance of ground controllers, the flight had napalmed extensive enemy entrenchments on a mountain ridge. The Reds were driven from cover and the flight returned to attack them again with machine-gun fire. Other large concentrations of troops were strafed and rocketed.

A post-operation assessment indicated that all the *Princeton* fliers did well during the day. Skyraiders and Corsairs knocked out two spans from a highway bridge at Pachung-jang. Morning flights attacking a train had severely damaged the engine and two cars and had destroyed two others. Seven trucks and seven ox carts had been damaged. Bombs and strafing had damaged one artillery position, and undetermined damage had been inflicted upon a breakwater at Sonpyong-ni in a similar attack. The aggregate results were top-flight for the "new" CAG-19 on its first full day of activity.

Results for all TF-77 air operations were most impressive, as nine bridges — most on the rail line between Hamhung and Wonsan — had been wrecked, or heavily damaged, before noon. On the east coast between Kosong and Kansong, Navy fliers also attacked troop and artillery positions, inflicting casualties and much damage during strafing runs on ten gun positions northeast of Inje. Air operations supplemented heavy bombardment by surface ships of targets northeast and east of Kosong, Wonsan, and Songjin, north to Chongjin.

Air operations on Monday, 4 June, were much like Sunday except that the *Boxer* detached from the Task Force and headed for "R & R" in Yokosuka. She was expected to rejoin us in ten days. R & R is a military term referring to the temporary detachment of personnel, or vessels, from combat zones. Assignment to more peaceful ports, or other rear areas, allows for rest and recuperation of soldiers and sailors, and resupply or repair of equipment. Recreation usually is a big component in this package.

Once again, on the 4th, a full day of flying was on tap for our pilots, but with one less air group. Operations were launched mid-morning into overcast skies and Task Force pilots struck at obscured targets over the length of Communist-held Korea. The series of close air support and interdiction strikes were scheduled to continue until 2100. Corsairs and Skyraiders, flying in a prebriefed strike, placed 250-pound bombs inside a tunnel far to the north, at Chowhan-dong. Another strike destroyed a rail bridge near Pukkan-dong with 250- and 500-pound bombs. Later, despite closing weather, Corsairs and Skyraiders battered marshaling yards and rail facilities with bombs, rockets, napalm, and strafing. A boxcar, building, and section of track were destroyed. Other strikes damaged rolling stock and rails. Near Sinpo, Panthers flying an armed reconnaissance mission fired rockets and damaged a Russian-built T-34 tank.

During the day, squadron pilots were assigned to three flights of two planes each to close air support in the Kojo area. One flight of six planes launched a bridge strike around Songjin. Two flights directed naval gun-fire at Wonsan, and one flight of four planes was sent on combat air patrol. It was a busy day for VF-871 and all *Princeton* fliers! In addition, the battleship *New Jersey* blasted away at coastal targets much of the day. And air group crew on the *Princeton* got a first look at the shores of Korea as we steamed close enough at times to clearly see beaches without the aid of field glasses.

Rumors and fact about our future status continued to swirl wildly about the ship. A sailor from VF-821 advised me that he had good information projecting our arrival back in the States around 10 September. The *Princeton's Morning Press News* reported that General Headquarters, Far East Command, had announced a Reserve phase-out program whereby enlisted personnel would be shipped to the U.S. in time to be released from active duty no later than 31 December. The catch was that this release would not apply to Reservists recalled involuntarily as members of Reserve units.

News of the release program did not stir up much chatter because it did not appear to apply to anyone in our unit. Most of us were content to finish our sea-duty tour, even if it amounted to six months, and then worry about release. We had been aboard the *Princeton* for only a short time but had already acquired a certain comfort level. The "Sweet Pea," as our ship was known, was generally believed to be the most non-regulation ship in the Task Force, because there were no annoying regulations regarding dress, other than safety, and no overly restrictive rules regarding eating or sleeping. Most importantly, we didn't have to wear hats. And even during air operations, food could usually be obtained in the chow hall, almost anytime, day or night. On a personal level, the afternoon of the 4th, after 1630 Mass, the Catholic Chaplain, Commander R. F. McManus, spotting my name on my shirt, made me feel at home by calling out, "Well, how are you, Coop?" This type of easygoing greeting — in contrast to the usual rigid military protocol — was commonplace aboard ship and helped to instill a sense of camaraderie and minimize the usual anxiety.

Our air group's first three days of combat air operations had been successful and without losses. On Tuesday, 5 June, *Princeton* aircraft began another long day of flying at 0900, targeting Red troops, gun positions, and rail facilities. Strike operations were scheduled to continue until 2230. One flight of Skyraiders and Corsairs joined up with a destroyer to attack four gun positions near Sang-ho, destroying one, with undetermined damage to others. Strikes near Puin-ni damaged a locomotive, two rail bridges, and an antiaircraft position. Another strike bombed a railway station, damaged eight boxcars, and started oil fires in a marshaling yard. Panther jets strafed lumber piles, gun positions, and damaged a rail bridge near Togsang. One flight of six VF-871 planes made a railroad strike at Sinpo. One flight of four made a strike at Chowan, and a flight of four flew combat air patrol; two planes in one flight provided close air support near Pyongyang. Most flights encountered antiaircraft fire, but all squadron aircraft returned safely from the day's missions.

A returning F9F-2B (Bureau number 123618) from our air group crashed while attempting to land, chilling the satisfaction of an otherwise successful day. At 1942, while on its final approach, the plane's altitude relative to the deck was too low. The pilot received a wave-off, a signal from the Landing Signal Officer to climb and go around again, but the low-flying Panther jet lacked necessary airspeed. The nose and cockpit section of the misaligned aircraft made contact near the edge of the flight deck ramp, on the after starboard side. The fuselage was shattered by the impact, and trailing sections of the broken craft dropped onto the fantail (stern) gun mounts below the flight deck. General Quarters was still in effect and the gun mounts, unfortunately, were still manned. The jet's exploding fuel tanks splashed burning fuel across the stern of the ship, including the flight deck. VF-871 mechanics on the flight deck saw a crew member jump from the flames into the sea, where a hovering helicopter quickly recovered him. Several onboard personnel were severely burned, and were immediately transferred to sick bay. The eight injured men included those who were at their fantail gun stations. The pilot, Ensign Philip S. Randolph, Jr., USN, who was believed to have been thrown into the water, was not sighted and presumed lost.

Although my duty station was well forward of the accident area, Jim Blyler, at his aircraft status board station in the island, clearly heard the crash described over his headset link with flight deck arresting gear crew. Jim looked out of the connecting hatch to the flight deck and saw flames spreading along the wooden deck from the impact point to forward of the arresting gear section. After viewing the devastation, he returned to the board and marked "strike" next to the number of the destroyed jet. A *Newsweek* magazine journalist aboard at the time witnessed this definitive action. Jim's father later mailed him a copy of the article reporting this act of finality. (*Time* magazine also reported a before-dawn launch of a Cor-

sair off the port catapult into the sea, producing a similar chalk-board notation in the air operations office below decks.)

Well-trained firefighters from ship's company responded quickly to the
Panther mishap, and, after some effort, extinguished the fire at 1951. The
flight deck was then promptly inspected for damage and debris was
removed. The burned hulk of the jet's forward section was pushed from
the flight deck over the side. Aircraft recovery operations, necessarily suspended during the cleanup period, were completed at 2007. The tragic
incident reminded us of the dangers inherent in shipboard flight operations.

We were advised that another plane would not make it back — VF-821
had lost an aircraft while making a forced landing in Korea. The pilot was
uninjured, but the Corsair was wrecked.

On Wednesday, the 6th, I found the need to visit sick bay to obtain treatment for my left shin, injured while I was climbing down a ladder. The
wound had become infected and I had developed a high fever, but the
medics had to attend first to the many critically burned patients from the
day before. The pungent odor of scorched flesh permeated the close air in
the ward. The sight of many men, bandaged as if they were mummies, was
overwhelming. My feelings of sorrow and pity were strong for these men,
whose pain was doubtless excruciating. I was thankful I could be treated
as an outpatient and return to duty. Despite the excellence of facilities and
care, one of the burn victims died during the morning, and his body was
flown back to Japan.

The *Princeton*'s sick bay had the latest and finest equipment to perform
all but the most specialized surgery. Commander J. O. Thatcher was the
Medical Officer for the Task Force, and seriously afflicted patients came
from all Task Force ships. Doctors, technicians, and key corpsmen of the
ship's H Division provided support to the vital medical department. At
sea, the 50-bed ward averaged 30 patients.

Flight operations on the 6th continued at a hectic pace that produced
accelerated aircraft maintenance requirements. Seven squadron flights,
involving 17 planes, flew a variety of missions during the day including
combat air patrol, naval gunfire spot, railroad and highway strikes, antisubmarine, and even a message drop.

A rash of instrument failures seemed to occur all at once. I was able to
procure a variety of instruments and other aircraft parts; however, one
necessity presented a challenge. I was requested by Lieutenant (JG) Miller

to get a left Corsair wing, a major component not likely to be easily found in — or transported from — an average ship's storeroom. Although the wing to be replaced was not battle-damaged, it had three unrepairable broken struts and flying the aircraft in this condition would be dangerous. A replacement wing was not available aboard and thus had to be ordered from a special Task Force supply ship, the USS *Jupiter* (AVS-8), the only aviation supply ship in the entire Fleet. The day's operations concluded uneventfully, except for a mid-day ditching, followed by a landing incident. At 1244 an AD4 Skyraider (Bureau number 123931) was reported down in the water about 40 miles north of the formation. The pilot was in a life raft and not apparently injured. Then later in the day, during recovery operations, an F9F (Bureau number 123600) missed the arresting cables and crashed into the barriers. The impact had damaged the right wing and tip tank, but the rest of the plane and the pilot were okay. Flight deck crash crews quickly cleared the damaged plane and debris, repaired the barriers, and recovery operations resumed.

Thursday, 7 June, dawned, not as another day of hectic air operations, but one that air group personnel looked upon as a holiday. The entire Fleet was at rest from combat because the time was reserved for major replenishment. Continuous day, and occasional night, operations required tons of fuel, ammunition, food, and other supplies, which had to be quickly replaced. Large attack bombers such as the Skyraider, and newly introduced jet aircraft, presented new storage problems. These bombers could carry five times the load of World War II naval aircraft, and the new jets often consumed ten times the fuel of the largest piston engines — thus replenishments were required more frequently to maintain continuous combat operations. The 7th, therefore, was set aside for rendezvous with tankers and cargo vessels; lines were shot across the sea, and fuel and supplies transferred. Once supplies had been moved from ship to ship over the lines, they were hauled primarily by the hand labor of ship's crew. Bombs, rockets, and boxes were lifted, pushed, or dragged over deck space to reach designated storage areas. Early in the process, bombs of many sizes covered most of the hangar deck. Large bombs, including some 2,000-pounders, ended up being stored in the chow hall until needed and were occasionally seen being used as foot rests during meals. In addition to the time-consuming transfer of fuel and ordnance, aviation and general supplies were also loaded.

Some of our long-awaited mail was brought aboard in late morning, and in mid-afternoon, we were greeted with a second mail call. My mail included a package from home containing photos, candy, cigars, books, and a compact peg game set, which Blyler and I played later in the day. The weather during replenishment was sunny and the seas calm and beautiful. I enjoyed looking at the many ships nearby, including the rarely seen battleship *New Jersey* and cruiser *Helena*, gliding lazily on the glassy sea. There were no flight operations on any carrier, but in late afternoon various ships participated in defensive drills. Antiaircraft guns were fired at targets towed by Air Force planes. The small, spreading, black blobs created by exploding shells disturbed the tranquility and filled the blue skies. Virtually all the ships' planes were spotted securely on the flight deck at the time, and portions of the hangar deck not occupied by bombs were then used for basketball games.

Replenishment day presented an excellent opportunity to pass on the latest rumors. The hottest was word that Captain Gallery would be relieved in August, and that the ship could return early to the States, still under his command. Speculation centered on whether or not the air group would also return or remain in Japan for assignment to another carrier.

Friday, 8 June, began with chilly overcast weather and rough seas. Our ship had assumed the role as carrier number one for the rest of the week. This meant that air operations commenced at 0430 and would continue until 1830. Our flight deck was required to be open to planes from other carriers at all times during those hours. The day's operations were preceded by an all-night loading schedule for the ship's ordnance men. A large strike required six hours of labor in ordnance preparation alone. Squadron ordnance men were required to be ready for commencement of flight deck loading as early as 0230.

Air operations rolled along smoothly during the day, with each scheduled flight of planes launched off the bow being quickly replaced at the aft end by a recovering flight that had been launched three hours before. Daylight continued until around 2030, when darkness began to set in and the ship commenced blackout conditions. All 21 planes involved in our squadron's seven flights returned safely. No air group losses were reported for the day.

Air operations resumed Saturday morning, 9 June, in dreary, dismal skies, but the weather improved by the time six of our planes had recovered safely around 1415 from their late-morning mission. A total of 18 squadron planes had flown missions before the day was over. The feverish pace of air operations affected almost everyone aboard in one way or another, though air group personnel felt this most directly. Pilots bore the brunt of the physical and emotional stress with repetitive missions and their inherent dangers. Despite the risks, many pilots sought to complete 30 missions and automatically become eligible for the Air Medal. Our maintenance personnel, especially aviation mechanics and metalsmiths, worked long hours getting aircraft ready for each day's operations. The mechanics concentrated on engine work while the metalsmiths handled a wide range of tasks aft of the engine. These men often worked until 0200 or 0300. Aviation Storekeeper Colwell and I were responsible for getting the required parts to them, so that they could do their jobs. Our work flow was anything but predictable and had many peaks and valleys. While most parts chasing occurred during the day, wake-up calls at night were not unusual during lengthy air operations.

After a little more than a week at sea with the Task Force, we discovered that replenishment days were not always free days for an air group. On Sunday, 10 June, a number of squadron personnel were scheduled for work-party loading assignments. Although replenishments usually occurred every three to four days, we found that some periods were shorter than others. We also noted that with the intensive wear and tear on aircraft, maintenance efforts and related activities had increased. In order to handle the increasing volume of work in our area, Colwell and I created an alternating schedule for handling parts requests during sleeping hours. Although replenishment days permitted crew members some time to recover physically between air operations, the increasing volume of primary work consumed much of our so-called "free" time. We realized that air operations would resume like clockwork each morning, or possibly later in the day, and we had to be ready.

As we settled into this new combat routine, we became more efficient and better prepared for the unexpected. We anticipated, and were able to respond to, assignments arising at unusual times, and came to recognize that war does not follow a predictable pattern. During the "valleys" in our work schedules, we also discovered the need to deal with administrative matters. Lower-rated enlisted personnel were directed to hit the books in order to pass upcoming, Navy-wide, promotional exams. Matériel Officer Lieutenant Ed Reed requested that I prepare for the Aviation Storekeeper 3rd class exam. I complied, but not with a whole lot of enthusiasm. This classification was, by Navy standards, an "essential rating," and thus one that could perhaps extend my active-duty time.

Squadron personnel taking the scheduled July exams for 1st, 2nd, and 3rd class ratings were also required to become familiar with the new Uniform Code of Military Justice — the body of laws governing members of the U.S. armed forces — which had become effective 31 May. Another subject of the exam was Military Requirements — basic rules of military procedure for dress, bearing, discipline, responsibility, etc. Thirty-five percent of the 265 men from the ship, who took similar exams in January, had failed to pass the Military Requirements element.

But skill improvement was not limited to enlisted men only — a squadron bulletin also reminded pilots of areas in need of attention. Pilots were reminded to be positive of their positions and certain that their targets were enemy before attacking, because there had been reports within the previous month — during which our squadron role was minimal — citing F4U, AD, and F9F aircraft attacks on U.S. boats and ships. The pilots were also directed to muster quickly in the Ready Room, especially at the sound of General Quarters, and their full attention was to be given to the Intelligence Officer who would brief them on targets, weather, and enemy defenses. Pilots were requested, especially after a flight, to provide information regarding the target or other mission data. Survival hints and navigation aids were also brought to their attention.

Flight operations on Monday, 11 June, were not as hectic, and the squadron flew only four flights, involving 10 planes, though one plane, bearing Bureau number 81939, was hit on a propeller blade. The oil cooler was also damaged by intense antiaircraft fire, but the plane was recovered safely with the pilot uninjured. The flights included combat air patrol, naval gunfire spot at Wonson and Songjin, antisubmarine patrol, and close air support at Chorwon.

Being ready for the unexpected was on the minds of all Task Force personnel early Tuesday morning, 12 June. The Fleet was watchful for enemy aircraft, and the sonar ears of escorting destroyers circled constantly to detect submarine sounds. Mines, most probably released from shore and carried out to sea by currents, were sighted on occasion. Once discovered, they were routinely disposed of. However, early this morning, one slipped by undetected. A destroyer, with crew members still in their bunks, suffered a disastrous hit and several men were killed and others injured. It was later speculated that the floating mine may have been mistaken for debris previously jettisoned in the area. Henceforth, no garbage was to be tossed over the sides of Task Force ships in combat operating areas.

The mine scare also reminded the *Princeton*'s Damage Control crew to vigilantly ensure ship watertight integrity. Large carriers were intricately compartmented to seal off ruptures into the smallest areas possible, and no *Essex*-class carrier had ever been sunk by enemy action. Efforts of Damage Control staff, diligently inspecting and repairing watertight compartment fittings, and air testing every small cubicle, was the key to this enviable record. During General Quarters, permission was required from Damage Control Central before any storeroom or other closed space below deck could be opened. A layout of the ship's deck plan noted the number of spaces that could simultaneously be open in any one portion of the ship.

Despite the anxieties created by the destroyer episode on the 12th, upcoming night air operations drew the excitement of some of us. Landings were expected around midnight and a group of us climbed up five levels in the island structure to watch the blacked-out recovery operations. Although it was cold, I waited with anticipation on a porch-like vantage point, high above the flight deck. Successive brief flashes from shielded deck-edge lights were shortly followed by previously invisible aircraft suddenly dropping out of the darkness to catch an arresting-gear wire. Daylight landings on the pitching deck were incredible enough, but night landings were truly something to behold. I marveled at the skills of these pilots who routinely set down their planes under such seemingly impossible conditions. Our squadron only flew two daylight flights, totaling six planes, during this relatively quiet day.

Air operations always dictated the scope and pace of most daily activities of squadron personnel. Less visible but essential administrative tasks, not directly tied to flight operations, were routinely performed almost without notice. Despite their relative anonymity, some administrative personnel volunteered spare time to the overall operational effort. One such crew member was Yeoman 3rd Class Ralph C. Tarleton, the designer of the squadron insignia adopted shortly before we had left the States. Tarleton, a graduate of San Francisco State College, had majored in fine arts and dramatics and been a Reservist for more than six years prior to recall. Recognizing that almost one-third of the activated squadron were natives of Oakland, and the rest from nearby areas, he designed the insignia to emphasize an acorn, the symbol of Oakland. The emblem featured the gold wings of Naval Air, and a silver helmet of the Conquistadores of old

Spain in California, emblazoned on a two-tone blue acorn. Light blue was intended to represent the Navy and the state of California. The dark blue was symbolic of carrier aircraft. Large replicas of the distinctive emblem were carefully painted below the cockpit on both sides of each aircraft. Tarleton devoted much of his free time to painting smaller versions of the insignia on the right side of each plane, representing missions flown, instead of more conventional images such as a bomb. Located forward of the cockpit, the symbol represented a combat mission flown by the aircraft — thus 15 missions called for emblems to be arrayed in three groupings of five per line. Tarleton further distinguished the pilots who flew the various missions, by painting the conquistador helmets with different color combinations. Each pilot was identified by exclusive colors, and could count his missions in any plane by the number of helmets representing his colors. The emblem, adopted as our official unit patch, was also evident on squadron flight jackets.

Yeoman Tarleton was kept very busy responding to the fast pace of missions flown, but soon expanded his efforts. He added the plane captain's name below the cockpit of each plane and then adorned the engine cowling with the plane's unique nickname. The plane captain was the rated enlisted man responsible for the fitness of each aircraft. One plane, squadron number 302, displayed the name *Louie's Love Nest* with a miniature bird's nest painted neatly beneath. Plane number 310 featured *Don's Hopped Up Model A* and included a cartoon of a small car. Not satisfied with these exemplary efforts, he branched out yet further by painting two green eyes on engine cowlings and two huge red lips on the chin scoops below the four-bladed propellers. This latter effort took more time, but by 13 June, he had already completed two aircraft. As of that date, we were the only squadron in the air group to aggressively display such uniquely adorned planes. I often wondered what the emotional impact was to enemy troops on the ground when these fearsome red lipped Corsairs, flying only 30 or 40 feet above the ground, came roaring at them!

As the combat days mounted, the skills of both pilots and crew members were sharpened by the repetition. The tedious pace of missions, however, sometimes produced a sense that each day was just like the one before. Yet there were breaks in the sameness, as on 13 June, when heavy operations resumed with our squadron flying nine flights, involving 21 planes. Plane number 316 (Bureau number 81057) was hit by .50-caliber fire, with loss of the lower left cowl; the pilot was uninjured. The squadron pace subsequently slackened, between 14 and 16 June, as only 10 flights, totaling 29 planes, spanned these three days.

Although the routine was usually broken only by replenishment days, there was some time for recreation. Evening movies were presented often on the hangar deck. Early June features included *Destination Murder*, *The Black Rose* (with Tyrone Power), and *The Conspirators* (with Elizabeth Taylor and Robert Taylor), among others. The movies were a welcome retreat from reality and were reasonably well attended. Although the showings were sometimes disturbed by peripheral distractions from ongoing aircraft maintenance and repair, these served to remind us that we were, after all, aboard a warship, not a civilian liner.

Sections of the hangar deck were also occasionally opened up for basketball games, apart from ship replenishment days. But dribbling the ball proved to be a real challenge, as welds on the steel decking often caused the ball to bounce wildly into unwanted areas. I was never much of a dribbler anyway, but the bumpy deck clearly highlighted my lack of skill.

Letter writing and reading well-worn books that circulated throughout the ship were the basic free-time activities. The remotely located matériel office proved to be a quiet hideaway for reading or writing, and was soon discovered as such. Increasingly, we were frequented by visitors. A long work table became the location sought after by a growing number of writers. Generally our guests conducted themselves with respect for each other's common quest for peace and quiet, but sometimes, after the evening gathering had settled in, someone would blurt out, "What do I write about tonight?" This stimulated discussion on an extensive array of possible topics, some serious — some crude.

On replenishment days, a few of our visitors would use the adjacent gun tub as a sun deck. Others would throw baseballs around on the flight deck if it was free of aviation activity. Card games were always going on, including a roving evening "serious" poker game that materialized in various unannounced locations.

At sea, with no access to sports broadcasts, we relied upon the *Princeton's Morning Press News* to provide sports highlights including baseball scores from the Major Leagues or, on occasion, Pacific Coast League games.

Some of the men engaged in hobbies, and Jim Blyler and I began cultivating beards. We attempted to grow goatees, but there was little progress evident — both of our minuscule beards emerged a similar, invisible blond.

On Sunday, 17 June, the *Bon Homme Richard* departed for Japan, to return in about 14 days. The carrier was replaced on line by the returning *Boxer*. During the morning, prior to flight operations, many of us visited the ship's Bazaar. The *Princeton* was said to be the only ship in TF-77 to bring aboard a variety of quality Japanese merchandise for purchase by the crew, and because the ship was scheduled to return before long to the States, there was an accelerated effort to reduce the inventory merchandise. Most of the stock had been pretty well picked over in previous months, but some unusual items remained. I spotted a barrel of 20 to 30 authentic Samurai swords remaining out of a total of 200 collected during World War II — beautiful and well-crafted, selling for $3.50 each. I purchased one to send home to my folks; some guys bought two or three. I had no idea of the age or designer, but admired the craftsmanship of this symbol of Japan's warrior aristocracy.

Flight activities during the day were moderate, with five Squadron flights, totaling 14 planes. One plane (Bureau number 82117) received a hit on the starboard wing tip and through the belly tank while on a strike at the Tanchon area. The pilot was uninjured.

An identical number of flights and planes went out the next day, the 18th. However, two more planes were hit by groundfire. Bureau number 96866 received a hole in the right aileron on a strike to Kilchu; Bureau number 81293 had two prop blades nicked on an armed reconnaissance flight in the Chorwon area. Neither pilot was injured.

On 19 June, only two flights went out, involving four planes, with no damage and uneventful results.

Our third week off the coast of Korea mirrored the routines established in earlier weeks, except for an accelerated number of missions. Ten flights, involving a total of 32 planes, were flown on Wednesday, 20 June. The rapid-paced schedule was suddenly broken when Ensign Moody was shot down while flying an afternoon bridge strike. Moody was forced to bail out of his damaged plane (Bureau number 81057) into waters near Wonson harbor. While flying a low-level mission, his aircraft had been severely damaged by groundfire, contact with power lines, or a combination of both. Whenever word was received of a downed pilot, anxiety immediately escalated among squadron members. Although each pilot was highly respected for his individual skills and courage, Moody, a former enlisted

Marine, was particularly revered by the crew. Many sighs of relief were heard when news came down that he had been picked up safely by a Navy landing craft and transferred to a destroyer.

Two other planes were also hit during that difficult day. Bureau number 82094 received fragment damage in the leading edge of the port wing, on a Songjin rail strike, and Bureau number 96755 was hit on the horizontal stabilizer and right flap, by a .50-caliber bullet. Neither pilot was injured. Air group successes for the day included an attack by Corsairs and Skyraiders on a previously undamaged bridge near Sinpung-ni. The bridge was situated between two 6,000- to 7,000-foot mountain peaks, and was almost impossible to attack. CAG-19 pilots flew through a narrow canyon, knocking out one span and severely damaging another with 1,000-pound bombs. Two other bridges were damaged, as was the approach to a third. Other flights hit marshaling yards and rail cars with undetermined results.

Pilots were not the only members of the squadron with specific duties to perform in Korea. A specialized contingent of maintenance personnel was launched from the flight deck on a mission key to our continued combat effectiveness. A detachment of four selected personnel was led by Lieutenant (JG) Miller and was assigned to salvage usable parts from accessible, downed Corsairs. One aircraft targeted for the mission was located at K-18, the emergency air field where the Skipper had crash-landed, once again in Allied hands. The objective was to recover what they could from the Skipper's downed plane. Miller was supported by Chief Petty Officer Alvin L. Harris, and Petty Officers Kenneth C. Ferry, Victor Koss, and Joe N. Olguin. The highly skilled men were issued rifles and side arms for their personal protection while on the ground.

Because many Corsair parts were not readily available at sea, this scavenger hunt had been under consideration for some time. A number of maintenance crew members had been actively promoting a mission of this sort, in the hope that they would be selected. The competition was keen and those not chosen openly expressed disappointment. But, although the assignment promised an exciting challenge, it also presented unknown risks inherent in land combat operational areas, and thus feelings of disappointment were tempered by a sober recognition that the ship was probably a safer place to be. However, risks or not, the team of selected personnel welcomed this opportunity to play a more active role in combat operations. Meanwhile, eight flights, involving 23 squadron aircraft, were launched on missions of destruction in Korea that day.

The TF-77 air operations and replenishment cycle rolled on without missing a beat. Between 22 and 28 June, the squadron flew missions totaling 28 flights, involving 87 planes. On 22 June, aircraft Bureau number 81293 received a .30-caliber slug in the right aileron. Early operations during the period included rail-line attacks with more than 100 feet of repaired track destroyed and roadbed supports mangled. Damage was also inflicted on antiaircraft positions and highways. Bombing and napalming of several troop positions resulted in 10 enemy killed and 5 buildings destroyed. UN actions for one day alone, involving American and British naval aircraft in attacks against enemy front-line positions and rear areas, totaled 260 sorties.

Navy pilots had also caused heavy enemy casualties during close air support strikes north and east of Chorwon and Kumhwa. *Princeton* and *Boxer* pilots attacked gun positions, buildings, and vehicles, in addition to destroying or damaging seven bridges at east coast rail and transport networks. *Princeton* Corsairs and Skyraiders crumpled three target bridges with direct hits, and destroyed additional sections of railway track. Jets strafed and bombed roads, disturbing transport and creating highway craters, rendering them unusable. On Monday, 25 June, four squadron planes assigned to a railroad bridge strike in the Pyongyang area destroyed three loaded ammo cars. A flight sent to strike near Koksan also destroyed three houses and a fuel dump.

During the period, Task Force fighters and bombers were also launched for close air support missions in the central and eastern sectors. *Princeton* and *Boxer* pilots reattacked coastal supply routes between Wonsan and Hamhung. Low-level napalm and strafing sorties on enemy positions north of Inje and northeast of Kumwha caused heavy losses, both in supplies and personnel. Heavy surface ship bombardment, during both night and day, shelled troops, gun positions, bridges, and supply dumps.

While the day-to-day drama repeated missions and shipboard support activities continued, we received important visitors aboard. Rear Admiral Albert K. Morehouse, Deputy Chief of Staff to the Commander Naval Forces Far East and soon to become Chief of Naval Air Advance Training at Corpus Christi, Texas, boarded for a "tour of familiarization" and observation of combat carrier operations. The *Morning Press News*, during his visit on 26 June, highlighted the Admiral's favorable impressions of our ship's company and air group personnel. Late in the afternoon of the 28th, the Chief of Naval Operations, Admiral Forrest P. Sherman, flew aboard our flagship as part of his visit to Fleet units. Upon his helicopter arrival, all hands then on the flight deck stood at attention, an event rarely seen at sea on the *Princeton*. However, our usual relaxed style of military etiquette continued to prevail throughout most of the ship during both visits, and many hardly knew either Admiral was aboard. There were no Stateside-style dress inspections, or any other unnecessary military rituals. The emphasis seemed properly to focus on the objective at hand, namely, fighting a war. Admiral Sherman later issued a commendation to TF-77 for setting new records in sustained carrier operations at sea.

During June, TF-77 aircraft had participated in "Operation Strangle," begun by Far East Air Forces (FEAF) at the end of May. The objective of the operation was to attempt to paralyze North Korea's road network through interdiction of all main supply routes, within a narrowly defined area. Supply routes lying within a band across the peninsula between 38° and 39° 15' north latitude were selected. Intelligence and targeting staffs designated particular "Strangle Areas" on roads within gorges and constricted passes where detours would be difficult or impossible to construct. Fifth Air Force, 1st Marine Wing, and Navy aircraft operated within specified sectors. Tactics included dawn and dusk heckling attacks, night strikes under flares, daytime interdiction, and armed reconnaissance sorties. Roads were seeded with delayed action bombs and FEAF B-26 Martin Marauder bombers and Marine and Navy aircraft planted anti-personnel "butterfly" bombs to hinder repair.

On 28 June, two VF-871 flights of four planes each had struck targets in the Koksan area and had cratered roads in numerous places. Strike reports also indicated they had destroyed two trucks, seven ox carts, two large warehouses, and had killed five oxen. They also reported heavy damage to two large warehouses and three trucks.

On Friday, the 29th, another flight of four squadron planes again cratered a road in the Koksan area and did considerable damage to camouflaged vehicles along the road. The "Strangler" strategy ultimately proved useless, as enemy repair crews repeatedly filled the holes and rapidly reopened roads. Despite the overall results, our pilots successfully carried out assigned missions within this combined service operation.

Also, on, 29 June, while four squadron flights of 14 planes were in action over Korea, Lieutenant Miller and his band of dismantlers returned with an array of usable Corsair parts. Members of the team were tanned and appeared physically fit with no ill effects from their adventure. Some wondered, however, whether the major gains from the expedition were the reclaimed parts or their luxuriant tans!

Our joy in welcoming back the ground detachment was quashed the following day, when we received word that Lieutenant (JG) Gordon C. George had been forced to ditch his plane in the sea near Wonson harbor. While returning from a mission, engine problems from a small arms hit in an oil line prevented him from making it back to the ship, and necessitated ditching. George, a former Cal Engineering student, was picked up safely after spending a few cold minutes in the sea. His plane (Bureau number 97004) became the fourth lost by the squadron but he was recovered uninjured. This month's final day concluded with a total of eight squadron flights, involving 18 planes.

Saturday was also payday, but this one was busier than usual for ship's disbursing personnel. Most crew members routinely let their pay accumulate on the books, having little use for cash aboard ship. With an eight- to ten-day rest period coming up, including liberty in Japan, many suddenly found a need for funds. Around 0930, members of the crew lined up to withdraw their pay, distributed in the form of military occupation scrip. These small currency-like documents, officially designated Military Payment Certificates, assured a later exchange for U.S. money or could be exchanged immediately at U.S. military establishments ashore for Japanese yen at current exchange rates. The scrip was periodically recalled and reissued with a new series to counteract industrious Japanese counterfeiters. Series number 481 had been issued to us, replacing one recently recalled.

Heavy air strikes on Saturday, 30 June, had reported destruction of six buildings and damage to rail, highway connections, and docking facilities, and had knocked out gun positions.

The 243 June offensive sorties were broken down as follows: 70 close air support, 137 strike, 8 armed reconnaissance, and 28 naval gunfire spot. These numbers reflect the effects of the opening phase of TF-77's interdiction campaign, which began in May. The 133 defensive sorties involved 106 combat air patrol and 27 anti-sub patrol. Our losses during the period, unlike the preceding month, thankfully included no personnel losses. Aircraft losses or damage, however, were certainly not insignificant. A total of 12 aircraft required minor repairs to surfaces due to small holes from .30-caliber antiaircraft fire and small fragments. One aircraft required replacement of an oil cooler. Two damaged aircraft — of Lieutenant George and Ensign Moody — were ditched at sea and lost.

Around noon on Sunday, 1 July, the *Princeton* left the Task Force and headed for Yokosuka, Japan, accompanied by two destroyers. Our carrier would be replaced on line by the returning *Bon Homme Richard*. After 31 days at sea and the stress of constant air operations, the entire crew aboard CV-37 was ready for a rest. That same morning, Lieutenant (JG) George was welcomed back aboard and appeared to be no worse for wear, despite his unplanned dip in the sea.

As we adjusted to the less frantic pace, we reviewed the activities we had carried out to sustain our successful air operations. Aircraft wear and tear increased with continuing operations, as did maintenance and supply activities. Colwell and I often found ourselves frequently adjusting our day-to-day tasks to meet the heavy demand for replacement parts. In recent weeks, I had handled most of the day and early evening orders of parts, while Ken dealt with frequent late-night requests. Often when I would report in the morning, he would be asleep on the matériel shack cot after having worked far into the night. Lieutenant Ed Reed, both a pilot and our supply officer, often spent extra time with us when not flying combat missions. He usually helped us organize our records and procedures, and each time he did so, I marveled that this officer, who was regularly getting shot at, would take time to assist his subordinate enlisted staff. Jim Blyler, who had by then returned to his primary electronic shop duties, also helped us by chasing after parts during critical periods. Occasionally, my duties took me onto the flight deck during flight operations where I would remain with the mechanics or other squadron crew until launch or recovery operations were completed. When all planes were in the air and the flight deck clear, we sometimes would sprawl out on the teak deck and enjoy the warm sun. These were welcome opportunities to recharge our personal batteries.

Shipboard life did have light enjoyable moments. My duties took me to the pilot's Ready Room on occasion and I, like other visitors, would linger, vainly trying to strike it rich playing the pilots' old nickel slot machine. Another especially enjoyable time was mail distribution. It was a pleasure to get a note from my NavCad friend Jim, who wrote that he was completing his flight training at Whiting Field, and expected to solo soon. And chow call was always welcome on any day, especially for Blyler and me; we regularly went to dinner together. We found that our

already voracious appetites had increased at sea, and we routinely demonstrated our satisfaction with the quality and quantity of the cook's shipboard cuisine. Eating didn't seem to accelerate the growth of our respective goatees, however, as both remained pathetically puny.

Our last full day at sea on Monday, 2 July, before returning to Yokosuka, was uneventful for most in the squadron. It was hot and humid, and
most men sat around on deck or in compartments with their shirts off,
writing letters and playing poker, as the *Princeton* plowed through the seas
toward our R & R destination. A number of us had been scheduled to take
the Petty Officer qualifying examinations, and thus morning hours were
mainly devoted to last-minute studying. I reviewed again the materials relevant to my Aviation Storekeeper 3rd Class exam. After lunch, I reported
with a number of others to the pilot's Ready Room, and at 1315 started on
the first of three test sections. The first dealt with Naval Military Requirements, and was comprised of 100 multiple-choice questions to be completed in two hours. The second involved 100 multiple-choice questions
relating to the rating being sought, and also allowed two hours. The third
part was a skill test for the rating, which, in my case, meant a typing test.
This test had a minimum passing requirement of 20 words per minute,
with no more than five errors, and was the only part of the exam scored
immediately. With my two nimble typing fingers blazing across the key-
board, I easily managed to pass, with 24 words per minute and only four
errors! All completed tests were then sent to the Naval Bureau of Education for scoring, and candidates were expected to receive results within
two months. My total test time took a little more than 3½ hours, but the
more technical tests, such as Jim Blyler's for Electronic Technician 3rd
Class, took longer.

I left the Ready Room with ambivalent feelings, principally because the
rating I sought was considered essential by the Navy. Success on the test
might mean a longer stay on active service, but I decided not to worry one
way or the other, because what would be, would be. After the exam, I did
some supply work, returning excess parts and obtaining others. After dinner, with anticipation of upcoming liberty in Japan, I joined many others
on the hangar deck for the evening's movies: *The Underworld Story*, star-
ring Dan Duryea, and *Kansas Raiders*, with Audie Murphy.

As we prepared for an 0900 arrival in Yokosuka, our spirits were further brightened by news that a recently proposed Soviet cease fire might soon be discussed seriously. The U.S. State Department had been seeking details of the plan, and Monday's news reports suggested that the Communists had agreed to discuss the matter further aboard a Danish ship, with General James A. Van Fleet, then Commander of the Eighth Army. Despite the recent on-again-off-again reports concerning the proposal made by Jacob A. Malik, chief Soviet delegate to the UN, the latest news accounts inspired hope. Recognizing that our ship would be returning soon to combat, we collectively wished that a diplomatic solution would be found to end the fighting quickly. I hoped that during our rest period the diplomatic process would produce an acceptable forum for debate of the underlying issues, and result in a negotiated end to the senseless killing.

Chapter 6

Rest and Recreation
July 1951

DURING THE EARLY *morning hours of Tuesday, 3 July, the* **Princeton***, en route to Yokosuka, quietly reentered the waterways of Honshu, the largest of Japan's four main islands. Honshu covers an area of 88,976 square miles and is the most heavily populated of the islands. Later, as we entered the 30-mile-long Tokyo Bay with its familiar sights, sounds, and smells, the thoughts of the 3,000-plus men aboard shifted from war to the mental and physical recharging of R & R. Obviously, physical rest from the rigors of air operations could be obtained aboard our idle ship in port, but* few, if any, considered spending their free time in that way. Most of us eagerly looked forward to recreational opportunities ashore.

By 0840 on Tuesday morning, the *Princeton* moored again at Yokosuka Naval Base. Our mooring operation was aided by tugboats that gently eased the huge ship into the dock. We were greeted by a Naval Station band and local Japanese girls performing a parasol dance, in traditional costumes. Our ship's band joined in with a few conventional musical pieces, thereby adding to the welcoming festivities. Liberty commenced shortly after the ceremonies ended, and many crew members quickly headed for shore. I remained aboard for a while to read mail from home, including another letter from Cadet Haughian who had asked me to buy him a Japanese Nikon camera. He neglected, however, to accompany the request with essential funds.

Around noon, I joined Stein, Young, and three of our yeomen — Ralph Tarleton, Ed Watson, and George (Frank) Musso — and went ashore. We set out to further explore the nearby city of Yokohama. When we arrived by rail at the Sakuragi Station, the three of us somehow got separated from the yeomen contingent. My trio headed for the large downtown Post Exchange, which had been closed during my first visit to the city. The PX was located on "5th Street," a designation no doubt created for the convenience of Americans. We browsed around the interesting six-story building for a while, and then decided to visit some nearby shops. I bought some silk handkerchiefs for family members at the Sun Brothers Silk Co., a shop on the opposite side of the street, about a block away. While there, we met a Merchant Marine officer who offered to show us some other interesting shops. We hailed rickshaws and followed him to a narrow street where the shops specialized in beautiful jewelry pieces of intricately carved ivory or jade. Stein purchased earrings and a brooch for his wife at a small shop offering particularly interesting carvings.

We joined the officer for dinner at the Seamens Club, a private facility reserved exclusively for merchant seamen and — after 1600 hours — their Allied Forces guests. The club was located on the periphery of a large square-block business area centered on 5th Street. The market area included a theater, gym, hospital, Yokohama Club, bus terminal, and snack bar, in addition to the PX. Our steak dinners were served with salad, fresh vegetables, dessert, and milk. The opportunity to eat a first-class meal, and drink fresh milk, was a treat unappreciated by landlubbers.

We thanked our host and headed by cab to a haunt we had favored dur-

Squadron VF-871 planes 306 and 310 on the flight deck of the USS *Princeton* in port at Yokosuka Naval Base, July 1951.

ing our last visit. The club, often referred to as the Service Club, was known officially as the Cabaret Sakura Port. Located on 8th Street, off D Avenue, it was within walking distance of the Sakuragicho rail station. We leisurely drank Japanese beer and listened to American tunes until 2130, then headed back to Yokosuka. Our first evening ashore was most enjoyable. We were pleased that we had made it back aboard ship shortly after midnight, and without disgracing ourselves, our squadron, or the U.S. Navy. We never did catch up with the yeomen, so we had no idea when they got back, or in what condition.

Liberty in port has always been a treasured occasion for seamen. Earlier in this cruise, *Princeton* crew members had visited the port at Sasebo, but had become involved in an awkward personnel incident while there. During the unfortunate post-Christmas R & R visit, prior to CAG-19X's arrival, a clash involving *Princeton* personnel broke out in the Officers Club. During the wild fracas, a brass spittoon struck the head of the Army Major in charge of the club. All personnel were restricted to the ship by shore authorities as a direct result of the incident. Rear Admiral Ofstie, who flew his flag on the *Princeton* — an indication that the Admiral is aboard — intervened and through his efforts the restriction was later lifted. As a result, however, the ship subsequently avoided that port and traveled instead through the Van Diemen straits to Yokosuka. After the Sasebo incident the crew explored urban Japanese life more peacefully in the new location. The alternate port on Honshu provided superb naval facilities as well as easy access to major cities. During the post-World War II years, beginning with the U.S. military occupation in August 1945, a gradual evolution in traditional political and cultural life began. The presence of our ship's crew members, along with other UN military personnel in Japan, would influence this gradual reformation.

During the early days of the occupation, the Japanese government essentially served to carry out the directives of General Douglas MacArthur, Supreme Commander for the Allied Powers. The General, for more than 50 years a professional soldier, suddenly was charged with the civil responsibility and absolute control over nearly 80 million people. His profession-

al military training and knowledge had not necessarily been designed to accomplish the different objectives of this new expansive role. MacArthur was called upon to direct sweeping governmental responsibilities embracing political science, education, technical, economic, and even religious areas. The initial objectives were to demilitarize Japan and to foster the establishment of a democratic government. The first would clearly require his military training and skills, and the latter would challenge his leadership abilities in sensitive and difficult new areas.

After demobilization of the Japanese military, MacArthur took the first steps toward accomplishing the governmental objectives. He issued what later was referred to as the "Civil Liberties Directive," which provided that all restrictions of political, civil, and religious rights then existing would be immediately lifted. This also prohibited any censorship of the press and mandated the release of political prisoners. Criticism quickly followed, especially from Soviet Union leaders who demanded more participation in the occupation and control of Japan. There was also some criticism at home for initiating this local action without referral for a decision by the State Department. Britain joined the Soviets in calling for a division of the unilateral powers then being exercised by the U.S. Both insisted that Japan be divided into spheres of Allied responsibility. General MacArthur argued against such a course, on the basis that it was evident that the division of Germany had been a mistake. He further pointed out that during World War II, neither nation had provided troops to assist the U.S. in fighting the Pacific War.

Despite his arguments, a Far Eastern Commission, consisting of representatives of all 11 nations that had been at war with Japan, was authorized during a Moscow conference that included participation by Secretary of State James Byrne. During that meeting, the U.S. surrendered its unilateral authority to the Commission. Commission meetings were held in Washington, D.C., and orders were transmitted to an advisory group called the Allied Council for Japan, which met in Tokyo. The Council consisted of the U.S., the British Commonwealth,

Nationalist China, and Soviet Russia. The Commission failed as an effective organization largely because of its composition and procedures. Scheduling of meetings was time consuming, and decisions took even longer as each of the four major nations had a veto. The Commission thus evolved into a debating society, and later quietly disappeared.

Early steps to revise Japan's Meiji-era (1867-1912) constitution, to bring about democracy, actually had started in October 1945, by appointment of a Constitutional Problem Investigating Committee. The Committee was appointed by then-Prime Minister Baron Shidehara, one of Japan's most respected diplomats. Advice was received from the people chiefly through editorials, letters, and calls on members. The content of the proposed new constitution was widely debated, because there no longer was censorship, and by the end of three months, a split had developed between those advocating an extremely liberal constitution and those who wanted little change at all. The first draft, submitted in January 1946, produced little significant change other than rewording the old constitution. MacArthur then directed his staff to assist and advise in the formation of an acceptable draft. The Prime Minister became active in the final preparation of a new draft that was ultimately submitted to, and approved by, the Emperor. It was widely circulated and debated by the Japanese people for a month before being submitted to the Diet — the country's two-house legislature — for debate and approval. After thorough exploration of all potential consequences, and after making many changes, both houses of the Diet approved the document with the basic principles intact.

The new constitution was adopted by proclamation of the Emperor on 3 November 1946 and placed into effect on 3 May 1947, and although it was generally referred to as new, it was really an amendment to the old constitution. The amended text, however, contained major changes in the form of government in Japan. Most important was the removal of supreme political power from the Emperor and the transfer of this authority to the people, represented by the Diet. The role of the Emperor was changed from that of an absolute monarchy to a constitutional

*role. The new constitution also abolished the army and navy,
and declared that Japan would give up the use of war as a political weapon. Economic and land reform programs were initiated, and women were given the right to vote. The document
completely altered the structure of government and, like the
U.S. Constitution, provided for executive, legislative, and judi-
cial branches. Overall, the new constitutional form of government combined basic elements of both the American executive
and the British parliamentary systems.*

American and other UN servicemen visiting Japan during the Korean
conflict were unaware of the gradual transformations that were taking
place in the occupied country. Along with the dramatic changes in the
basic structure and form of government, the people had also begun to
assimilate some Western social concepts and integrate them into their own
traditions and customs. Crew members on liberty were exposed to Oriental customs, dress, and religions that had melded with Western influence.
The nature of post-World War II work in urban areas, coupled with exposure to Western people, had stimulated changes in the way people related
to each other in a new, non-belligerent environment. Men were engaged in
work on new, modern highways and buildings, projects designed to
remove the scars remaining from the air raids of 1944 and 1945. Cities in
the large Tokyo Bay area, as in other locations, were heavily populated
with industrious Japanese citizens, but the average male employee earned
only the U.S. equivalent of about $40.00 per month. These Japanese usu-
ally related to each other and to foreigners with poise and courtesy despite
any animosity about the war. Our ship's crew had numerous chances to
mingle with Japanese citizens, including former military personnel, on the
streets, in clubs, in shops, or in train stations, and these contacts provided
opportunities to heal old wounds and build new relationships.

The physical environment of the cities I visited was noticeably different
from the U.S. in that few Japanese used automobiles as part of everyday
life. Taxis with smoking exhausts, however, were everywhere — many of
which were older American cars — burning any available fuel. Gasoline
was so expensive that it was common to find vehicles using various flam-

mable liquids, as well as some autos that had been adapted to burn wood or coal. It was common for a cab driver to shut off his engine, disengage the gears, and coast down hills to save fuel, a practice that often produced sweaty palms for uneasy passengers like me. Drivers would also sometimes confuse passengers by announcing only a building or place name, rather than a street or number location. In some cities, taxicabs competed with three-wheeled, bicycle-powered rickshaw carriages. Two-wheel manually drawn rickshaws were often seen around military installations.

The Japanese built their first railroad between Tokyo and Yokohama in 1872. The major mode of interurban transportation for citizens and military personnel, therefore, were the trains that ran along the coastal corridor between Yokosuka, Yokohama, and Tokyo. For Californians, this system might be compared with the Pacific Electric Railway that once operated in the Los Angeles area. Japanese commuters, during rush hours, could be seen patiently waiting for trains in orderly lines strung back and forth across platforms. The small, numbered pasteboard tickets, similar to those routinely used in American theaters, were marked on one side with the destination city, and on the other with the notation "Available for 1 day — Allied coach only." The stations were clean, schedules punctual, fares affordable, and Allied military occupation coaches comfortable. The only shortcoming on the trains was a lack of rest rooms, which on long runs presented painful occasions for us passengers who had downed a quantity of fine Japanese beer.

In good weather, Tokyo's well known Ginza shopping center was crowded with small portable stands, set up by independent merchants in areas between the street and sidewalk. Although a number of large buildings were damaged during the war, the Ginza still could be compared to stateside urban shopping regions such as New York's Fifth Avenue. The Japanese, like the French, are noted for their contributions to the development of the modern department store. Major Ginza department stores, similar to those found in the U.S., such as Macy's and Bullock's, were well patronized. The large Tokyo PX, formerly known as the Matuya Department Store, was the magnet store for military personnel. One other giant store, the Takashima, contained items usually found in U.S. stores but, in some departments, the traditions of the Japanese people were sharply emphasized. Clothing, dolls, art, and china all reflected the delicate workmanship of the culture. Although most products were Japanese,

Charlie Stein
aboard a Squadron
VF-871 Corsair on
the deck of the
USS *Princeton* in
port at Yokosuka
Naval Base, July
1951.

some Western household items were beginning to become available on a limited basis, as importers reopened.

Although the Ginza and the PX were must-see attractions, many other Tokyo sights were visited by the *Princeton* crew. The moated walls of the Emperor's Palace, the Dai Ichi building, the General Headquarters Club (GHQ), the Ernie Pyle Theater, the Marinouchi Hotel, and a favorite night spot, the Komatzu, all drew our attention. The shrine city of Kamakura, not far from our port in Yokosuka, was a major attraction for those interested in Japanese religion, history, and culture.

Wednesday, 4 July, was spent aboard ship with my duty section but I didn't have to perform much work; my only task was to sweep out the crew sleeping compartment. Except for that detail, most of my time was spent reading mail from home and friends. In the stack of envelopes received during our two mail calls were letters from my two Air Cadet friends reporting on their flight training, and from a high school friend stationed with the Air Force near the Cadets in Florida. After reading my first batch of mail, and before picking up the second, I played basketball on the hangar deck for nearly an hour. All in all, with the news from home and the generally relaxed pace, it wasn't a bad holiday — even if I did have to spend it aboard ship. I looked forward to the next day and the start of a 48-hour pass that would allow me again to travel around and stay ashore if I wanted to.

On Thursday morning, the 5th, however, my hopes for an early start were frustrated by an unexpected assignment to a work-party until noon. After lunch, I completed packing a few overnight items, primarily shaving gear and another set of whites, and prepared to go ashore. I was joined by Charlie Stein and John Young, and at 1330 we boarded a train bound for Tokyo. After a transfer stop in Yokohama we arrived at the huge central station around 1530 and took a cab to the large Tokyo PX where we wandered about for hours, shopping for gifts for our families and friends. I purchased four colorful lacquered oil paintings of Mt. Fuji, depicting four different seasons, for placement in our future home.

After having been confined to the ship's limited space for so long, it was exciting to explore different surroundings. We stopped for a veal cutlet dinner in the PX restaurant, and then continued our shopping spree until the store closed at 2000. The spacious dining room, similar to those found in swank U.S. hotels, featured a band playing soft dinner music. A beautiful atmosphere complemented the excellent food.

We left the store laden down with bags and boxes, with no idea where we would go next, but we decided to take a cab to the Red Cross Headquarters to see if we could locate a hotel room for the night. The office was closed, but we were able to check our packages in the building. At that point, we set off to explore some other sights in the city. Earlier, at the PX, Stein had met up with an old high school friend, stationed on Kwajalein, taking a five-day leave in Tokyo. Charlie and I went to a prearranged location to find him, while John sought us lodging. Four major hotels — the Dai Ichi, the Imperial, the Kaijo, and the Teito — were designated as "Occupied," presumably meaning available to personnel of the Occupying Forces.

We quickly found Charlie's friend in the New Tokyo Beer Hall, a busy club adjacent to one of many canals running through the city. Similar large canals were interlaced among commercial buildings in the Tokyo Bay area. The big, newly furbished club was a favorite hangout for military personnel from UN countries. A slogan painted on one of the club's walls posed the question, "What is life without love and beer?" Fellowship among the military personnel of diverse nations was akin to a generic love of man, and no animosities were evident in this happy gathering place. Plenty of beer no doubt helped foster the cordiality.

Charlie's friend was engaged in conversation with a member of the U.S. Air Force, another from the Australian Air Force, and five British soldiers, all just back from Korea. We joined the group and were welcomed warmly. Two of the Brits were recalled Army Reservists, so we had something in common. We also compared differences in speech and customs, thoroughly enjoying the friendly banter about our similar, yet different, cultures. We began signing Japanese and American currency notes in a manner similar to the "Short Snorter" notes signed by GIs in World War II — a roll of paper currency from places visited. I ended up with a 100 yen note and a U.S. "Silver Certificate" dollar bill covered with signatures from hometowns in Australia, Britain, and the U.S. To commemorate the occasion, the Aussie took a photograph of the group.

John joined us around 2145 with the news that it would be unlikely that we would find a hotel room at that hour, and thus it was decided that we would catch a train back to Yokosuka. After vigorous handshaking and numerous "cheerios," we bid farewell to our new friends and started our trek back to the ship. We retrieved our packages at the Red Cross and took a cab to the downtown train station, brightly illuminated by a large neon sign, "RTO - Tokyo Central." We managed to catch the 2240 train to Yoko-suka, and from there boarded a Navy bus and returned to the ship. Although we could hardly compare our itinerary to that of a typical tourist, we had thoroughly enjoyed our day.

On the following day, the 6th, I decided to go to Tokyo with a couple of other guys from the squadron. My two friends wanted to spend an hour or two in Yokosuka first, so I left them to their pursuits and headed solo for Tokyo. I met a soldier on the train, and upon arrival in Tokyo we hired a cab and rode together to the PX. I spent the afternoon shopping for family gifts and having myself sketched by two different sidewalk artists, for a total of 400 yen.

On the way to dinner I ran into Raymond Dreyer, Howard Kovakka, Joseph Vizena, and Kenneth Wolfe of our squadron, on their way back from a rest camp stay. After a shrimp dinner, we all headed back to Yoko-suka. We shopped a little more there, then Dreyer, Vizena, and I felt com-pelled before reboarding to dally briefly at the Enlisted Mens Club over a 15-cent Pabst Blue Ribbon Beer. We made it back aboard ship at 2315.

The most pleasing aspect of traveling by rail in Japan had been observ-ing the people as I passed through big cities, towns, and hamlets. I formed some impressions about their dress, housing, industry, transportation, and — even to a degree — the areas of greater or lesser affluence. For the most part, homes blended harmoniously with the surroundings, whether coun-try or city, and reflected the general living conditions of the community. In rural areas, people usually lived in single-story houses, with one to four rooms. In cities, although many lived in apartment buildings, traditional single-story homes were evident as well. On one occasion I happened upon workers constructing a home in Yokohama. Prefabricated light-weight walls were quickly erected, and sliding paper-covered screens were commonly used in place of doors between rooms. I watched in amazement at how quickly a small, but functional, family dwelling could be put in place.

It was also interesting to observe the variations in dress of the people we encountered. I saw women wearing traditional kimonos as well as Western-style clothing. Farmers, and less affluent city workers, most often wore cotton pants and jackets. People in the cities mostly wore leather shoes; however, we observed some still using traditional wooden san-dals.

New York Governor Thomas E. Dewey and dignitaries near a fully armed Skyraider on the deck of the USS *Princeton*, at Yokosuka Naval Base, 7 July 1951.

The Hospital Ship *Repose* in port, anchored near other U.S. Navy ships at Yokosuka Naval Base, July 1951.

Because only about 15 percent of the flatland was available for farming, land was used carefully and creatively. Cultivated terraces could be seen carved out of hillsides and small mountains for the small farms that grew rice, wheat, barley, and soybeans. Postwar land reforms had reduced the number of tenant farmers so that more land was being cultivated by the owners.

Saturday, 7 July, began as an uncomfortably warm duty day brightened only by morning mail call that included a letter from Father Lloyd, Chaplain of the *Weigel*. Although it was a routine day for me, it was significant for the *Princeton* because we received an important visitor, political figure Thomas E. Dewey, Governor of the state of New York and former candidate for the presidency of the United States. He was greeted warmly by the ship's band and all hands, standing at attention. The Governor, accompanied by Navy and local Japanese political dignitaries, was provided a brief review of the ship, planes, and crew as part of his inspection tour of the Far East. One exhibit prepared for him was a close-up look at a Skyraider fully loaded for action. The imposing aircraft, armed with the maximum ordnance, was positioned on the flight deck not far from my work location gun tub. From my vantage point about 20 feet away, I could easily see the Governor and the others viewing the powerful single-engine plane capable of carrying more tonnage than a four-engine B-17 bomber. I was able to take an excellent photo of the visitors standing in front of the ominous Skyraider. The Governor's party departed shortly thereafter and boarded the TF-77 cruiser *Helena* moored nearby. I concluded my duty day walking a boring flightdeck watch by reflecting on an ALNAV — a military term for a letter to all Navy personnel — regarding Reserve release policies stating that recalled Reservists would remain on active duty a minimum of 15 to a maximum of 24 months.

As our days in port dwindled, I tried to combine my few shipboard tasks with a half day of sightseeing, and thus after Sunday Mass, Blyler and I headed for Tokyo. Typical weather on the island of Honshu is similar to the middle-Atlantic states in the U.S., with warm, humid summers. The difference between the two areas is that though all of Japan receives ample rainfall, heavy snow falls mostly in the northernmost areas, but rarely does it snow in Tokyo.

After arriving in Tokyo around 1445, we walked in a steady summer rain to the Imperial Palace grounds. My California upbringing had conditioned me to dry climates, with occasional high temperatures, but virtually no exposure to humidity. This new experience — walking in warm rain and not feeling cold from damp clothing — was surprisingly pleasant. At this stage of our visit, we had completed most of our shopping and wanted to see as many historic and cultural exhibits as money and time permitted. No one was allowed on the palace property but we were able to walk the perimeter of the beautiful grounds. A huge moat circled the palace and restricted us to the visitors side. Blyler and I approached two Imperial Guards for information, and an interpreter helpfully provided data regarding the palace and the Imperial Family. We purchased some photos and had our picture taken by a professional, with the Double Bridge in front of the palace as background. Four copies of the photo were ordered and could be picked up the following day.

Despite our best intentions to see all the sights, we reverted to what was becoming a habit — returning to Ginza Street and our bit of America, the Tokyo PX. One of the main attractions of the PX was the availability of good food. Being in a strange land, and accustomed to an American diet, we were reluctant to try the Japanese restaurants because of language difficulties and general uncertainty about the dishes available. We had also been cautioned to dine out with discretion because of unstable occupational health standards. After a short stop to exchange military scrip for yen and eat a PX hamburger, we spent the bulk of the afternoon visiting shops and stores along the Ginza. Around 1800, we checked into the PX dining room for another high-quality dinner, in my case — again — veal cutlets. After dinner we strolled over to the Red Cross to check a few packages, and from there went on to the New Tokyo Beer Hall to enjoy the music, beer, and comradeship with GIs from many places in the world. Our return trip seemed shorter due to a lively discussion with a Marine we met on the train.

I did a little work in the personnel office on Monday morning, 9 July, and set out for a sunny afternoon in Tokyo. The main purpose of my fourth visit was to retrieve the photos Blyler and I had taken the previous day. I was accompanied this time by Stein, and after arrival at 1600, we walked directly to the Imperial Palace grounds. The day was beautiful in contrast to the rainy conditions when the photos were taken. The photographer had the prints ready and they turned out well. Because this was Charlie's first visit to the palace we walked around the impressive grounds for awhile, bought some postcards, took a few more photos, and hailed a cab. We intended to eat dinner at the PX, but finding it closed, elected to walk to

Jim Blyler and Paul Cooper near the Imperial Palace Double Bridge, Tokyo, 8 July 1951.

the nearby General Headquarters building to try the snack bar. The imposing GHQ, located downtown in the former Dai Ichi Mutual Insurance building across from the palace moat, provided an awesome experience for two fellows outside the mainstream of power. The "spit and polish" U.S. Army sentries standing rigidly at the entrance, wearing shiny silver helmets and white gloves, were impressive and intimidating. Entering the eight-story building, I could almost sense the spirit of General MacArthur in the corridors. The General, who had displayed his tactical military genius in Korea, was greatly revered by the Japanese people for his civil leadership; posters and signs expressing sorrow at his departure were observed still hanging on structures in the downtown area.

But before we got too inspired by the solemnity of our surroundings, we found the humble snack bar. Although the ambiance of the snack bar was not as impressive as the elaborate PX dining room, the food was good. I put away fried chicken, salad, potatoes, milkshake, and chocolate cake with ice cream, all for $1.35 in U.S. Military Payment Certificates (scrip). The aura of a powerful military command headquartered in this most significant building did not in any way inhibit our appetites!

Following dinner, we strolled around the Ginza shops until 2015 and went back to the GHQ club for a couple of beers. The patrons were almost exclusively Army personnel, so we headed for the New Tokyo club and a more diverse military clientele. After another congenial visit in the friendly surroundings, we called it a night at 2200. On the sidewalk outside the club, we met a British sailor — the first I had encountered — and walked with him to the train station. His unique brand of humor filled our stroll with laughter. Our train ride, in an almost empty Allied car, was uneventful, and we arrived back aboard ship around midnight.

Tuesday, 10 July, was a quiet duty day and I spent most of my time writing letters and taking photos of people and planes on the serene flight deck. I also hand-washed some white uniforms as the ship's laundry service was not available. I looked forward to a little more sightseeing the next day, our last in port; however, Wednesday morning started with chasing parts — an omen of things to come. After completing my work, Blyler and I dealt with the domestic duty of pressing our whites. We finally departed the ship, in regulation shape, at 1330 and dallied about in Yokosuka for awhile before boarding a train for Kamakura, a small historic coastal city with a mild climate, 50 km west of Tokyo. Situated near sandy beaches, and with a multitude of significant religious and cultural attractions, Kamakura was a frequent destination of occupying forces. Charlie Stein had suggested that we visit, and that we make sure to see Daibutsu, the giant statue of Buddha. We were delighted to find that this ancient little city had a number of attractions and landmarks.

The Kamakura period in Japanese history covered the years from 1185 to 1333. Kamakura in 1192 became the seat of a Shogunate government and, during the years when Samurai warriors dominated the Imperial government, the city served as the capital of Japan. During this period, Japanese art and literature experienced significant development and the city contained a great number of ancient shrines and temples as well as old artistic treasures. The huge statue of Daibutsu, the Great Buddha, was erected by artists in 1252. The culture of those times was reflected in many tree-shrouded old temples, simple tombstones, and stone Buddhas standing along small paths.

We rented bicycles in order to see as much of this picturesque city as possible, and initially joined a couple of other sailors and headed off to view the shrines, temples, and statues: Tsurugaokahachimangu shrine, in the historic center of town; Enkakuji, an old temple typical of the town; Kenchoiji, an example of Zen culture; and Meigetsuin, known as the "hydrangea temple." Our first stop was at famous Tsurugaokahachimangu. On a hill behind a smaller entry structure, and up a steep flight of more than 50 stairs — each about 24 feet wide — the red columns and siding of the large shrine contrasted with the green of the heavily forested surrounding hillside.

A unique, small, arched wooden bridge was nearby. I thought that it would be fun to ride my bike over the relatively short bridge and quickly peddled up one steep side and rolled easily down the other. As I was looking around for Jim, a uniformed Navy Chaplain approached me. He advised that the bridge was reserved for the Emperor's use only! I was very embarrassed, and concerned that I may have offended nearby Japanese citizens by my disrespectful act. I offered my apologies to the Chaplain and departed the bridge area as unobtrusively as possible.

It was so late in the day that we did not enter the temple itself, but could see priests moving about within. Visitors were permitted and all, including Occupation military, were required to remove their shoes. The beautiful temple had been the Emperor's primary place of prayer in times past. In view of my bridge *faux pas* a few moments earlier, I made a point of looking for signs so that I would not make any more irreverent mistakes. A wooden sign with the heading "Kotoku-In Monastery" contained a message printed in Japanese and English. The translation read: "STRANGER WHOEVER THOU ART and whatsoever be thy creed, when thou enterest this sanctuary remember thou treadest upon ground hallowed by the worship of ages. This is the temple of BUDDHA and the age of the Eternal and should therefore be entered with reverence. BY ORDER OF THE PRYOR." I was very careful to be respectful as we walked these hallowed grounds.

As we returned to our bicycles, Jim and I encountered a stooped, slender, gray-haired old man dressed in traditional black clothing standing near our bikes and gesturing vigorously while attempting to speak to us in Japanese. Unable to communicate with him, we tried to leave the area as politely as possible and move on to other sites. We finally eased ourselves away and rode to the side of town where the colossal bronze image of Buddha was located. This incident with the old man had left me with uneasy feelings.

The statue of Daibutsu sits on a large pedestal dominating a broad plaza. The imposing hollow structure, standing over 43 feet high and 97 feet in circumference, was cast in September 1252 in sand-mold sections. The length of the face is 7.7 feet, the eyes 3.3 feet, the ears 6.6 feet, and the nose 2.8 feet. The breadth of the mouth is 1.8 feet and the length, from knee to knee, 30 feet. The circumference of the thumb alone is 2.8 feet. The total weight of the statue is more than 92 tons. This mas-

sive creation is considered a marvel of man's handiwork, and a major work of art. The statue had withstood many natural disasters including major earthquakes over the centuries. Despite damage by a tidal wave that swept over the site in 1495, and years of wear from the elements of nature, it was in an excellent state of preservation when Jim Blyler and I were there.

The floral background for the impressive Buddha was similar to that of the shrine, a backdrop of green trees. Visitors were permitted to enter the hollow body of the statue and climb up an interior circular staircase almost to the head. Jim and I marveled at the artistic skill that went into crafting the statue, as well as the engineering genius that enabled it to survive virtually intact, with the exception of some cracks, over many centuries.

After completing our tour, we were about to leave the site when we spotted an unexpected attraction on the grounds — a beer vendor. Surprised that such beverages would be sold in a pious environment, we each bought a warm, but tasty, Nippon brew. We took a few photos of the statue and returned to our bikes to resume our unguided tour to a statue about 20 feet tall, named in English, "Goddess of Mercy." The statue was carved from the wood of a huge banyan tree and covered in gold leaf, intricate facial features and designs surrounding her symbolic headpiece. The clothing of the statue contained tiny, artful designs that conveyed an impression of solid gold.

Upon returning to our bikes Jim discovered that he had misplaced the key to his lock. He had unsuccessfully searched through the limited storage space available in his enlisted naval uniform. Suddenly, the need to mount our bikes and depart increased significantly. While glancing around the area, I spotted the unsettling figure of the old man in black heading directly toward us. His appearance in this far location of the city made us both uncomfortable. Although we had traveled quite a distance and had been on our bikes for over two hours, he had somehow followed. We had no idea why he was pursuing us or had an interest in us. But the sight of his rapid approach accelerated our desire to leave.

The old man was almost upon us when Jim finally located the key. We hastily departed and peddled directly back to our first point of entry to the city. We were so unnerved by the specter of this ancient man following us that we returned our bikes and concluded our visit. Although I was probably more bothered by the spooky patriarch than Jim, we both looked over our shoulders, fearing his reappearance, as we hurriedly walked back to the train station. Relieved that he had not followed us, we caught the 1828 train back to Yokosuka.

Our visit to the historic city was one of the high points of this visit to Japan, despite the eerie and confusing experience with the old man. Jim and I capped off our final day in port with a dinner at the Golden Pheasant Restaurant in Yokosuka, an American-operated eatery, and pondered again and again what the strange old-timer may have wanted with us.

As *Princeton* personnel straggled back to the ship on this final night in port, it was clear that the brief interlude between air operations had been rejuvenating but that it was time to shift mental emphasis — from tourism to action — in whatever manner might ultimately be required. Refreshed by the relaxing stay and our glimpses of Japan, we were physically and mentally prepared to return to work. Come what may, we were ready to sail on the morrow to resume our assigned mission.

Although news reports received from the war zone while we were in port had been sketchy, we were aware that Task Force fighter and attack aircraft had been flying armed reconnaissance missions along roads and railroads. These actions continued while United Nations representatives followed up on Soviet proposals for talks seeking a peaceful solution to the conflict. Some progress had been made during our final week in port. Preliminary discussions aimed at ending hostilities had begun the previous day, 10 July, in Kaesong, North Korea. Motivations for the proposed talks, however, were viewed with suspicion by some of the Allies. Some military Commanders saw them as being nothing more than a delaying tactic designed to allow time for the enemy forces to recover from massive losses suffered in their earlier offensives. But, despite these misgivings, discussions had, at least, begun.

Chapter 7

Back to Korea
July-August 1951

THE USS *Princeton* pulled away from the familiar *Yokosuka pier promptly at 0700 on Thursday, 12 July, with supplies replenished and crew refreshed. The mood of the air group crew was more relaxed than during our first deployment from Yokosuka, when most had experienced a fear of the unknown. We had been exposed to the stress of combat and felt fully confident about our ability to effectively resume our TF-77 assignment. Despite our belief that we could perform whatever mission assigned, hope remained that these efforts would not long be required. Most crew members were* encouraged that the diplomatic efforts finally underway might produce a solution to end the hostilities.

As the *Princeton* sliced through tranquil waters en route to the Sea of Japan, shipboard work routines quietly resumed. Prior to sailing, all units conducted formal musters to ensure that every crew member was aboard. Shortly after our 0730 squadron muster, I began a busy day of parts-chasing as our maintenance crew readied planes to resume action. Between runs, I found time to read mail received before our departure. I especially appreciated a package from Aunt Vi that enclosed two Western novels, licorice candy, miniature cigars, and a small checker set. The checker set was immediately put to good use that evening.

Friday's routines mirrored the previous day, as almost everyone aboard, except pilots, resumed normal shipboard duties. Our mechanics worked steadily throughout the day repairing planes for upcoming air operations. A non-routine activity — promotional Petty Officer exams — was again scheduled for a few additional squadron members. Administrative space was scarce at the time, and it was necessary to conduct some of these tests in our cramped supply office. Test-takers had to put up with occasional traffic in the office during the busy parts activity.

Late Saturday morning, 14 July, we rejoined TF-77 and participated in replenishment operations then underway. During the evening ship's news broadcast, it was announced that the *Princeton* would be relieved at sea by the *Essex*, our old shakedown ship, no later than 1 September. We also found our that a committee from the ship — including Father McManus, the Catholic Chaplain — had already been dispatched to the States to plan a homecoming party in San Diego. Festivities tentatively under consideration included a two- to three-hour open house aboard the ship, followed by an evening dance party at the El Cortez Hotel. It also appeared certain that the air group would return with the ship rather than be reassigned to another carrier.

Official news, as usual, produced an accompanying rash of not-so-official reports. Latest rumors had it that, after returning, our squadron would switch to jets and be stationed at either NAAS Santa Rosa, or NAS Moffett Field. An article from the 27 May *Oakland Tribune* appeared to lend some support to this. Copies of the newspaper, which had been received from home by various squadron members, reported that an undesignated air group then in the Pacific would be stationed at Santa Rosa. Because our air group was the only one likely to return soon, this was widely interpreted to mean us. It had long been anticipated that our pilots would be retained on active duty for an extended period following return. A transition to jets would take six to eight months before pilots would be ready to go to sea again. The rumors further predicted that our squadron would remain intact during the transition period but Reserve enlisted crew would be released to inactive duty before the squadron shipped out again.

During the *Princeton*'s absence, early peace talks had begun, but the war rolled on and death and destruction continued. Although the attack emphasis had gradually shifted to interdiction strikes, many missions flown by air group pilots during the tour had been in close support of infantry units. Pilots were repeatedly cautioned against a general practice of pressing attacks to extremely low altitudes that resulted in a greater loss of lives and planes. Many close air support missions were flown by pilots who routinely pushed their flying skills to the maximum in an attempt to save the lives of others on the ground. These pilots continually balanced the prevailing risks with prudence, while seeking to effectively carry out these difficult low-level missions. The offensive attack missions targeted enemy rail lines, truck and troop movements, bridges, supply dumps, and buildings. The objective of the increased strategic missions was to restrict enemy freedom of movement. As a result of these persistent air strikes, North Korea shifted most of its rail operations to a west coast network. A rail link from Samdong-ni terminated in Kowon, a small railroad town north of Wonson, which became a particularly significant target. While the interdiction campaign was costly to the enemy in terms of losses of vehicles, rolling stock, supplies, and buildings, it was also very costly to maintain. The intensive campaign was expensive in terms of aircraft and crew losses, and the thousands of tons of munitions and supplies consumed. Aircraft were becoming increasingly vulnerable to the growing sophistication of enemy defensive capabilities. North Korean use of early-warning, gun-laying, and, most especially, ground-control interception radars was of growing concern to USAF B-29 night operations crews. During July, TF-77 tactical aircraft also began to note the increasing effectiveness of North Korean antiaircraft defenses. Our squadron had suffered high losses — one pilot and four aircraft — and it was apparent that this second full tour would not be any easier.

On Monday, 16 July, the **Daily Press News** reported that the Communists had accepted demands made on the previous Friday by General Matthew B. Ridgway, for resumption of cease-fire negotiations. The reply, which was delivered to a UN liaison officer at an enemy outpost near Kaesong, was under study by Allied headquarters. The liaison officer, Colonel Andrew Kinney, flew to the outpost by helicopter at 0640 Saturday, more than nine hours after the note was first broadcast by Pyongyang radio. Kinney was one of three Allied colonels who made the original arrangements for ceasefire talks. The formal reply to Ridgway's virtual ultimatum, written in both Korean and Chinese, was hand-delivered to him at the Communist outpost at 0700. Two South Korean officers orally translated the note to Colonel Kinney before he quickly sent it on to Headquarters for official translation. Early speculation was that the Kaesong discussions might be resumed that afternoon or the following morning.

The same issue of the **Morning Press News** also reported that a House of Representatives Armed Services Subcommittee had attacked the Defense Department's Reserve recall policy as "inadequate, unfortunate, negligent and almost unbelievable." The Subcommittee declared that Reserves had been ordered to active duty "at the expense of heartaches, broken homes, closed businesses and lost jobs." It urged an early release of all Reserves serving involuntarily on active duty, but conceded that this would have to be a gradual process to prevent disruption of the armed forces. The Subcommittee concluded that "the entire program has been handled in such a way to cause our reserves to feel that the military departments have failed to keep faith with their reservists." Despite these statements, which validated the long-held views of squadron members, the consensus was that "we are here now, let's get on with it."

Our pilots returned to the skies in clear sunny weather and on Tuesday, 17 July, Lieutenant (JG) Donald E. Frazier accomplished a milestone by successfully making the 10,000th landing aboard the *Princeton*. Following flight operations, traditional cake-cutting ceremonies were held in the officers' wardroom. These informal occasions brought the ship's officers, air group pilots, and staff officers closer together. Lieutenant Frazier became the third VF-871 pilot so honored, preceded by Ensign Moody, aboard the *Essex*, and Lieutenant Robert Kennedy, who accomplished the *Princeton*'s 8,000th landing.

Frazier's beginning with VF-871 had been somewhat unusual. Prior to hostilities, he was affiliated with the squadron only in an associate capacity, because no pilot billets in the unit were then available. Not recalled, he soon volunteered for active duty, was accepted, and was assigned to a night fighter squadron in San Diego. Upon reporting, the assignment officer questioned his former Reserve affiliation and he mentioned his unofficial status with VF-871. He was advised that his former buddies were housed in that very hangar and asked if he would like to join them. Without hesitation Ensign Frazier said, "Yes," and was quickly transferred, on an official basis, to the squadron. Opportunities to be the pilot to achieve a symbolic landing were largely controlled by chance, but Frazier's accomplishment, like those before him, produced surges of pride among squadron personnel.

On Wednesday, the 18th, our rejoicing was put on hold when around 1800 we anxiously awaited recovery of two of our planes. Before dinner, I had remained on the flight deck with Blyler while he waited to check the radios of the two overdue aircraft. Lieutenant George, who had been pulled from the sea prior to our return to Japan, returned late but safely. His wingman, Lieutenant Frank Martin III, did not. Martin, of San Carlos, was hit by groundfire on a napalm run near Kumsong. His plane failed to pull out of the bombing run, dove straight into the ground, and exploded. There were no indications of any attempt to bail out after the plane was hit, and he was presumed seriously wounded or dead before impact. Martin, 29, was one of our original pilots from Oakland and, as the Operations Officer, was third in command of the squadron. He was married, with three children, and had commented to a mechanic prior to taking off that his oldest boy was doing well in school; he had also remarked that he was weary of the repetitious three-hour missions.

A deep gloom descended upon the squadron with the loss of a second pilot, and fifth plane. Planes were expendable, but pilots were not. That same day, another of our planes returned with a large hole in the tail assembly, and an aircraft from another squadron returned with jagged holes along one side and bottom. Improvements in enemy groundfire defenses clearly made them more difficult to avoid. Despite the resumption of peace talks, there existed the grim reality that the war continued unabated. It was particularly difficult to accept the loss of another of our squadron family only four days after rejoining the Task Force.

Thursday, 19 July, was just another routine replenishment day but was significant to me because mail call brought a letter from Marie announcing that we were going to become parents! I quickly relayed the joyous news to all my close squadron friends. Ed Watson and Charlie Stein were already each the father of two. Stein, however, had not yet seen his new twin sons. We discussed the difficulties of military parenting during wartime.

Thursday was unusual for the rest of the squadron, too. We were surprised to learn that we would immediately be losing two of our original enlisted crew because their enlistments, and one-year mandatory extensions, had expired. They were to be transferred at sea that very day. Freight, mail, and personnel often were transferred over thin strands of connecting steel cable between the fan-tails of respective ships on the "bos'n" (boatswain) chair — a basket device hanging from a cable. Our Leading Chief, Chief Petty Officer Ray F. Derry, and Airman John H. Boysen were shuttled above the waters for transport to Japan and then home to the States. The destroyers that made up the screen of the Task Force handled special calls, like this one, for transfer of personnel. Both men would be missed. Chief Petty Officer Alvin L. Harris was designated to assume the role of Leading Chief, replacing Derry, and Lieutenant Walter "Gam" Gamboni was named Operations Officer, replacing Lieutenant Martin.

Flight operations were canceled when the weather turned foul on Friday, the 20th, bringing a low ceiling and rain. After dinner, the storm cleared briefly and for about 90 minutes the *Princeton* participated in gunnery practice along with other ships. During the practice, most if not all the *Princeton's* 40 millimeter and five-inch guns were fired. As the exercise continued, the ship rocked with earsplitting noise. Bad weather on Saturday forced cancellation of flight operations for the second day in a row, but afternoon skies were filled with antiaircraft fire as gunnery exercises were repeated. While bad weather usually resulted in easier work days for most, the real benefit was to the pilots who were given a needed respite from deadly enemy groundfire.

On Sunday morning, 22 July, flight operations resumed in clear, sunny skies. A replacement plane, flown aboard the previous day from Japan by the Skipper, was taken up for a test flight. The test pilot brought it back aboard after a three-hour hop, with the distressing assessment that it needed a new carburetor. No carburetors of the type were available aboard ship, so the disappointing end result was a replacement plane that couldn't be flown in combat. The plane was designated as "hangar queen #2," as we already had named another disabled aircraft "#1." The balance of our planes seemed to be in pretty good shape and available for full duty.

Around 0930, on an otherwise bright day, the mood of our squadron was tragically devastated by news that we had lost another pilot. Ensign John P. Moody, Jr., 24, from Coronado — but originally from Proctor, Minnesota — flying wing with the Skipper, was picked out of the air by antiaircraft fire over Kumsong. The first blossoms of black smoke were spotted as the flight approached the target. These deadly black puffs contained flying pieces of metal — ack-ack, as the pilots called it — launched from enemy antiaircraft guns. One of the first bursts hit Moody's plane in the belly tank. It immediately blew up. The plane remained structurally intact at first, but crashed shortly thereafter, and at the time, it was unclear whether or not the pilot went down with the plane. It was believed he may have been blown out of the aircraft by the explosion of the external fuel tank.

Ensign Moody, who had joined the squadron after it was activated, had also been flying wing with the Skipper when he had been shot down earlier, on 20 June. His safe return from that mission had produced great relief within the squadron. Confirmation of the loss of this much-loved young pilot affected all of us in individual, deeply personal ways. A former enlisted Marine, he had been a commissioned naval aviator for just a short time, and had been married only six months. Some of the enlisted men with whom he had worked closely quietly handled their private grief. The young ensign had been extremely well liked for his good nature and cheerful smile. His former enlisted status created a special relationship with the enlisted men and his lighthearted manner endeared him to all. His sudden death, coupled with the loss of Frank Martin only four days earlier, was a stunning blow to squadron morale.

Our squadron had by then suffered more combat losses than any other in the air group, and our tour was not yet over. The significance of the grim statistics — three pilots and six planes lost — was impressed upon the remaining pilot cadre. Anxiety affected all of us as the pilots prepared to carry out their remaining missions. Uncertainty about whether a pilot's next mission would be his last weighed heavily on everyone. I wondered why my two friends, Jim and Vince, then in the final phase of flight training, wanted to become pilots.

My duties on that sorrowful day concluded with a 2000 to midnight watch that didn't start until 2130, when flight operations secured. During the watch, I was joined by another sailor who had a portable radio and we listened to recorded American music transmitted by a Tokyo station. We also picked up programming from stations originating in Vladivostok, Russia, and Hawaii. This unusual reception of voices and sounds from distant locations helped to take our minds off the sadness of the day.

Monday, the 23rd, was fortunately uneventful in terms of air operations. During the morning, conversation centered on rumors that a dispatch had been received outlining new Navy policy regarding release of Reservists. It had been reported that all veteran World War II enlisted Reservists in organized units involuntarily recalled would be released in October. This would affect 26 men in our squadron. Those who had been in inactive Reserve were required to remain on active duty for a total of 17 months. Non-World War II Reservists, totaling 15 including me, were required to remain on active duty for 24 months — essentially one more year. Officers were expected to remain on active duty for a full 24 months, with pilots to be retrained in jets before release.

Before dinner, I visited the squadron personnel office to verify the rumors with our yeomen who always seemed to have the "straight poop." I was allowed to read the ALNAV dispatch that confirmed the reports heard earlier. Reactions in the crew compartments depended on an individual's circumstances. Any grousing, however, served as an escape from grief over the two recent pilot losses.

Tuesday, 24 July, was a quiet day generally, with no calamitous events reported. Miller dropped by our office during the day to chat and commented that, as things currently stood, we would remain on station until 10 August. A return to Yokosuka for 10 days would be followed by a short phase-out tour of five or six days with the Task Force. The *Princeton* would then briefly participate in joint operations with the *Essex*, the *Bon*

Homme Richard, and the *Boxer*. The *Princeton* would then detach, return to Japan, unload excess gear and most aircraft, and begin the journey home. All of these plans, of course, were subject to change as dictated by combat circumstances. Later in the day Charlie Stein, on duty in the Chief's mess hall, told me that he was scheduled to be discharged in November. Needless to say, his day had been brightened considerably by this information. He hoped to bring his wife from Pennsylvania for a couple of weeks, following our return to San Diego, to show her a little of California before they settled down as parents. His discharge, he thought, might take place in Pennsylvania, at a base near his home in Sumert. In any event, he would not be with the squadron for long after our return.

Replenishment day on Wednesday, 25 July, brought the usual load of supplies and ordnance, and the primary commodity sought on such days — mail. I received one letter from Jim, my friend at NAAS Whiting Field, Florida. During the course of morning replenishment we said goodbye to two more squadron mates, Chief Andrew Winfield and Airman Allan H. Hong. This second pair from the Oakland contingent had also completed their enlistments and obligatory extensions. They were being transferred, along with 72 other similarly affected Task Force personnel, to a nearby ship for return to Japan, en route to home and discharge. Around 1700, with replenishment completed, we suffered through another noisy session of gunnery practice.

The grinding pace of air operations was resumed on Thursday, the 26th, with a resultant toll on aircraft and pilots. During the afternoon, our Exec, Lieutenant Commander Cooper, had difficulty bringing his plane aboard during recovery due to severe oil leaks caused by enemy groundfire. The plane had been hit in the right wing and a main hydraulic line had been severed. During approach, he had experienced a loss of hydraulic pressure, and had trouble lowering his landing gear. But before completely losing pressure, he managed to get the gear down, and although the damaged plane splashed hydraulic oil all over the flight deck during landing, we were grateful that it wasn't more serious, and that he got back uninjured.

After dinner on Friday, 27 July, an old TBM torpedo bomber, modified to provide Carrier-On-Board-Delivery (COD), came aboard. These planes, affectionately called "Turkeys," functioned almost like a scheduled airline flying to and from Japan. COD flights routinely carried passengers and bills of lading and manifests for cargo varying from newspapers to engine subassemblies. The "Codfish Airline" passenger on this day was a female reporter by the name of Kate Holliday, the first woman to land aboard an aircraft carrier in the war zone. Her visit was to collect data for magazine articles concerning life aboard a carrier. Admiral Forrest P. Sherman had issued a dispatch to the Commander of Naval Forces in the Far East authorizing women correspondents to sail aboard a ship underway.

As she climbed out of the plane, the flight deck was lined three deep in places, with curious crew members taking photos. She got right into shipboard life that very evening. While preparing to watch night landings from Primary Fly Control in the island, she handled the announcement "white flag" — a signal from the air officer that the flight deck was ready — over the public address system. The reaction throughout the ship was one of surprise; hearing a feminine voice was a bizarre experience! In subsequent days, Kate was oriented to many other significant elements of carrier operations. While attending mission debriefing sessions, she heard the grim descriptions of pilot losses. She was a guest in the general mess, Chief Petty Officer mess, and the wardroom. Officers and crew talked with her about their jobs, including the intricacies of landing an aircraft aboard a carrier. After having experienced the personal terror of a carrier landing, Kate decided to stay aboard for the remainder of our tour and return with us to Japan. There was speculation that she had feigned fright at having to fly off the ship, and thus got to stay. Whatever the circumstance, she became a welcome addition to the ship's crew.

Before Kate's arrival that afternoon of 27 July, Lieutenant Killingsworth's Corsair was severely disabled by enemy fire, and he was forced to bail out offshore. A Navy destroyer picked him up shortly after he had safely parachuted into the water. Word of his recovery was received with relief by squadron personnel who, by then, were reacting to all damage reports with anxiety. Killingsworth was expected to be transferred back to the *Princeton* on the following day. His fatally wounded plane was the seventh squadron aircraft lost to enemy action, but we were relieved that we had lost only a plane, and not another pilot.

Parachute rigger John T. Young was especially pleased, as Killingsworth's safe bail-out was the second successful jump with a chute that he had packed. Riggers were always pleased when their careful preparation of a chute resulted in the saving of a pilot's life. Tradition also dictated that the rigger be presented with a bottle of whiskey by the returning pilot, and Young anticipated getting his second bottle soon. He had shared his first — resulting from Ensign Moody's successful 20 June jump — with me and one other friend. That earlier occasion, indeed, was no longer as meaningful, with the subsequent loss of Ensign Moody.

John had then awakened me after midnight with news that after all the dry days at sea, he had received a bottle, and offered to share some with me. Neither of us particularly were whiskey drinkers, much less straight shot types, so we headed for the galley to obtain a mixer. Unfortunately, no soft drinks were available at that hour, and the galley staff could offer only a powdered orange drink mix. We poured the mix into a borrowed metal water pitcher, filled it with ice cold water from a nearby drinking fountain, and added a liberal amount of whiskey. Having no stirrer available, John thrust some fingers into the mixture and swished it around briskly. After we arrived at our "cocktail lounge," the matériel office beneath the flight deck, we tried out the concoction. The results were distressing; the mixture tasted absolutely foul. We made several futile attempts to acquire a taste for the repulsive potion, but soon dispatched it over the side with the hope that nearby marine life wouldn't be harmed.

Later that day, Saturday, the 28th, it was evident that the intensifying enemy groundfire began to be reflected in pilot performance. As Jim Blyler and I watched the late flight return around 1900 hours, our Exec again had difficulty landing aboard the *Princeton*. In relatively calm seas, Lieutenant Commander Thomas G. Cooper was unable to bring his plane in at an attitude acceptable to the ship's Landing Signal Officer, and took four wave-offs. Finally, on the fifth pass he landed safely, to the relief of all watching on deck.

Crew members often gathered at various observation posts in or around the island structure to observe returning planes during recovery operations. Recoveries of late afternoon or night flights were particularly popular because most duty assignments had been completed and the crew had free time. On some nights, it was estimated that 300 to 400 officers and crew of the *Princeton* watched from various locations around the flight deck. Many remarked that they enjoyed observing, but sweated out the difficult landings by tired pilots. More frequently, landings were hindered by battle damage, as was Cooper's that Saturday. Some crew members remarked that, after that incident, Cooper began to experience wave-off difficulties, leading some to believe that the Skipper, who routinely flew numerous missions, was also beginning to show signs of stress. I hoped that replenishment, scheduled for the next day, would afford our pilots some measure of rest.

The evening news broadcast Saturday provided insight into what might be in store for our ship in the next month. The *Princeton* was tentatively scheduled to return to port at Yokosuka around 13 August, remain the usual 10 days, and then rejoin TF-77 for five or six days. The *Essex* was to depart Pearl Harbor on 19 August, and arrive in Yokosuka five or six days later, and relieve us at sea during the last week of August. Our date of departure from Yokosuka and expected arrival at a port in the States yet to be revealed were uncertain. The newscast also included a commentary from Kate Holliday describing the purpose of her visit and what she had hoped to accomplish during her remaining time with us. Since her arrival, she had already become the first woman to fly in a close air support mission over Korea. Her flight, in a Navy prop plane, consisted of napalm and rocket runs on Communist positions eight miles east of Kosong. Her participation in the mission certainly did not indicate a reluctance to fly off a carrier deck!

Replenishment day, Sunday, 29 July, began for me with a wake-up call at 0415, as I was one of 15 lucky squadron members assigned to a work party. Following early breakfast, we watched our supply ship pull alongside and secure lines. Bombs and other reinforcements soon swung in cargo nets through loading openings, and into our hangar deck. We placed wooded platforms or skids under each net so that materials could be moved by forklift to predesignated hangar deck holding locations. Work continued steadily until 1000 when we broke for lunch and religious services. Cigliutti and I attended both. A Catholic priest had been brought aboard from another ship during the morning, and many in the large congregation were overheard saying they were glad to be able to attend Mass again.

Work resumed at noon and continued until mid-afternoon. I was assigned to install tail fins on bombs and dispose of resupply debris. Disposal methods were simple because cardboard, wood, and metal scraps were simply tossed overboard. Some crew members amused themselves by trying to hit empty oil drums that had been thrown from the bow of the ship. I had noted since joining TF-77 that trash and disposables were routinely tossed into the ocean, and was bothered at first, wondering about the long-term effects of this method of waste disposal, but I couldn't think of any reasonable alternative for a war zone. The work party secured at 1500 and I quickly settled in to read letters received during the day's two mail calls. A welcome letter from my wife reached me in only nine days, which was pretty good delivery time, given the circumstances. A letter from Cadet Haughian described his first solo flights, and a boat ride, complete with strange bugs and an alligator, that he had taken in the marshes of Florida. He was well on his way to receiving his wings.

The long day concluded with a small, informal cocktail party for selected guests, hosted by John Young in the matériel office. John had just received the bottle of whiskey from grateful pilot Killingsworth for packing the chute that had worked. Blyler somehow obtained a can of powdered lemonade, which he offered as a mixer, and around 2230 a small party was ready to begin. I was sent below to get Charlie Stein, who enthusiastically accepted the invitation and hopped out of his bunk. The lounge under the flight deck provided an appropriate secluded atmosphere for quiet socializing. Our group was joined by Ingebret Fagerlie, who contributed a large pitcher and a number of coffee cups. Blyler and I carried two cans of ice-cold water to our hideaway, where we prepared the lemonade. On this occasion, a screwdriver from the shop was used to stir the mix, and the work table bar got pretty sloppy during the whole process. No sugar was available, and the tart lemonade produced a drink similar to a whiskey sour. Unfortunately, the lemonade overwhelmed the flavor of the whiskey, but with the ingredients available, we were able to allot two drinks each.

It was widely believed among the enlisted men that officers had access to alcoholic beverages aboard ship. These suspicions generally arose on those unusual occasions when the squadron Ready Room was secured and locked. Although crew members wondered about the effects on flying performance, all agreed that with the stress the pilots were under, they were entitled to an occasional swig. Some highly speculative reports that certain pilots actually flew better after some libations the night before were, however, never confirmed.

It was a rarity for alcoholic beverages to be privately made available to enlisted personnel, and although we enjoyed our impromptu party, no one was anxious for any more pilot bailouts in order to have repeat celebrations.

Monday, 30 July, was routine with moderate parts requirements and, except for an unexplained 0900 call to General Quarters, the quiet day concluded around 1100. Air operations produced no unusual or untoward events.

On Tuesday morning, the 31st, we were hit by bad weather; flying operations were canceled and an early replenishment was substituted. We took on another load of bombs, and five sacks of precious mail, including letters and a package of newspapers for me. Later, an unexpected event occurred in the matériel office. Word of our cocktail party on the previous night had leaked out, and a gathering of new patrons arrived, promoting another party. But, cocktails for this one were restricted to straight lemonade, as no other ingredients were available. Previous mixing problems were solved by replacing the inadequate screwdriver with a much more effective tool — a new paintbrush, which swished the brew around quite well. The first batch met with disaster, however, as one of the guys dropped his cup into the pitcher and then, without thinking, stuck his unwashed hand into the mix to fish it out. The contaminated batch went over the side and a replacement quickly prepared. The second brew, although blended in a more careful manner, was not given time for a fair evaluation, because some guests, revolted by the lack of hygienic conditions of the first attempt, left before the second was ready! Interest in our social hours tapered off sharply thereafter.

The beginning of what I hoped would be our last month in the war zone began on Wednesday, 1 August, with foggy weather that forced another cancellation of air operations. We had been at sea for 21 consecutive days during this tour and seemed to be encountering an increasing number of bad weather days. I obtained some materials for our engineering crew in the morning and, after lunch, visited Stein in sick bay. Charlie had come down with a bout of respiratory illness, and had been relieved from duty. He was confined to sick bay, but looked like he would recover.

After more parts-chasing in the early afternoon, I joined Ralph Tarleton and Frank Musso in the personnel office to help them develop a squadron cruise book. The book was to include data on our unit's background, training, and performance, accompanied by photos and a few articles. I wrote a short piece about liberty in Japan.

Squadron scuttlebutt during the day focused on a dispatch regarding disposition of our planes and surplus equipment after we would be relieved by the *Essex*. We were directed to leave in Japan all aircraft having less than 14 months combat duty. Combat-ready planes were in short supply because so many were being lost in battle. Only the older, most battle-weary planes were to return with us. Ceasefire discussions were continuing, we were told, but were stalled over where the line for temporary cessation of warfare should be placed. Actual armistice talks had not yet begun, and so far, even the preliminary dialogues did not appear to be going anywhere.

Foggy weather prevailed again on Thursday, the 2nd, but lifted enough to launch a single flight of planes in late morning, many from our squadron. The unpredictable blanket of fog settled in again not long after launch, making a return to the ship impossible. All planes were diverted to landings at various emergency airfields in Korea after the mission. Our squadron was directed to K-18, the familiar forward airstrip bordering the village of Kangyoung. The pilots landed at speeds normally appropriate for a carrier but a little fast for a short landing strip with no arresting gear. The fast approaches required full use of the runway for most and, although one plane ran out of field, all arrived safely. All 14 planes returned intact to the ship in late afternoon after the foggy conditions had cleared.

Although the rumor hotline was continually active during the bulk of our tour, the periodic assignment of some squadron personnel to K-18 went virtually unnoticed. The primitive airfield was a bare-bones operation staffed by a limited number of station personnel on temporary duty from various operating units. Our own crew had been assigned to the field for purposes of servicing planes needing emergency repair and included squadron members Ira Williford, Alvin Harris, and Victor Koss. Some of these men had also been part of Lieutenant Miller's scavenger hunt in June.

The K-18 airstrip had been built to accommodate only a few planes at a time, and was equipped to do little more than get disabled aircraft flyable enough to return to their ships. Facilities could be considered something more basic than simply "no frills," with battle helmet washbasins and clothes laundered by hand in cold water. Ten-man tents were usually occupied by no more that two or three men each. Yet contrasting with the otherwise austere conditions, social clubs built by station personnel out of scrounged materials housed cocktail bars available to both officers and enlisted men. During those summer months of 1951 at K-18, enemy planes were not as much a threat as were mosquitoes. All personnel were ordered to take antimalaria pills at least once a week. But, despite such precautionary treatment Chief Petty Officer Williford contracted the disease while stationed at the base, and was later hospitalized.

The work pace at the air field was light, averaging only one disabled plane per day. Planes that could not be repaired were pushed into a dump at the side of the airstrip — which is where the Skipper's plane had ended up after his emergency landing on 18 May.

Life was somewhat boring at K-18. Baseball and swimming in the warm waters on nearby ponds occupied some time, and there were occasional visits from USO troupes, but off-base liberty was limited to the nearby village of Kangyoung. The only U.S. military personnel stationed in the town was a single ammunition disposal technician, who was called upon occasionally when an unexploded bomb fell off a crippled plane. The village had been overrun by North Korean troops earlier in the war and remained badly damaged. Dwellings were principally two-room houses, most with bullet holes in the windows. The principal occupations of the citizenry were rice farming and fishing. Airstrip personnel were leery of eating the local food, however, and usually returned to base for the standard, but safe, dehydrated "gourmet" menu. Those assigned to shore duty at this delightful station never mistook the environmental ambiance for a garden spot of the Orient!

Marginal weather conditions prevailed again on Friday, 3 August, but two flights were launched during the day. Flight quarters, however, continued until 2100 to complete the recovery of planes from the second flight. Rumors circulating during the day indicated that some dates had finally been determined for our arrival back in the States. After my watch ended at midnight, the duty Chief Petty Officer confirmed that a clarifying dispatch had been received stating that we were to arrive in San Diego during the week of 9 September. The seven-day range was given to allow for a possible stopover in Pearl Harbor to pick up personnel or equipment left by the *Essex*. In any event, we knew with some certainty our destination port and the week of arrival.

We awoke on Saturday, 4 August, to clear weather, allowing for a schedule of flight operations — the first time in many days. Busy operations produced more work for virtually everyone, and parts were in demand off and on all day. In late afternoon, the Task Force steamed close to the shores of Korea, bringing mountains and coastal terrain clearly into view again. Someone estimated that we were 38 miles offshore of Korea, and only 200 miles from Russia. The Chaplain had returned to the *Princeton* the previous evening, and Catholics aboard were pleased with the resumption of the 1630 daily Mass in the library.

Sunday, 5 August, was a routine replenishment day but because Colwell was assigned to a work party, I was busy handling all supply duties.

Between parts-chasing runs I managed to attend the 1115 Mass on the hangar deck and to read some of my incoming mail. Another letter arrived from my friend Jim who was keeping me regularly posted on his progress in flight school. After lunch, the continuing demand for parts kept me hustling until dinner. Our evening concluded, as usual, in the matériel office, but with a different guest population. Since word of our private cocktail party had leaked out, a number of new visitors had arrived each evening, a few with unrealistic expectations. Although no similar parties again materialized, many enjoyed just coming to this out-of-the-way place to visit and talk. Our new guests sometimes brought a pot of coffee, cookies, or some sandwiches from the chow hall, and the ever-popular lemonade was also frequently provided. This particular evening, however, one of our ten or more guests brought a box of goodies from home. We concluded that the camaraderie found at these gatherings must have been the attraction, rather than expectation of a sip from the nectar of the gods. We could think of no other reason why anyone would clamber up many ladders and catwalks through a blacked-out ship to crowd into the small compartment with no windows or portholes!

A bright sunny day greeted us on Monday, 6 August, and flight operations resumed on a fair-weather schedule. I was very busy with parts activity during the morning but paused at 1000 to listen to what turned out to be the long-awaited "going-home" announcement over the PA system. Beginning with the usual "This is the Captain speaking," Captain Gallery, with dramatic suddenness, advised us of a dispatch, just received form Admiral Radford, Commander-in-Chief Pacific Fleet (CINCPAC), stating that we would be relieved by the *Essex* two weeks earlier than originally planned. We were to be detached on 10 August and immediately head back to Yokosuka. The *Essex* would relieve us in port rather than at sea. The originally contemplated phase-out return to the combat zone would not be necessary. We were scheduled to depart Japan for the final time on 17 August, and head for a two-day stopover in Pearl Harbor. Our arrival home in San Diego was tentatively scheduled for Tuesday, 28 August.

The abrupt news caught me and most others by surprise. After it finally settled in, spontaneous cheering and shouts of joy engulfed the entire ship. All but critically essential work paused for a few moments while crew members expressed their wild exuberance, then ship routines resumed in support of the air operations underway. It had been busy, but it was a happy day for me that concluded watching late flight-recovery operations from a lofty island perch.

Tuesday, the 7th, was also busy, as squadron mechanics worked steadily to get our aircraft in good shape for Fleet reassignment after our arrival in Japan. The entire air group was expected to offload virtually all aircraft there, as most were not yet ready for overhaul. Our squadron did not expect to bring back more than six of our uniquely marked planes.

I got a haircut during that afternoon that I expected would see me through my return to San Diego. Also in the afternoon, before the late launch, two TBMs came aboard, making what appeared to be normal delivery runs. One of the planes, however, off-boarded a very important person, the next Captain of the USS *Princeton*. Captain Paul D. Stroop had arrived to relieve Captain Gallery; he was officially scheduled to assume command on 11 August. Earlier, we also received a Royal Navy pilot, a flight officer who compared in rank to a U.S. Navy Lieutenant Commander. He visited from one of the British carriers and shortly made his presence known by making a flight deck PA announcement. In a crisp British accent he directed the flight crew to "spot all planes forward and prepare for landings." Needless to say, his unusual accent generated reactions similar to those produced by Kate Holliday's earlier announcement! I was able to enjoy the late afternoon sun, sitting in the gun tub watching the 1730 launch of jets. Blabbing with Blyler about how nice it would be to see the Bay Area again, I concluded my day in the matériel office.

Our last TF-77 replenishment day — Wednesday, 8 August — began with the sun seemingly brightened by the detachment news. Despite the general euphoria, work went on at a "let's wrap things up and go home" intensity. Parts activity was hectic in the morning, although there was no flying. It seemed almost like a normal operating day, though I paused briefly to receive letters and a package of licorice and books from home. Activity continued during most of the afternoon, but Blyler, Stein, and I took advantage of a subsequent lull to sit in the warm sun for a couple of hours before dinner. Later, while eating, an announcement was made that the air group was eligible for the Korean Service Medal with one battle star, and the Navy Occupation Medal. In addition, a pending United Nations Medal was a certainty when formally authorized. A Presidential Unit Citation was also a possibility. I closed the day in the matériel office, and engaged in horseplay with Charlie Stein. The fun progressed from tossed wads of paper to a full-fledged ink fight involving multiple pens. The skirmish ended only after both of us had to go below for a shower.

On Thursday, 9 August, our final full day of combat flight operations began at 0400 in clear weather. Work in the morning was surprisingly light, permitting me to do a little more sunning. Around 1600, things picked up when one of the returning flights produced a number of parts requests. Evening flight operations secured around 2000, as all our remaining planes landed safely. Sadly, however, our air group failed to get through this last full day without a casualty. Corsair squadron VF-821 lost a pilot when his plane crashed in flames during an afternoon mission. The *Boxer* also experienced a difficult afternoon when a landing jet crashed and exploded on the flight deck. *Princeton* crew often watched takeoffs and landings on the other carriers during breaks in our own operations. On this occasion, the *Boxer* was very visible as weather conditions were clear and the distance between us not great. Although we could easily see the entire sequence of the accidental event, and the aircraft flames were quickly extinguished, we could not see whether the pilot was safely removed from the plane — but we assumed he was, because the wrecked plane was pushed over the side shortly thereafter. A secondary major flight-deck fire, caused by the crash, disrupted further landings on the *Boxer*. Spilled fuel continued to burn, and the smoke obscured our view of most of the flight deck, making it some time before the crew of the *Boxer* was able to complete the interrupted recovery operations.

Although most aboard the *Princeton* were upbeat as we came to the close of this meaningful final day of combat operations, I was personally troubled about one aspect related to the upcoming withdrawal from TF-77. As we geared up to sail under noncombat conditions, a subtle "shaping up" of the entire ship had already begun. Small and large duty-station areas were being cleaned up, and valuable, excess parts and equipment replaced into inventories. However some disposals were made that were, in my way of thinking, very questionable. After dinner, during the darkening hours, while gazing at the sea and the ships at rest, I noted some surplus materials being tossed over the side. I watched as .50-caliber machine guns were hurled into the ocean from the hangar deck level — and assumed they may have been defective weapons destined for the scrap pile. My concern intensified, however, when the guns were followed into the briny deep by substantial amounts of belted ammunition. It seemed to me that ammunition — most likely belted by hand aboard the *Princeton*

— should have been transferred to one of the nearby carriers. The *Boxer*, on this night, lay close to us, yet the expensive and presumably usable ammunition was consigned to the sea. This practice conflicted with my personal distaste for waste, and I was aware of the long, sweaty hours that men had spent belting the ammunition. On a few occasions, I observed our squadron's ordnance crew working well past midnight, tediously preparing ammunition for morning strikes. I regret that I did not, at least, question the propriety of this jettisoning operation. But at the time, I reasoned that it did not seem advisable for a 21-year-old "white hat" airman to question decisions made in another command. I watched the disposal operation with continuing dismay for about 30 minutes and then went below to bed.

VF-871's early morning and final flight over Korea returned safely just before 1000 on Friday, 10 August. While our air group was flying its closing forays over enemy targets, the ship was already preparing to disengage from the Task Force. On the flight and hangar decks, previously recovered aircraft were stowed away for more sedate sea operations. Remaining squadron surplus, or obsolete parts and matériel, were turned in to stores or the engineering department. Shortly after 1000, with all planes then aboard, the *Princeton* detached from TF-77 and headed for Japan. Crew members promptly geared up for an activity seldom seen during combat — a change-of-command inspection — scheduled for the following day. Wherever I looked, men were feverishly shining shoes, pressing whites and neckerchiefs, or, in the case of the Marine detachment, cleaning and polishing weapons.

The frantic activities continued right up to dinner and resumed immediately thereafter. At 1930, weary crew members happily reported to the flight deck for a gigantic celebration enhanced by the clear weather and comfortable evening temperature. The purpose of the gathering was to commemorate the completion of our Task Force duty and to formally honor those pilots who had completed the 10,000th and 11,000th landings on the *Princeton*. Our own Lieutenant (JG) Frazier was honored for making the 10,000th landing and said a few words, as did an esteemed pilot from another squadron. A skit, composed principally of players from our squadron, entertained a large, appreciative audience. Yeoman Tarleton and pilots Alton Donnelly, Francis McCue, Ed Reed, and Stewart Smith played major roles in a comedy of sorts. Tarleton was especially noteworthy in his Royal Navy sailor role of Heathclife Windersmear, as was Donnelly, playing Russian pilot Igor Beverski. Donnelly, being a former teach-

Lieutenant (JG) Donald E. Frazier at shipboard ceremonies honoring his 10,000th landing on the USS *Princeton* and completion of Task Force duty, 10 August 1951. (Courtesy, J. Edward Watson)

er of the Russian language, was particularly effective in his role. After the applause quieted down, Captain Gallery, our very popular outgoing CO, said a few words of appreciation to the officers and crew for a job well done. Captain Bill was cheered for at least ten minutes by the appreciative and respectful audience. The entertainment was followed by an ample supply of ice cream and cake. The party concluded around 2130 and few left unsatisfied.

Most men returned to their compartments to complete preparations for final inspection. After all was done that could be done, Stein and I sat on the fan-tail until 2300 to enjoy the stars, moonlit water, and the realization that we were going home. In anticipation of that happy event I went below, showered, and shaved off my long-nurtured, but still scraggly, beard. Though it had become a familiar part of my face, I felt ambivalent toward the dirty blond appendage, and considered how it might be assessed during our formal inspection. Fellow beard grower, Jim Blyler, was not consulted before I took this drastic step, because he might not have understood my motivation to remove the beard. Beside which, Blyler's growth was neater and longer than mine, and I wanted to conclude the embarrassment of daily comparisons!

Reveille at 0530 Saturday morning, 11 August, was treated with more attention than most other early-morning wake-up calls due to the looming 0900 change-of-command inspection. For many, there were still uniform, equipment, or personal details in need of serious attention but feeling confident about our own preparations, Stein and I went out to the fan-tail after breakfast and watched the sun rise over the nearby Pacific islands. We went below at 0730 for some final touchups before squadron muster at 0830. Finally, our squadron merged with nearly 3,000 officers and men on the hangar deck for the most formal inspection any of us had been subjected to since shipping out.

The inspection party consisted of an Admiral, two Captains, and a number of Commanders and Lieutenant Commanders, scrutinizing the military appearance of each of us. After standing in ranks until 1000, we received word that our squadron had survived the ordeal in good shape. The inspection was followed by a brief awards ceremony where Air Medals, Purple Hearts, and Good Conduct Medals were presented to ten eligible officers and men. Additional awards were expected to be presented following our return to the States. All hands were greatly relieved when the tedious ceremonies finally concluded at 1030. The sleeping compartments were suddenly congested as thousands of men hurried to change into more comfortable uniforms.

We steamed toward our final visit in Japan before heading home, and life aboard ship assumed a calm, relaxed routine. While each crew member had ongoing tasks to perform, the urgency and hectic pace of combat operations was gone. As we went about our duties, the ship's orchestra entertained on the hangar deck during the afternoon. One selection — "California, Here I Come" — was highly appreciated by all.

During the afternoon, I was advised that I was one of the lucky squadron members selected to go to a rest camp in Japan for three days. A total of eight resort camps had been set aside for Navy R & R use, with each ship arriving from Korea allotted a specified number of reservations. Also selected, among the 13 spots allotted to our squadron, were Stein and Perez. Stein and I were assigned to the Kanbayashi Hotel, but Perez was booked elsewhere. We looked forward to visiting the best resort hotels in Japan. It would be fun to live like tourists — for a short time, anyway. Accommodations reportedly included a private room with shower, bath, and meals, for no more than one dollar per day. The balance of the costs were paid by the U.S. government. Guests were welcome to play ball, swim, or just sleep in during their stay. Blyler wasn't selected, unfortunately, because of his current duty assignment, but would get a 48-hour pass during the final stay in port.

While life aboard ship had shifted to a new relaxed pace, we did not go unreminded of the war. In late afternoon, the ship's crew conducted gunnery exercises again, because although we had technically been relieved from combat, an aircraft carrier in open waters remained an inviting target. Noisy though gunnery practices were, all of us recognized that the maintenance of defensive skills was essential to our well being. Nearing the relative safety of Japan, we also could not help thinking of those who were not returning with us. As we concluded this final return from the war zone, we mourned for our missing shipmates and hoped that their lives were not lost in vain.

The Defense Department, in early August, reported a new total of 80,079 American battle casualties in Korea. This stag-

*gering number included 13,407 deaths. Three members of our small unit alone had perished over Korea during our short tour of duty. A total of 32 deaths, including our losses, were reported by the **Princeton** during the ship's first post-activation combat tour. We were saddened at these statistics, especially because the "non-war" went on, and the dying continued on both sides. Ceasefire talks had been stalled since General Ridgway broke off negotiations on 6 August because of Communist violation of the neutrality of the meeting place at Kaesong.*

Chapter 8

Homeward Bound
August 1951

SUNDAY MORNING, 12 August, seemed sunnier
and clearer than the many preceding Sundays at
sea. A larger number of crew members turned out
for breakfast, and afterward many went on deck
to watch the landscape of Japan come into view. For the
last time, we entered Tokyo Bay en route to the Yokosuka
Naval Base. The day was, no doubt, brightened considerably by the recognition that after this brief stay in port we
would not return to Korea. The combat segment of our tour
was complete, and we had nothing ahead but intermediate
stops on the way home. Despite the rumors that had varied

from week to week regarding the possibilities of our return, we were actually on the first leg of our voyage home.

As the *Princeton* approached our assigned dock, a rarely used berthing procedure was ordered to counteract wind conditions hampering maneuverability of the guiding tugboats. Propeller pilots were instructed to prepare for a "windmill" operation; the flight deck was quickly spotted on the port side with F4U and AD aircraft; and more than 15 aircraft were lined up, with noses pointed into the wind and tails pointing toward the pier. The pilots were ordered to "start engines," and shortly thereafter, the propeller backwash began to slow the *Princeton*'s approach into the quay. The rpm's of the engines were gradually increased to offset wind pressure blowing the ship toward the pier. As the huge ship gently eased into its berth, the order was given over the bullhorn to "cut engines." Although the windmill procedure was effective, it was infrequently used because of the potential for damaging expensive aircraft by racing their engines without the cooling benefits of flight-generated winds.

Another warm reception was provided to us by the Naval Station band, and a group of local Japanese dancers. Many aboard were preoccupied with anticipation of this final visit, and those selected for one of the rest camps anxiously awaited liberty call. Shortly after attending 1100 Mass, Stein and I, armed with our leave papers and property passes, happily departed for our destination resort, the Kanbayashi Hotel. Upon arrival at the Yokosuka train station information booth, our enthusiasm was dampened by basic logistics. Our leave papers stated that we needed to check in at the hotel within six hours or our reservations would be canceled. We anxiously inquired when the next train would depart and were informed not until 1945. To make matters worse, we would have to board a sleeper because the journey, involving three transfers, would take between 11 and 12 hours! We pondered whether it would be worthwhile to travel such a long distance for a relatively short stay. To be safe, however, we called the hotel and requested that our reservations be held beyond the six-hour limit. Although assured of the extension, we again mulled over the pros and cons of going through with the long trip. After lunch at the Naval Station Enlisted Mens Club, we called our squadron duty officer and asked whether or not we were required to accept the scheduled tour. The duty officer, after clearing with CAG, advised that because we were on an approved R & R leave, we could select a predetermined alternative destination. After discussion of preferred locations, we accepted the duty officer's recommendation — the Green Hotel in Tokyo. Although disappointed that our rest camp trek didn't work out, we were relieved that we could more effectively use our remaining time in Japan. We finally got underway and boarded the 1600 train for our new destination.

After arrival in Tokyo, we decided to handle first things first — namely, to get something to eat. Replenished by a solid meal at the PX, we headed by taxi to the Green Hotel but were greatly frustrated trying to describe it, or its location, to our driver. After being driven aimlessly around the huge city, we abandoned the cab and hailed another. Our new driver delivered us without delay to the hotel, which was of moderate size and located some distance from the major hotels and the central Ginza area. Although under Japanese management, the clientele was principally military personnel from several UN nations. The management sought to offer "proper" lodging only, and a prominent sign posted near the entrance cautioned "no professional women allowed." The hotel's architecture was traditional but not of a stereotypical style. A standard Oriental roof on the two-story, gray stucco building was highlighted with light green tile. The building fronted carefully manicured gardens surrounded by a backdrop of stately pine and cherry trees.

After registering in the lobby, we were escorted to a clean second-floor room costing 1,500 yen per night. The small, boxy, double room seemed odd to us, with its thin silk-covered walls, fabric-clad sliding hollow doors, and detached, shared bath. The serene surroundings and lovely gardens, however, helped us first-time travelers adjust to this different style of lodging.

Before turning in that first night, we went downstairs to the small coffee shop for ham sandwiches and beer. The tranquility of our repast was soon disrupted by a tipsy soldier from New Zealand who loudly entered the dining area and proceeded to entertain with a variety of jokes. Believing that he had an appreciative audience, he expanded his impromptu act by going into the lobby and returning with a potted palm. He centered the huge plant atop a table and inartistically performed a dance around it, to the delight of his audience.

Later, we met Private F. M. (Flip) Hedgewood, an Air Force enlisted man on leave from Korea, and spent the evening with him drinking beer, chatting, and playing American jazz music on a hotel record player. Hedgewood had been stationed in the Far East since 1948, and in Korea since the start of the war. We enjoyed the peacefulness of the hotel, and the camaraderie of others, including the entertaining "Kiwi," as the New Zealander was affectionately dubbed, but decided to call it quits at 0100 and headed for what we hoped would be a restful night.

On Monday morning, the 13th, we slept in enjoying our non-military accommodations without having to worry about reveille. We had a leisurely breakfast around 1100, and spent the balance of the morning and early afternoon exploring the ponds, lawns, and general beauty of the hotel grounds. We took photos and visited with other GIs, some of whom were from foreign UN forces. At 1600, we met up with Flip Hedgewood and took a cab to the downtown Air Force Airman's Club. After an early supper of steak sandwiches and beer, we walked about a mile to the more exclusive GHQ Enlisted Mens Club, in the Dai Ichi Building. Charlie and I had visited the club briefly during our last stay in port. Although patronage was sometimes restricted, we were allowed to enter after presenting our R & R leave papers. We had a photo taken of the three of us sipping 25-cent mixed drinks in the lounge, and after paying 100 yen each for the three prints, we went upstairs to explore the GHQ ballroom. I marveled again at the decor of our beautiful surroundings. So luxurious was this ballroom that it exceeded anything we had seen in stateside hotels. The huge dance floor was designated the "Starlight Room," and adjacent areas were covered with carpet that looked at least an inch thick. We listened to American tunes played by an excellent 16-piece Japanese orchestra until 2300, when we called it a night. After returning to the hotel by cab, we met two men from our air group and talked on until midnight. It was a very warm night and, after going to bed, we battled mosquitoes and a noisy Mitsubishi fan until 0400.

After a very restless night, we awakened on Tuesday, 14 August, not with a sense of leisure as before, but exhausted. A breakfast of bacon and eggs with toast, washed down by numerous cups of coffee, helped to restore some life to our tired bodies. The day was much like the previous one except for a PX dinner, after which we returned to the GHQ Club to pick up copies of the photo taken the previous evening. On the way we livened things up by dropping firecrackers out the windows of our taxi. Some of the harmless — but noisy — fireworks didn't explode until we were almost a block away. After more Starlight Room music, we picked up our photos and departed for our hotel. The prints turned out well, and we mailed one off to Private Hedgewood, who had already returned to Korea.

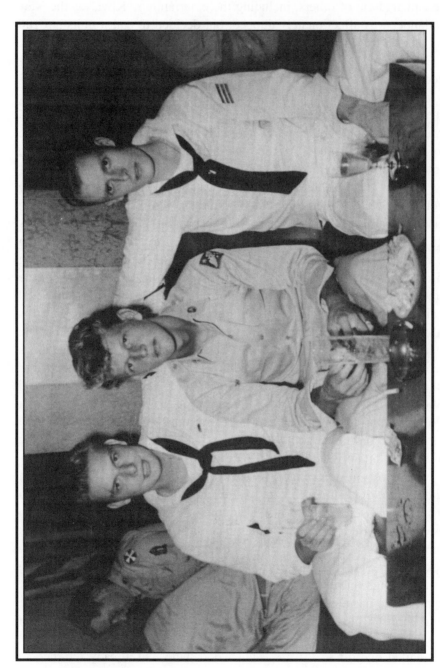

Charlie Stein, F. M. (Flip) Hedgewood (U.S. Air Force), and Paul Cooper, at the GHQ Enlisted Club, Tokyo, 13 August 1951.

A large party was well in progress at our hotel when we arrived, and the place was jumping with excitement. We joined the festivities and had a couple of Canadian Club-and-Cokes in the garden while we were treated to a spectacle of clumsy attempts by an Air Force officer to woo a Department of the Army Civilian — a DAC. He failed and she left. We joined a couple of Air Force guys, an Army "groundpounder" (infantryman), and a British merchant seaman for conversation until 0200. Rather than spend another miserable sleepless night, we stopped at the front desk and requested bug spray from the woman in charge — the "mama-san." After a liberal dose, our room was mosquito-free — and we went right to sleep. Wondrous stuff, that DDT!

On Wednesday morning, the 15th, we arose at 1000 after a restful final night of leave, but immediately faced a serious problem. We had enough yen to pay our hotel bill, but not enough for breakfast. This was an awful situation because as usual, I was hungry. We packed our bags, checked out, and headed for the PX where we could exchange some scrip for both food and yen. As we traveled downtown, we chatted about our stay and the interesting servicemen we had met. We didn't quite make it to the PX, however, as our disappearing yen left us about a mile short. After toting our bags through crowded streets, we finally arrived, checked the luggage, and quieted our growling stomachs in the restaurant. We exchanged some scrip for enough yen to get us through the day and back to the ship. I estimated that five dollars' worth should handle my needs without a lot left over.

That day, 15 August, was a Catholic holy day as well as my sister's birthday, and I planned to solemnize both by attending Mass. The previous day I had called the General Headquarters to locate nearby Catholic chapels, and was advised that the GHQ Chapel Center was the closest. After Mass, I made my way to the street and started to enter what I believed to be a cab, with two others I had seen inside at the services. It turned out that the vehicle was a limousine from the Spanish Embassy! The couple inside were the Ambassador and his wife. I was most embarrassed and apologized profusely for my diplomatic *faux pas*, and quickly stepped back onto the sidewalk, where I belonged. I was joined shortly by an officer from the Philippine army, and we shared a cab back to the PX. During the ride he said that he, too, was a recalled Reservist, and a Certified Public Accountant in civilian life.

That afternoon, Charlie wanted to shop for jade, so we visited some shops near the PX. He found a ring for his wife, but we couldn't put together enough yen between us to pay for it. Back to the PX we went, and while there, we stopped for a chocolate ice cream float. Later on, with jade shopping finished, we strolled at leisure along the busy Ginza thorough-fare. During our walk we practiced a custom common then among GIs — bumming smokes. We had been out of cigarettes for some time, and with-out ration cards, were unable to buy any in Tokyo, even at the PX. As we turned a street corner, I bumped into one of the tallest uniformed people I had ever seen. The soldier, whose shoulder patch identified him as Ethiopian, appeared to be about seven feet tall. After apologizing, I noticed he was clutching a full carton of Phillip Morris cigarettes, so I politely offered to buy a pack. He couldn't understand English well, and, of course, I could not understand him, but we attempted to communicate by pointing our fingers or using other, charade-like signals. He finally grasped our desperate situation and graciously gave us a pack, refusing any payment. We were touched by this clear affirmation of the cooperative UN spirit. We were also very glad that he was on our side!

As we meandered back to the PX, I ran out of yen — again. I managed to buy a dollar's worth from a sailor we encountered on the street, but he required a commission and I received, therefore, only 340, rather than the standard 360 to 1 rate of exchange. Street entrepreneurs, even uniformed ones, were present everywhere.

We concluded our visit to Tokyo with a cab ride to the Railway Trans-port Office where we boarded the 1555 train to Yokosuka. In spite of the fact that Tokyo was headquarters for the Allied war effort, and essentially an Army town, we had enjoyed it. Although we were not due aboard until 2000, we decided not to linger in the comfortable Navy environment of Yokosuka. We had satisfied our tourist objectives, and when we stepped onto the gangway around 1800, we left Japanese soil for the last time. Charlie and I were part of the first liberty party off the ship, and the last to return. We were ready to go home.

While we had been away, the crew aboard had engaged in a flurry of pre-departure activities. Materials critical to the war, including aircraft, had been off-loaded for use by other ships or units. Fresh paint had been applied to the superstructure of the ship in many areas. One unique touch was the transformation of the huge "37" on the stack from standard regu-lation block numbers into quasi-Oriental characters. The new Oriental look suggested that the ship and crew had indeed spent some time in the vicinity of Japan and Korea. Our journalist guest, Kate Holliday, also had departed the ship during our absence, armed with a lot of basic information about wartime carrier life.

Goodbye parties in the Yokosuka Officers Club, and last rounds of local nightspots, had been completed during the final days before departure. Many, like Charlie and I, had made a final combing of PX and other shopping centers in search of bargains. One of my last purchases in Tokyo was a souvenir recording of a song very familiar to most then serving in the Korean War. The tune, played over and over in Japanese clubs, was commonly know to GIs as "She ain't got no yo yo." This colloquial title was influenced, no doubt, by the Japanese lyrics, which have a similar sound. I bought the recording, published on the Nippon Columbia label, under its correct title of "China Night." The flip side of the 78 rpm disk contained "Hill of Pure Heart," a song rarely, if ever, heard by military personnel.

My return to the ship was accompanied by a certain sadness at departing so soon from a land and a people that had been most hospitable. This feeling was soon dispelled, however, by eight letters from home that had been received during my absence. Later in the evening, our squadron had a couple of visitors from our replacement ship, the *Essex*, which had arrived during the morning. The familiar carrier had come to relieve us in port, and had brought some familiar faces. Two members of the *Essex* crew were former members of our squadron, detached earlier for medical reasons. Both recovered from their ailments after we had deployed and were reassigned to units in the *Essex*'s air group. Unfortunately, the tour of sea duty beginning for them would last until March 1952.

Most aboard the *Princeton* arose early Thursday, 16 August — our departure day. After breakfast, a muster was held for all CAG-19 personnel to be sure that all hands were back on board. Following a send-off by local Japanese officials and a delegation from the Naval Station, the *Princeton* pulled away from the quay for the final time during this deployment. Our next stop would be Pearl Harbor, some 3,400 nautical miles from Tokyo Bay. The officers and men of the "Sweet Pea" had endeared themselves to the local Japanese community during our routine visits to port. On one occasion, the ship had played host to a group of Japanese orphans; crew members had functioned as guides, served up Navy chow, and entertained the children as guests at an excellent Japanese vaudeville show. Regularly in the evenings when in port, the ship had provided excess food from dinner meals to needy residents from neighboring communities.

The replacement carrier USS *Essex* (CV-9) at anchor in Tokyo Bay, 16 August 1951.

These gestures of kindness to our former enemies did much to heal the memories of World War II and garner respect for the crew of the *Princeton*.

As we departed Tokyo Bay shortly after 0900, we passed a number of other U.S. ships anchored there. It was difficult to believe that only a few short years earlier this same body of water had sheltered the mighty Japanese fleet. The most noticeable ship in the harbor at that moment, as far as we were concerned, was the majestic *Essex*, CV-9 — our former shakedown, and now our relief, ship. The *Essex* was temporarily anchored out in the harbor, and would shortly pull into the berth we had just vacated. As the *Princeton* moved slowly past the portside of our somber replacement, we noted many new Banshee aircraft crowding her flight deck. The tail symbol "S" adorned the planes of her air group, CAG-5, soon to go into action over Korea. As we moved past the ship that we had nicknamed the "Reluctant Dragon," her signal lights flashed us a message of parting good will. For us, the day seemed sunny and bright as we approached the channel and open seas. But for the *Essex* crew, perceptions might have been somewhat different. Once we had moved past her we realized that we were officially relieved, and on our way home.

On the high seas once again, we rapidly adjusted to non-combat shipboard routines. Other than drawing a little cash during pay hours that afternoon, I had little to do. I cleared up the debts incurred during shopping sprees when I ran out of yen, and paid six dollars for a ship cruise book to be published later. After an uneventful afternoon and early evening in the office, I went to bed early.

On Friday, 17 August, our first full day at sea, work assignments began to gradually emerge. Around 0830, I received a request for a replacement aircraft tail elevator assembly. Somehow in the pre-departure movement of planes, a tail had been smashed. The assembly was of significant size and had been stored well below deck, in a remote storeroom. It took almost two hours just to get authorization to open the applicable hatch and, it seemed, with two helpers, just about that long to get the cumbersome unit onto the hangar deck. Parts requirements were not nearly as demanding during the afternoon, however, and there was time for some letter writing. Later that evening, we were advised that we were about 800 nautical miles away from Japan and watches should be set back one hour. The first phase in recapturing time lost during our trip west, aboard the *Weigel*, was underway.

Jim Blyler in front of the USS *Princeton*, moored at Ford Island, Pearl Harbor, Hawaii, 21 August 1951.

On Saturday, we were informed that the estimated date of our arrival in Pearl Harbor was 21 August. The mild, sunny day was disturbed only by a moderate work load. Aircraft parts demands had reduced to a trickle, as we had ceased flight operations. Late afternoon brought out plenty of sprawling sunbathers, myself included. And I capped off my generally quiet day with an uneventful midwatch.

The two succeeding days were truly unique, in that they were both Sunday, 19 August. The first Sunday was a routine, almost boring day. We crossed the International Date Line during that night at 0300, and consequently awakened to another Sunday. Activities on the second Sunday, however, were much different than the first. After breakfast we mustered at 0800 in the Ready Room for special work assignments, and I was sent with one of several painting parties where I spent a monotonous morning chipping loose paint from deck and bulkheads. This traditional Navy activity is one that most sailors get exposed to at one time or another — like it or not. Before lunch, I chased a few parts, and after lunch briefly listened to the ship's band on the hangar deck. This respite ended at 1300 when it was back to the Ready Room for an exciting afternoon of more chipping. The quality and quantity of my work was hampered by a severe cold, which I had been treating with the all-purpose Navy cure-all pills, the APC aspirin-type product. Following dinner, after setting my watch back the nightly one hour, I hit the sack but found I couldn't get to sleep until around 2230.

Although there were no air operations, the daily work pace didn't necessarily decrease, it just changed. Monday found me, Perez, Stein, and others back in the Ready Room for yet more paint work. Shortly after reporting, Perez and I were sent to the paint locker where we stood in line for more than an hour waiting for supplies. Standing in lines — slow-moving, or almost stationary — was also an established Navy custom, at sea and onshore. Finally, at 1100 we returned to the Ready Room and began a new assignment, painting the deck. This was immediately hampered, however, by the availability of only two paint brushes. After brief individual orientation flings with a brush, we mostly spent the morning standing around watching the others take their turn at the job. Many compartments aboard ship, including our matériel office, were being freshly painted, as the ship was scheduled for a thorough inspection upon return to the States. Following lunch, at 1300 we returned, and again took turns brushing on gray paint until 1500. After admiring our handiwork, I went below and

joined Jim Blyler on the hangar deck, where we watched a pickup basketball game until dinnertime. Most of the evening was spent writing letters
for mailing the next day in Pearl Harbor. The bulk of remaining letters
home most likely would be written before leaving Pearl, because anything
written later would not reach the mail system until we arrived in San
Diego.

A high level of anticipation was present throughout the ship on the
morning of Tuesday, 21 August, as we neared the Territory of Hawaii. I
arose at 0630 for early breakfast and some horizon watching, hoping for a
glimpse of these fabled islands. A total of 122 islands, all formed by vol-
canoes, made up the Hawaiian Island group. Many had been eroded by
centuries of waves and ocean currents until only atolls remained above
water. Our destination was Oahu, in the chain of eight main islands to the
southeast that included Hawaii, Maui, Kahoolawe, Molokai, Lanai, Kauai,
and Niihau. These particular islands were once described by Samuel
Clemens — Mark Twain — after his 1886 visit, as "the loveliest fleet of
islands that lies anchored in any ocean." Cool trade winds kept the climate
pleasantly mild all year with little temperature difference between night
and day, or summer and winter. It is understandable why the islands, 2,000
miles from the U.S. mainland, were already becoming a major vacation
attraction.

*The Hawaiian Islands were virtually unknown until Captain
James Cook of the British Navy had reached them in 1778.
Local chiefs ruled during the period of Cook's visits, until the
main island area was united under chief Kamehameha in 1795.
He ruled the island group, except for Kauai and Niihau, as
King Kamehameha I, with local chiefs serving as governors of
their islands. The two remaining islands accepted Kamehameha's rule in 1810, and all eight islands became a republic in
1894. Politically, these islands have been an integral part of the
U.S. since annexation as a territory in 1898. They were used by
the U.S. Fleet during the Spanish American War, and served as
the shipping and assembly center for the armed forces in the
Pacific during World War II. In the postwar period, they were*

being developed as a major training center for the armed forces.

Situated a little more than 2,000 miles to the southwest of San Francisco, the islands seem to have little military significance. Yet, any aggressor seeking to attack the U.S. West Coast from across the Pacific would necessarily have to take into account the Hawaiian Island group. This may have been a consideration in the Japanese attack on Pearl Harbor in 1941. Thereafter, the islands demonstrated their significance by becoming the hub of U.S. military operations in the Pacific. After passage of the National Security Act of 1947, the three armed services in the Pacific area were unified into one military defense and security command. Known as the Pacific Command, it included Army, Navy, and Air Force personnel under the administration of the Commander-in-Chief Pacific and U.S. Pacific Fleet, Admiral Arthur W. Radford. Headquarters for the joint command was located in CINCPAC's Fleet administrative headquarters on Oahu atop Makalapa Ridge, overlooking Pearl Harbor. The islands became a critical strategic headquarters for naval operations again during the Korean conflict.

We mustered on the *Princeton*'s hangar deck at 0800 in preparation for our imminent arrival in Pearl Harbor. All first-timers aboard eagerly looked forward to sighting this historically significant naval port, situated in what had been described to us as an island paradise. On schedule, we entered the harbor formed by two mouths of the narrow Pearl Stream. Named for the pearl oysters that once grew there, the harbor was one of the largest and best sheltered naval anchorages in the world. The nearly ten square miles of navigable water included three landlocked lakes. It was at Pearl Harbor, at 0755, on 7 December 1941, a "date which will live in infamy," that Japan launched its first attack of World War II. It was also the base from which reconstituted U.S. naval forces were sent to engage in the decisive battles of the western Pacific.

*Among the 92 U.S. Navy vessels anchored in the harbor on 7
December 1941, 18 were sunk or severely damaged. The Pacific Fleet lost eight battleships, three light cruisers, three destroyers, and four other vessels, but no aircraft carriers. About 170
planes were destroyed, and approximately 3,700 casualties
killed or wounded, including civilians. On 7 December 1950,
plaques were dedicated on the sunken remains of the battleships **Arizona** and **Utah** in memory of the men who went down
with their ships. The **Arizona**'s hull still contains the remains of
1,102 men who were trapped when the ship sank.*

Remnants of the devastating World War II assault were clearly visible
to crew members as the *Princeton* moved peacefully through the quiet harbor. We headed in the general direction of the Pearl Harbor Naval Base,
headquarters for the U.S. Pacific Fleet. In addition to the Pacific Fleet and
its various forces, the base housed a Navy shipyard, supply center, ammunition storage depot, and other major support facilities. The huge base —
covering 22,000 acres — was located five miles west of Honolulu, on the
south side of Oahu. Oahu itself is the third largest of the Hawaiian Islands,
with an area of 640 square miles and a population then of more than
318,000. Shortly after 0900, we pulled into our assigned dock on Ford
Island, a moderately sized but significant naval facility, in the harbor opposite the Naval Base. Although Navy facilities on this harbor island were
greatly damaged during the Japanese attack, any remaining effects were
not readily evident. We were greeted by dignitaries from Honolulu, and
officials from Pearl Harbor Naval Base and the Pearl Harbor Naval Air
Station. They were accompanied by a contingent of Hawaiian dancers,
dressed in colorful grass skirts and flower leis. Our beautiful tropical surroundings were made even brighter by their warm reception.

I was fortunate to receive a 24-hour liberty pass and was very anxious
to explore Oahu, "the gathering place," as it was once called in Hawaii's
ancient days. We were told to expect mail call sometime during the morning, and because this always took precedence, I waited to read the four letters and two cards from home.

After lunch with Stein and Blyler, Jim and I went ashore for the first time during this stopover in paradise. We boarded a liberty boat at 1345 for the 10-minute trip to the Naval Station. Although our crossing was uneventful, that definitely was not the case for those in the launch immediately behind us. A fracas unexpectedly broke out, and a number of sailors were observed scuffling wildly about. Some, with cameras swinging from their necks, dressed in immaculate white uniforms, were seen tumbling over the sides and into the harbor waters. The cause of the melee was unknown, and later we heard that a number of soggy sailors in muddy uniforms were seen returning to the ship.

Onshore, we climbed aboard a waiting bus destined for Oahu's center of activity, the city of Honolulu. En route, we traveled near the landmark Aloha Tower and the Honolulu Airport, which at the time was one of the three busiest air terminals in the world. During 1950, Honolulu handled more takeoffs and landings than did the airport outside of San Francisco. These runways handled ten scheduled airlines, seven from the mainland and three locals, which serviced the primary islands. Major U.S. mainland airlines included Pan American, United, Northwest, and Transocean. International carriers included British Commonwealth Pacific, Canadian Pacific, and Philippine air lines. The local carriers were TPA Aloha, Hawaiian, and Trans-Air Hawaii. Honolulu resembled many large seaport cities on the mainland, except for the magnificent tropical surroundings. Ships brought most of the food, manufactured products, and raw materials used on the island. Honolulu also was a regular port of call for luxury liners operated by Matson Navigation Company, American President Lines, and a number of freighter passenger lines, though the average flight time from the mainland was nine hours, contrasted with the 4½-day voyage by ocean liner.

We took the 15-minute bus ride downtown, and wandered near places reflecting the island's history — such as the Iolani Palace, where Hawaii's kings and queens had lived and ruled, and the old Kawaiahao Church, once the site of coronations. We also strolled the streets of Chinatown where shops contained unusual merchandise and a variety of foods. The local people, in each of the various shopping areas, reflected the different races and nationalities that had made Hawaii a melting pot. Although we each were considered a *malihini* (newcomer), we felt most welcome in the heterogeneous cultural environment. Most of those we encountered in the downtown areas were dressed in loose, brightly colored clothing, patterned after garments worn by early Hawaiians. A few women

wore the muumuu, the loose, floor-length dress introduced by early mis-
sionaries. Others wore a holomuu, a fitted version of a muumuu. Many
men simply wore shorts and an aloha shirt, a sport shirt with brightly colored, tropical, or oriental designs.

After exploring the downtown area, we took a bus to Waikiki Beach,
about which we had heard so much. This world-famous beach had been a
swamp until it was drained and improved after World War I. We reached
the Waikiki area from downtown Honolulu by traveling a short route that
took us along Kapiolani Boulevard to Kalakau Avenue; from there, we
spotted popular Kapiolani Park with its grandstand, tennis courts, and new
zoo. We walked on the sun-splashed golden sands, along a stretch of deep-
blue ocean, with a backdrop of graceful palms. We found it to be all that
we had expected, with the beach as the center of Honolulu's water sports
activities — swimming, surfing, outrigger canoeing, and spearfishing.
Gentle summer trade winds, blowing from the east or northeast, created a
balmy environment perfect for strolling or just enjoying the beach and the
warm ocean waters. Blyler and I were captivated by the beauty of the sheltered sea front whose boundary to the south featured yet another landmark, the extinct Diamond Head volcano. On its slopes was Fort Ruger,
headquarters for the Hawaiian National Guard. The beach area extended
from the mouth of the yacht harbor at Ala Wai canal to Diamond Head.
We resolved, right then, to come back and spend a lot more time at this
lovely spot.

A short walk up the beach in the opposite direction took us to another
storied landmark, the Royal Hawaiian Hotel. The stately "pink palace"
was clearly visible, jutting out from a point along the beach that was mostly free of other big buildings. The Royal Hawaiian and the adjacent
Moana, both fronting on Kalakau Avenue, were the only major hotels then
situated on the beach. The sandy pink Royal Hawaiian, built in 1927, was
not only noticeable but easily accessible from the beach. The main
Kalakau Avenue entrance, however, was partially hidden by an expansive
garden area, filled with native plants and palm trees, thriving in the sub-
tropical climate. An enormous variety of brilliantly colored flowers and
plants enhanced the lovely lush gardens, and the scent of plumeria was
everywhere.

Proper attire was required to enter the Royal Hawaiian from either front
or beach entrances. "Proper," at the time, essentially meant coat and tie or,
if military, a correct official uniform. Swimsuits were allowed only at the

beach entrance. We were thankful that we had dressed properly in our white uniforms, so that we could see the magnificent interior of that famous hotel. Rich furniture, placed tastefully upon thick, lush carpeting, surrounded by numerous arrangements of colorful island flowers, was the standard for all interior public areas. Rhythmic Hawaiian background music was heard almost everywhere, featuring the ukulele and the Hawaiian steel guitar.

After sightseeing through lobby, halls, and ballrooms, I suggested to Jim that it might be appropriate to stop for a drink in that beautiful establishment. We chose the Surf Bar, a comfortable open-air cocktail lounge on the beach side of the hotel, and sat beneath swaying palm trees at a table placed on a covered area of beach where ocean waves came gently hissing over the sands toward us. We sipped unique Polynesian drinks garnished with thick wedges of tasty pineapple. The comfortable, warm temperature, gentle breezes, and peaceful environment more than qualified this spot as a bit of paradise.

After mailing some postcards home, we decided to eat dinner nearby at the famous Don the Beachcomber's restaurant "on the beach at Waikiki." Wearing apparel at this highly popular bar and eatery was casual Hawaiian. Typical dress could range from the traditional Aloha shirt and pants to a formal coat and tie. The relaxed informal theme and laid-back nature of the place was appreciated by the customers. Proper dress for a *luau*, the traditional Hawaiian feast, served by Don "in the true Polynesian manner," however, was more restrictive. Don's printed invitations specified that South Pacific garb was mandatory. For the ladies, this meant that holokus, holomuus, muumuus, and sarongs were in order. Pareaus, lavalavas, and aloha shirts were considered acceptable for men.

Beneath graceful palms, beside a reflecting pool lit by flaming torches, Don sought to recapture the spell of the islands as it was during the days of the kings. The interior and exterior of the restaurant was accented generously with Polynesian artifacts; however, the Daggerbar cocktail lounge had its own very distinct emphasis. Don's hobby had been the collection of rare and old daggers from odd and interesting parts of the world. This interest was based on a belief that the daggers held secrets and intrigue from past centuries. The perfection developed by skilled craftsmen of the 15th through the 18th centuries was evident in Don's collection. Over 60 rare and valuable antique daggers from more than 20 cultures could be found in the bar. Each exhibit contained an identification number that could be used to reference a description printed in the cafe menu. A 14th-century steel cross-hilt dagger from the Roman Empire was the oldest. We so enjoyed the food, drinks, and environment that after wandering around the beach area following dinner, we returned to the Beachcomber and closed it up at 0100. Later, back aboard ship, after our return bus and boat rides, we were transformed by the "aloha spirit." Jim and I, both from urban Berkeley, had thoroughly enjoyed our first exposure to this cosmopolitan island city.

The following morning, still on my 48-hour pass, I slept in until 1100 and, after lunch, left with Charlie Stein for liberty. Our first stop in Honolulu's commercial district was a military uniform shop where we each purchased three campaign ribbons. We had decided that we wanted to look our heroic best when we returned. We were eligible for the "glory bars," so why not wear them? We placed the Korean Service, with one battle star, Navy Occupation, and United Nations Service ribbons in the proper left breast location on our jumpers and headed for Waikiki. We rented swim suits, towels, and lockers at a handy beach concession and went for our first Hawaii swim. The day was gorgeous — the sun hot, and the ocean beautifully blue. Water temperatures at Waikiki that August ranged from 77 to 82 degrees, significantly warmer than off California. We alternately sunned and swam until 1730 when we reluctantly decided that, as pleasant as the beach was, we had best use our limited time to see some other sights.

We walked to the Royal Hawaiian and visited the hotel boutiques, some of which were then referred to as "Servitor" shops. At one, I purchased a half-ounce bottle of white ginger perfume for my wife. Charlie bought a bottle for his wife, too, and we mailed them directly from the store. We found picture postcards featuring the hotel, hastily penned a note, and sent them on their way.

I found a public phone in a garden area of the Royal Hawaiian, and placed a collect call to Marie at her parents' home. After waiting about an hour to get a connection, I was overjoyed to hear her voice once again, soft and clear over the radio-telephone system. I alerted her that although we were still expected to arrive in San Diego on 28 August, she should keep an eye on the newspapers for any last-minute changes. It was great to talk with her again, but there was still an ocean between us.

Based on the previous evening's pleasant experience, I suggested to Charlie that we have dinner again at the Beachcomber. He accepted my "expert" recommendation, and we enjoyed another delicious meal, preceded by a couple of island drinks. We said *mahalo* (thanks) to the restaurant staff, took a cab to our boat landing, and were back aboard ship by midnight.

Although Thursday, the 23rd, was my duty day, I was technically still on my 48-hour pass during much of the morning so I slept in again. While on Ford Island, we took aboard a number of defective "dud" aircraft for transport back to the States. Some of these may have been those earlier rumored as off-boarded by the *Essex*; some may have come from carriers rotating through the port. Once the loading process was completed, the *Princeton* moved its berth from Ford Island to a dock at the Naval Station to board some passengers. A group of civilian VIPs, guests of the Secretary of the Navy, were scheduled to return to San Diego aboard our ship. These events resulted in a one-day delay of departure from Pearl Harbor and created consternation among some of the crew as to possible slippage in our San Diego arrival date. Our new departure date was set for Saturday, the 25th. Its impact on the projected 28th return date was then undetermined.

Although my section had duty, most of us had no specific work to do, which made being restricted to the ship particularly frustrating. We glumly watched one of our few remaining Hawaiian days slip away. Blyler, beginning his 48-hour pass, went ashore to spend the night with some friends living in Honolulu. I took care of my laundry, asked John Young to sew up a shirt, obtained a camera pass, and visited the Personnel office, but did nothing very meaningful during the day. After dinner, until going below around 2000, I gazed over the rail at the peaceful island paradise so far removed from the bloody war zone.

*The Thursday, 23 August, banner headline of the **Honolulu Advertiser** broadly proclaimed, "Reds End Peace Talks." The Communists had broken off armistice talks allegedly because UN forces had bombed and strafed the city of Kaesong. The UN claimed that the Communists had planted evidence and that the incident was a frame-up. The disappointing Communist action came after 43 days of fruitless negotiations. Peace talks had*

The rental convertible: John Young, Bob Perez, and Jim Blyler, Honolulu, 24 August 1951.

bogged down from the start over Communist demands for establishment of a 38th Parallel truce line and withdrawal of Allied troops from positions north of that line.

Our last full day in port on Friday, the 24th, began with muster on the hangar deck at 0800. Although some work details were assigned, liberty would be granted in the afternoon. After straightening up some of my things in the compartment, I joined Ken Colwell and Bill Norton, my fellow supply colleagues, on another work party to finish painting the matériel office. Motivated by the promise of early liberty, we completed the first phase of our project by 1130. After lunch, Perez and I departed the ship for our final look at the island. We walked to the Naval Station main gate and phoned Blyler at the home of his friends. By 1345, Jim arrived, as arranged, to pick us up in a jaunty green 1951 Chevrolet convertible he had rented — the top, of course, was down! Shortly before his arrival, John Young had joined us, so all three of us piled into the sporty car. Jim parked near the home of his friends close to Waikiki, and we headed for the beach. Some of us preferred to swim in something more fashionable than rental or regulation Navy-swimsuits, and a quick stop was made at shops on Kalakaua Avenue. In true island spirit, I purchased a colorful wrap-around swimsuit, which dazzled my shipmates and others on the beach. We spent the first hour and a half mostly frolicking in Waikiki shoreline waves. Feeling a little more adventurous, we decided to swim out into the ocean as far from the beach as possible. Young was the clear winner, managing to get out more than 150 yards. I managed, with my slow sidestroke, only about 100 yards and got very tired in the process. I was able to struggle back to within about 20 yards of the beach — to a breakwater that I had spotted on the way out — where I could stand on the wall. I was determined to hang on to the breakwater with my toes, despite heavy wave action, and to recover my lost strength. After resting in this awkward manner for a few minutes, I swam back slowly and dragged my exhausted body onto the sandy beach. It was evident that I lacked either the skill or the stamina to attempt this kind of nonsensical challenge. The other adventurers returned safely, at their own paces, and we sprawled in the warm sand for a long while, resting and taking photos for posterity.

Despite the foolish swim challenge, we thoroughly enjoyed our time on this marvelous beach.

We returned to the house, jumped into the convertible, and immediately set out for a driving excursion to the other side of the island. Still clad in our swimsuits, but comfortable in the mild, temperate weather, we headed toward the mountains through the beautiful Nuuanu Valley, famous for battles fought there by ancient Hawaiian kings. We ascended the tropical mountains to the Nuuanu Pali, the 2,000-foot gap in the Koolau range, at the end of the valley. The majestic view of windward Oahu overlooked the blue Pacific lapping on white beaches, acres of waving sugar cane, and neat patterns of far-reaching pineapple fields. We stood at the edge of a sheer drop at the top of the Pali, which represented Oahu's most famous scenic view — the spot where King Kamehameha the Great drove the defending army over the precipice, when he conquered the island in April 1795. We were surprised at the force of the steady wind blowing up from the lower valleys. It was so strong that we could almost lean over the edge without falling. We traveled along a roadway cut in the sheer face of the cliff, descended to sea level on the other side, and proceeded to the village of Kaneohe. We passed banana groves, coconut palms, and lushly colorful oleander and hibiscus. We noted thick growths of tropical plants and trees in areas of rich soil where rainfall had been particularly heavy.

Not having time to drive completely around the island, we headed east from Kailua Bay on a road that would take us back to Waikiki by way of the back side of Diamond Head. It was foggy on that side of the island and we decided not to swim at any of the unfamiliar beach areas. We passed near Hanauma Bay and the "Blow Hole," a natural hole in the lava ledge through which wave action forces ocean water up in geysers. Unfortunately, we did not see one of these events.

Our return took us to Koko Head, and then past several miles of residences, back to Diamond Head. Before returning to Waikiki, we took a side trip to the campus of the University of Hawaii, which was then the world center of sugar technology. The university, founded in 1907, was located in the lower Manoa valley and had an enrollment of about 4,700 students with a faculty and staff of about 850. The institution also excelled in the fields of tropical agriculture, marine biology, and Pacific and Asiatic cultures. John was so impressed with the campus that he vowed to return and enroll as a student. Although our tour only covered the east end of the island, it took us through the more natural, undeveloped, typical regions. The views from the mountains were spectacular, and at sea level the beaches were simple, uncluttered, and truly unspoiled.

After changing clothes at the home of Blyler's friends, Perez, Young, and I departed so that Jim could take his friends to dinner at Trader Vic's, the famous restaurant known for its Cantonese chow, and the home of such exotic drinks as the Scorpion and Fog Cutter. We headed instead for the Beachcomber, which had by then become my favorite hangout. After dinner, I attempted — unsuccessfully — to send a telegram from the Royal Hawaiian to Marie, advising of our delayed departure, while Perez and Young waited in the Surf Bar. After awhile, I walked back and picked up Blyler and we all had a night cap — a free round from our friendly bartender — before leaving at 1130.

Arriving at the rental agency to return Jim's car, a dispute arose over whether or not there should be charges for an additional day because it was a few minutes past midnight. Bob and I listened to the debate for awhile, but left in order to get back to the ship on time. Jim and John decided to stay and discuss the issue further. We made it back at 0100, but the two hagglers returned about a half-hour late. Fortunately, they were not put on report. Their tenacity in the quest for justice had prevailed. Our last liberty day in Hawaii closed on this satisfying note.

As we prepared to depart Pearl Harbor, the Territory of Hawaii's importance to the Korean War effort had become evident to many of us. We had been aware of the strategic and symbolic value of the Territory during World War II but had little knowledge of the magnitude of its role in the new Korean conflict. Multi-cultural Hawaii had, at that time, the largest Korean community outside of Korea and Japan, numbering about 7,000 persons. More than 5,800 of the residents within this ethnic community were U.S. citizens. The islands were also involved in the military transactions between the U.S. and the South Korean government. When the war began on 25 June 1950, three South Korean gunboats purchased from the U.S. were then moored in the Honolulu harbor. These boats were

immediately moved to Pearl Harbor where they were equipped with new guns and deployed to the Pacific in less than a week. Military support for the beleaguered South Korean government also had received prompt assistance from island personnel. The 24th Army Division, which had been formed in Hawaii, mostly contained men from the islands. The unit, bearing the taro leaf insignia, was among the first to go into action in Korea. Shortly thereafter, in early July, the 5th Regimental Combat Team, part of Hawaii's defense forces, also sailed to join embattled U.S. and South Korean troops. Within weeks of the departure of these units, about 200 Marine Reservists were also en route to Korea. In early March 1951, some eight months after the start of the war, casualties from Hawaii totaled more than 600 — including 132 killed, 379 wounded, 96 missing, and 2 prisoners of war. Residents of the Territory had paid a hefty price in carrying out the vital role of stemming enemy actions early in the war.

On the island home front, the pace of work had also intensified at the Pearl Harbor Naval Shipyard. Shipyard personnel increased by more than 85 percent over pre-Korean War levels. Shipyard ordnance shop personnel rehabilitated many worn-out Fleet combat ship guns to speed up operations in the Pacific. Some specialty occupations required recruitment from the mainland, but with the continuing influx of military personnel and stepped-up defense work, a housing shortage quickly developed. During calendar year 1950, about 90,000 Navy personnel arriving for duty in the Pacific passed through the Pearl Harbor receiving station, which could only provide lodging for approximately 2,000 men and women at a time. By February 1951, the shortage in naval civilian housing became so critical that mainland workers were refusing to come without assurances of housing. Plans to construct two privately operated military housing projects on Navy land rapidly moved ahead.

Transportation activities had also increased sharply. During the first six months of the war, the Military Sea Transportation Service (MSTS) in Hawaii handled more than 386,000 tons of cargo and more than 22,000 passengers. The Military Air Transport Service (MATS) serviced and refueled planes at a rate of one every 75 minutes. Operations were largely con-ducted from Hickam Air Force Base and the Honolulu Airport. In eight months, 11,500 tons of high-priority cargo and 44,600 persons were flown to the Far East. A reverse air lift eastward brought back 15,700 combat casualties and 4,700 non-battle patients. Tripler Army Hospital housed most of the patients for at least one rest day, before transfer to mainland hospitals near their homes; and Hawaii's own war wounded recuperated at Tripler as well.

*Late in 1950, President Harry S. Truman visited Hawaii en route to discuss Far East problems with General Douglas MacArthur. His arrival at Hickam Air Force Base on 13 Octo-ber, aboard his plane the **Independence**, marked the third time a U.S. President had visited the islands. He spent 16 hours on military matters, toured Pearl Harbor and military bases on windward Oahu, then left for Wake Island. He returned from his discussions with MacArthur on 14 October, and spent 32 more hours on Oahu. He conferred with military officials and began preparations for a major foreign policy speech in San Fran-cisco. During this visit, however, Truman found time to take an auto ride over the Nuuanu Pali and spend part of an afternoon at the Kailua beach club, then returned to Honolulu by way of the Blow Hole. He and his party departed aboard the **Indepen-dence** on the morning of 16 October.*

As on the mainland, the Korean War had intensified the urgent need for an effective civil defense system in Hawaii. But the Territory, ahead of most states because of statutory author-ity to establish such an organization, had the framework already in place and proceeded with plans and community-based activities. A volunteer ambulance program utilized in World War II was already organized, and before the close of 1950, an identification bureau began fingerprinting some 70,000 school children on Oahu. American Red Cross first-aid classes commenced in the evenings. Air-raid warning sirens were reactivated, and a block-warden system was in the process of being reformed. Evacuation plans, blood-bank establish-ment, bomb-shelter identification, medical-supply stockpiling, and other phases of civil defense were underway. The island *population, tested only a few years earlier in war, had shifted again to a war footing. The readiness of the military installations and the civilian population in Hawaii played a critical role in the early days of the hostilities. Were it not for the **Princeton**'s side trip to Oahu, I and many others would not have been exposed to the significance of these islands in the ongoing Korean conflict.*

Saturday, 25 August, had begun as did most every day in Hawaii — with beautiful skies and the scent of flowers. Unfortunately for us, it also began on the flight deck with a formal parade and muster. Our time ashore in this incredible place had ended. Our thoughts shifted to home. The return to San Diego, originally scheduled for 28 August, was now projected for Wednesday the 29th. I was glad that at least I had alerted Marie of this possibility. As we pulled out of Pearl Harbor at about 0800, bidding *aloha* to the islands, I resolved to return someday with Marie to this magnificent place.

As we headed for open seas, the decks of the *Princeton* were filled with the regular crew as well as a number of returning military personnel and the civilian VIP guests. The senior members of the three armed services and the secretary's 11 guests were all civilians and each was extended every courtesy from all ranks. During their short trip with us, they would be given an opportunity to learn firsthand about aircraft carrier organization and operation from the men who did this as a profession. Several destroyers, returning for overhaul, also accompanied the *Princeton*, creating the impression that we were back in the Task Force once again.

Life at sea resumed its normal beat, but on this first day we had little work to do. After lunch, I straightened up the office, then my locker. Because I was close to my bunk, I decided to lie down for a while to read. My reading lapsed into sleep around 1430, and continued until Stein finally woke me for dinner. After dinner, Charlie and I gazed in fascination from the fan-tail at the ship's beautiful wake, shimmering in the dusky waters. As darkness descended, we went below to the hangar deck to see a movie. We were entertained by the ship's band as a warmup for the film,

Mother Didn't Tell Me, which I had already seen, but enjoyed again. Later, we gathered with our cronies in the matériel office under the flight deck as we had done so often while at sea with the Task Force. We sat around chatting until 2300 about how much we had enjoyed the beauty of Hawaii, but now couldn't wait to get home.

After breakfast with Charlie Stein, my last Sunday at sea began with more painting. Ken Colwell and I prepared the remaining half of the matériel office for a fresh coat of gray, and following a religious services break, we wrapped up our prep work and straightened things for the rest of the day.

Personal plans for our arrival in San Diego were constantly discussed. Jim Blyler graciously offered to stand by for me on Wednesday, the 29th, my normal duty day, as I hoped to find my family members waiting upon our arrival. Stein and I set our watches ahead another hour and capped off an easy day with a spirited card game of Casino.

Monday, the 27th, was also a light day and devoted mostly to taking care of administrative details relating to our arrival. After the 0845 muster on the hangar deck, approved leave papers were passed out to those who had submitted formal requests. Most of the crew expected some extended liberty and preferred to defer submitting leave requests until they could get a clearer picture of what was to become of the squadron and air group. I decided, however, to submit a request for a few days of leave beginning on the 30th, depending whether or not my family was able to come to San Diego. I prepared the essential duty day "standby request" for our Wednesday arrival, hoping I would find them waiting on the pier. After dinner, Stein and I watched the movie *Abandoned* on the hangar deck, and concluded an uneventful day with another one-hour watch adjustment.

The final day of the reactivated *Princeton*'s maiden nine-month sea journey began with growing anticipation of our San Diego return. Cleanup activities were completed around the ship as all hands worked to present the "Sweet Pea" in the best light. I stood in a paint line for awhile after breakfast, but no more paint was available. The balance of the morning was devoted to photo sessions on the flight deck, for the ship's forthcoming cruise book. All hands in our squadron appeared for the session properly clad — officers in crisp tan uniforms and enlisted men in pressed undress blues. Despite the wind, which blew strongly across the flight deck, we managed to get suitable shots taken without anyone losing our seldom-worn hats. Although we had looked forward to such cruise-ending formalities, we were saddened that three members of our close unit would be missing from the photos.

The balance of our fourth and final day after departing Hawaii was uneventful, and most crew members dealt with personal matters. One event of significance to many squadron members did occur in late afternoon. An important piece of equipment in the pilot's Ready Room, unfortunately, had to be abandoned. A treasured recreational device, a five-cent slot machine inherited from our predecessor squadron, was not allowed into the state of California. In early January, President Truman, by signing Senate Bill 3357, had made it illegal to carry slot machines across state borders, and thus, also, illegal in state waters. Simultaneously with the President's action, the Navy issued ALNav 1-51, an order directing the destruction or disposal of all slot machines and similar gambling devices that paid off in money or property aboard ship or on any area under Navy jurisdiction. This stunning blow principally affected Officer and Chief Petty Officer Clubs, where food and liquor prices were kept low because of profits from hundreds of slot machines.

When it came time to carry out the directive, the impact upon the squadron was not financial but emotional. Despite the frustrating pleasure that the machine had provided officers and enlisted men during the long days at sea, it could not enter California with us! Most Air Stations had already taken drastic actions to implement the order for disposal of these gambling devices, including breaking up machines with axes or dropping them from aircraft into the sea. Some had been sold to private civilian interests, where state law did not bar them. In our case, California law did not allow them and thus they could not remain on government property. But it was felt that somehow the dedicated service provided by our functional, but ungiving, machine should be recognized, and the best means of disposition and recognition decided upon was burial at sea. Accordingly, at the proper moment and with appropriate solemnity, our lovable one-armed bandit was sadly dispatched over the side. Though the aft port corner of the pilot's Ready Room would never again be the same, we were comforted with the realization that, after the following day, we would have no further use for either the bandit or the Ready Room!

As the mighty *Princeton* concluded its long seagoing journey, which had begun with its rebirth at Bremerton, Washington, a tired and experienced ship's company was elated to finally be returning home. Air group personnel were relieved that the rigors of the shorter than normal tour of combat operations were over, even if the future remained uncertain. The civilian visitors aboard had explored the ship during the passage from Hawaii, and spoke freely with the crew regarding the intricacies of carrier life. And our military guests, especially those who bunked on the flight deck on warm evenings, anxiously awaited their return to stateside life and some personal space. All of the population aboard, estimated to be more than 3,000, were exposed to the noisy practice firing drills, which livened up the four-day cruise.

During the final days at sea, the last of the painting and cleaning was completed. The ship was bright and fresh, its passengers and crew proud, and all very eager to return to home and loved ones.

Chapter 9

Welcome Home
August-September 1951

*O UR FINAL DAWN aboard the **Princeton** on Wednesday, 29 August, produced many early risers eager for a glimpse of the beautiful California coastline. Both crew members and the guests from Hawaii busily packed personal belongings, and most crowded into the mess areas for an early breakfast. Although a moderate overcast obscured any distant views that might have been possible, island perches and bow rails were already crowded. The eager anticipation of returning to our San Diego starting point was clearly evident among air group personnel. Ships company, most of* whom had been at sea with the "Sweet Pea" since she came out of moth-balls, welcomed the cherished opportunity to return to any mainland port.

Shortly after 1100, an announcement blared over the PA system advising crew to prepare for flight quarters. Soon thereafter, both the hangar and flight decks were filled with motion and activities not seen since 10 August. Planes were brought up to the flight deck via the deck edge elevator, and plane pushers arranged them on the deck in desired pre-flight configurations. Then shortly before noon, pilots walked across the flight deck for the last time from their Ready Rooms and climbed into waiting planes. Immediately thereafter, the bullhorn at Pri-Fly (Primary Flying Control, the equivalent of the control tower on an airfield) announced "start engines" as the ship increased speed to 30 knots and began a slow turn into the wind. The bullhorn then announced "white flag — launch planes," and the first jets shot from the bow catapults into the sky. CAG-19's final launch from the *Princeton* had begun. Once the Panther jets were on their way, the flight deck thundered with a continuing launch of propeller-driven Corsairs, followed by Skyraiders. But all 33 aircraft left the ship on a peaceful mission, no longer encumbered with the heavy weapons of war.

Ten Panther jets of VF-23 broke off from the formation, departing CAG-19 for the last time, and flew directly north to NAS Moffett Field. The Corsairs of VF-821 and VF-871 and the Skyraiders of VA-55 headed for NAS San Diego, led by the CAG Skipper, Commander A. L. Maltby, who had assumed command of the air group when Commander C. R. Stapler was shot down on 10 June. Maltby, also in charge of VA-55, had suffered a close call himself, receiving a direct hit from a 37mm shell to the wing of his Skyraider during a bombing run. Shrapnel tore a gaping hole in the wing and cut his face, forcing him to land at an emergency field in Korea.

After the last of the air group planes were on their way home, the sense of anticipation increased among those remaining aboard. The mighty *Princeton* plowed steadily through moderate seas for what seemed an eternity, until at long last it moved past San Clemente Island and the carrier *Antietam* (CV-36), which was then on maneuvers. Finally, we were within range of Point Loma and the port of San Diego. Officers and crew rushed to quarters on the flight deck. Lines upon lines of sailors stood in formation, garbed in dress blues and our seldom-worn white hats, ringing the edges of the flight deck as we entered port. As we rounded North

Island, a great cheer rolled across the narrow waters toward us, from an estimated crowd of 3,000. Bands struck up music and banners waved, and we realized we were almost there! At 1430, as the 3,000-ton ship maneuvered for docking at NAS piers O and P at North Island, the formations, released from duty, shifted to the starboard side nearest the dock. We had earlier been advised that a system had been devised to spot loved ones by using large alphabetical cards. As we pulled closer and closer to the dock, all eyes aboard sought out faces or signs identifying family and friends. The throngs of visitors crowding along the pier could be seen trying to pick out their favorite sailor from those grouped high on the ship, all wearing identical uniforms. By this time, "bluejackets" — sailors — were crowded into every available nook and cranny from the hangar deck to the flight deck trying to get a clear view of the dock. The launch of planes had delayed us an hour, but we finally tied up at the quay wall at 1500. We were officially home!

Although abruptly out of mothballs and manned with a preponderance of Reservists, the ship had done her job well. During the nine-month deployment, she had conducted operations of a magnitude far overshadowing that of any other carrier operation. She had spent 186 days in the operating area, 124 of which were flying days. A total of 9,586 sorties had been flown; and there had been 9,796 launches and 9,788 landings while in the operating area. Targets in Korea had been hit with 8,920 tons of aviation ordnance and ammunition. A total of 54 replenishments had occurred at sea and, in addition to supplies and ammunition, the ship had taken aboard 12,845,297 gallons of bunker fuel and 4,022,575 gallons of aviation gasoline. Regrettably, a total of 32 deaths had been reported by the *Princeton* during the long deployment. Although our squadron, VF-871, was not aboard during the entire cruise, we were privileged to have served for a time with the officers and crew of this highly respected warship.

On hand that 29 August to give color to our return were the NAS band, the Marine Recruit Depot band, four majorettes from Coronado High School, and the Navy band's majorette, along with a banner proclaiming "Welcome."

Despite the promise of the card identification system, I had difficulty picking my family out of the huge crowd that spread the entire length of the ship. Innovative, if not funny, signboards dotted the pier, seeking to attract the attention of a particular loved one aboard. I finally spotted my family clustered together, off to the right — my wife and her mother, my father, mother, brother, and sister. The joyful sight of so many of my family gathered so close, all looking for me, produced a lump in my throat. I spent the next few minutes waving wildly, while running along the flight deck to get nearer their vantage point — until they finally spotted me, and all at once their many arms flew into the air.

Liberty call could not come soon enough! I was properly outfitted in my pressed dress blues and had a pass signed by Lieutenant O. D. Gilman, one of our pilots, allowing me to remove a box of souvenir gifts and my laundry bag. I was ready to go! But the bullhorn announced that official calls would be made first by the Commander of the San Diego area major Fleet and Shore Commands, present at dockside. The protocol ceremonies would then be followed — as soon as possible — by liberty. Smiling with delight from her wheelchair throne on the speakers' stand on the pier was 17-year-old Jane B. Taylor of San Diego, "queen" of the *Princeton*, who provided a warm "welcome home" to the crew over the public address system. Taylor was joined by her court of four attendants from local orphanages: Esther Chavez, 10; Judy Miekle, 9; Maxine Nichols, 10; and Linda Johnson, 8. Congratulations were also offered by Vice Admiral Thomas L. Sprague, COMAIRPAC; Vice Admiral Arthur D. Struble, First Fleet Commander; and San Diego Mayor John D. Butler. After the dockside functions concluded, Jane was carried aboard the *Princeton* where she was greeted by the Skipper, Captain Paul D. Stroop. The reign of the small, frail girl was just beginning; she was scheduled to preside over additional welcoming ceremonies the following day.

The idea for a homecoming queen had been suggested by a crew member while we were at sea. A gala ball had been planned and the decision was made to choose someone from home who had fought a battle of her own in life — symbolic of the hardships our men had faced in battle. Once the idea became known aboard ship, the feedback was overwhelmingly positive. Interest grew and in less than 24 hours — despite the fact that no drive for funds had even been suggested to the crew — more than $3,000 was quickly deposited with Chaplain McManus, as donors from all over the ship contributed savings to meet the anticipated needs of a queen not yet picked. In July, an advance committee composed of enlisted men and officers had been sent from the ship, then off Korea, to San Diego. Under the leadership of Father McManus, the committee had been assigned to arrange for the homecoming event and to select the queen and her court.

With the cooperation of officers of the Commander Air Forces Pacific Fleet, and the San Diego Chamber of Commerce, the selection committee found our queen, with the help of the Sunshine School for Crippled Girls. Handicapped virtually since birth with cerebral palsy, and without parents, Jane Taylor had been in and out of hospitals all her life, and had been taken into Mr. and Mrs. George Melmin's home the previous spring. Her warm smile and manner quickly convinced the committee that she would be perfect as the queen of the USS *Princeton* homecoming ceremonies.

But Jane Taylor's relationship with the crew of the *Princeton* did not end with the final event of the homecoming. The crew had also raised $5,000 for her education and welfare, placed in trust with the San Diego Chamber of Commerce.

The media carried nationally the heart-warming story of Queen Jane and the crew of the *Princeton*. It was noted that the majority of crew members aboard the ship were Reservists, and that most were married, with families of their own. Perhaps for these reasons, the *Princeton* was affectionately referred to by the NAS newspaper, *The North Islander*, as "the family ship of the Pacific Fleet." The written commentaries indicated a great deal about the spirit and character of the crew. Letters and resolutions were also received from organizations commending the *Princeton*'s action. The *San Diego Evening Tribune*, on 29 August, had noted that "what the *Princeton*'s crew has done will not solve the Iranian oil crisis nor will it end the Korean War. But it will go far to restore many an individual's faith in the eternal goodness of humanity." As the euphoria of our return and homecoming celebrations tapered off, all fortunate enough to have served on the USS *Princeton* held their heads high.

Shortly after 1600 the afternoon of our homecoming, we met the logistical challenge of expediently off-boarding the more than 3,000 people. The first of a continuous stream of men in dress blues began surging down the gangway into waiting arms. It took about ten minutes before I could leave the ship to be reunited with my family. As the numbers on the pier rapidly grew, so also did the emotional intensity of the reunions. Crying, laughing, and hugging — our jubilation was reflected by all around us.

After a few lingering minutes describing external components of the ship to my father and brother from dockside, we piled into my folks' gray 1948 Dodge sedan and headed for San Diego for dinner. We spent the night at the Harbor Travelodge, in anticipation of the busy afternoon and evening on tap for Thursday, when the *Princeton* homecoming celebration was scheduled to peak. And curiously, now that I was back home with my family, the thought of attending a Navy function seemed appealing.

Thursday, 30 August, was indeed different and exciting. I was back in the pleasant city of San Diego, surrounded by family, on a perfect day. After a leisurely morning, during which we didn't go anywhere or do much other than update each other on recent events, we squeezed again into the Dodge, then took the slow but scenic ferry to Coronado Island. An open house and reception for our homecoming queen was scheduled between 1500 and 1700 aboard the *Princeton*. We arrived early for the festivities so that my family could tour the ship, under my "expert" guidance. Midway during our visit our queen was wheeled onto the flight deck and officially crowned. That evening, all shipmates, family, and guests were invited to attend the formal homecoming party at the Pacific Square Ballroom in San Diego, with a dance featuring the music of Frank Duval and his orchestra.

Reality returned to the *Princeton* crew, however, the next day, Friday, 31 August, as we realized that we were still in the Navy with an uncertain future before us. Although we were free until Monday, 3 September, the location and duration of our next duty station was unclear.

I decided to wait until Monday before I concerned myself with the future. My family returned to their homes, and Marie and I recognized that we all had to get back to our individual lives and responsibilities at some point. We had no idea yet where we would be living, and hoped we could find suitable housing that coming week.

On Monday, the 3rd, I reported for duty once more aboard ship. We were informed that the air group would commence disembarking that morning, and began off-boarding personal belongings for transfer to NAS station barracks. Despite earlier rumors, inspired by wishful thinking, we were evidently destined to be located again at North Island. With the others, I hauled my seabag and personal items down the gangway and loaded them on a bus for transfer to the designated barracks. Work parties began removing squadron equipment for transfer to our assigned hangar. All squadron work at the time essentially revolved around these activities, although the projected duration of the shore assignment remained murky. Despite the uncertainties, I made a few exploratory inquiries regarding the location of suitable housing. Most married squadron members were in the same situation, and were similarly scurrying about attempting to find accommodations for dependents. Leads were shared, but often were found to be dead-ends, as vacancies were quickly grabbed up.

On Tuesday, the 4th, I was assigned to NAS Supply until further notice. I reported as instructed and was provided a pickup truck for use in carrying our varied parts activities around the Air Station. Some of my runs brought me to the hangar housing our air group, for pickup and disposal of excess or defective parts. During one of these runs, I ran into Vic Koss who informed me of a possible apartment vacancy, and after checking it out with Marie, we decided to take the place. We moved in that night with our few possessions.

The balance of that first week of shore duty was troubling, as the permanency of my detached station duty began to be a concern. By reporting daily to the NAS supply division I began to feel as I did while mess cooking — cut off from the squadron. It was almost as if I were — heaven forbid — a "Regular." The oppressive atmosphere of regulation, so unlike the *Princeton*, was still present on the station and, complicating my anxieties, I began to feel ill late in the week, aching all over with a fever and severe headache.

As this first disturbing week back home neared an end, and still feeling ill, I obtained a Special Request Pass, authorizing me to be away from the station on the weekend. I was the recognized squadron "expert" in such matters, able to quickly process and obtain an authorized pass. Perhaps this one small administrative success in an otherwise bleak week, in terms of my detached assignment and illness, was an omen of forthcoming good luck. Without knowing it, I had just submitted my last personal request.

Late Friday afternoon, 7 September, all squadron enlisted men were summoned together for an important announcement. A decision had been made to release from active duty all our enlisted Reservists called up in 1950. COMAIRPAC instructions 190.1, dated 24 July 1951, pursuant to ALNav 62-51, was the authority for this astonishing action. Officers were not affected and would be retained on active duty for an undetermined period, and the squadron itself would not be deactivated, but would remain an active operating unit. Administrative processing of affected personnel from active to inactive duty was to be initiated without delay, and all regular duty assignments were effectively suspended. Enlisted personnel were to be transferred for processing, effective 10 September 1951, to the Separation Center, Flag Administrative Unit, COMAIRPAC, NAS San Diego.

Who would have expected anything like this to happen? Certainly, the many of us who were hustling around the San Diego area trying to find housing did not anticipate anything like immediate release. Only isolated individual separations, such as Charlie Stein's, were considered likely during our return trip from Hawaii. The long-nurtured dream of squadron transfer to a duty station nearer to the Bay Area had lingered in our minds, but *immediate* release was not envisioned. We left the base that night shocked, but obviously happy. A homecoming celebration sponsored by the City of Oakland was already scheduled for Saturday, 15 September, in Oakland.

After many telephone calls home over the weekend to share the exciting news, Marie and I were thankful that we had arranged only interim housing. We contacted our former landlady and neighbors at the 7th Avenue apartments to advise that we would not be returning and to thank them for their kindnesses. Yet although the suddenness of this change in our future had caught us completely by surprise, instead of reestablishing ourselves in San Diego, we could happily shift our thoughts to setting up housekeeping for the first time as a Bay Area couple.

During the weekend, almost unnoticed in our personal excitement, came news that on Saturday, 8 September, Japan had signed a symbolic peace treaty with 48 nations, to be effective on 28 April 1952, when the Allied occupation, in which we had participated, would officially end. Although further combat was now remote for us, we hoped that as with the ending of World War II, there would be a similar peaceful end to the Korean conflict.

As Vic and I headed off to North Island Monday morning, it was strange to be doing so no longer as members of VF-871. As of 10 September 1951, we were officially under the command of the Separation Center. We had already moved our seabags and personal belongings from the squadron barracks, and shortly after arrival had been provided an overview of the separation process, which would largely involve paperwork and a physical exam. I was concerned that the exam might find physical problems that could delay my separation. Wouldn't that be a sad state of affairs? I would have preferred a physical similar to the one conducted upon my call into service at NAS Oakland — a non-exam, as I never saw a physician, only my file coming out of the doctor's office bearing the notation "physically fit for active duty."

The Navy had other ideas, however, and a more thorough separation physical was on tap. Thankfully, my injured leg had healed, and I had recovered from whatever malady had afflicted me the previous week. I was found "physically qualified for release to inactive duty."

In ensuing days, the obligatory paperwork began to peter out and so, thankfully, did the latrine-duty work assignments. We were provided a few lectures advising us of our responsibilities as inactive Reservists, including an individual obligation to remain in the Navy an additional nine months beyond expiration of our standard four-year Reserve enlistment period. We were also informed of the many advantages of reenlistment, but these, obviously, fell on deaf ears. Close attention was paid, however, to discussions of benefits available to us as veterans. Among the most attractive were low-interest GI home loans, GI educational programs, and conversion of military term life insurance policies.

On Thursday we reached the final stages, and each received remaining pay and allowances due and a personal set of orders. The subject of my orders read "Release to inactive duty class V-6, U.S. Naval Reserve." Somehow, this grouping of military words had a marvelous ring to it. The most significant element of the orders, however, was contained in point 3, which stated that I was "detached effective 13 September 1951" and directed to "proceed to your home." It also indicated that I was "granted one days travel time upon expiration of which at midnight of 14 September 1951 you will regard yourself released from all active duty." I read this point over and over, especially the final nine words, which were truly significant as far as I was concerned. One other item of importance, from a personal perspective, was number 10, which stated: "The Commanding Officer has determined that your service has been satisfactory." Although this was not what could be termed overly laudatory, it was gratefully appreciated.

As Vic and I left the Separation Center on Thursday afternoon and headed back to our wives at the apartment hotel, we were still adjusting mentally to our new status. We took our final boat trip from North Island and boarded a San Diego Transit Route 2 bus, near the pier on Harbor Drive. Finally, as we rode up Broadway and neared 11th Avenue, we realized we were actually out of the Navy! We were free men!

Rather than begin a long, tiring train trip to Oakland that evening, Marie and I decided to fly home the next day. On Friday morning, we excitedly checked out of our short-lived interim home and called a cab for the airport. As we waited in front of the building, I noticed a sea bag sticking up out of a garbage can with the cover sitting on top of the bag. Apparently, one of the other separated Reservists staying at the hotel had decided to unceremoniously conclude his naval career right there in the side yard. As our flight headed into the clear skies, we happily closed the San Diego chapter of our young married life.

But the saga of the men of VF-871 from the USS *Princeton* was not yet over. On Saturday, 15 September, 25 officers and 35 enlisted men were reunited at the Oakland Municipal Airport for a civic welcome and reunion. The 483 strikes against Communist forces in Korea had made for a long "weekend" for the men of VF-871 — these so-called "Weekend Warriors" — and we received a hero's welcome home in Oakland. Those present were recognized as members of one of the first naval Reserve units to be called to action in Korea and the first to return.

Because the enlisted men at the celebration had been officially released from active duty only a few hours earlier, they had mainly arrived separately. Most officers arrived by air from San Diego; after 30-day leaves, they were destined to remain on active duty, possibly an additional nine months to a year. A number of the squadron's uniquely marked dark blue Corsairs were flown north from NAS San Diego, led by the Skipper, Lieutenant Commander Harrison. The graceful planes, with gull wings folded, were parked in a row as a backdrop for the upcoming ceremonies.

VF-871 Squadron members were welcomed at the Oakland Airport by Captain Edward C. Renfro, Commanding Officer of NAS Oakland; Clifford E. Rishell, mayor of Oakland; Dudley W. Frost, president of the Port Commission; and Walter Eggert, president of the Oakland Chamber of Commerce. After a few brief welcoming remarks and complimentary

The "Welcome Home" ceremonies at Oakland, 15 September 1951. (Courtesy, Del Fuller, Jr.)

words for the crew by the Skipper, group photos were taken near the planes. Squadron members were then ushered to a fleet of 15 waiting convertibles for a parade through town. Because there was no preassigned vehicle seating, the bluejackets dashed to the cars, and I managed to join John Young and Ingebret Fagerlie in the white lead vehicle. Through downtown streets, we slowly followed two Oakland Police motorcycle officers and a black Cadillac containing dignitaries. The doors of the cars were marked: "Oakland's Own Home From Korea," "Welcome Home Navy Fighting 871," and "Oakland Welcomes Its Weekend Warriors." Crew members waved to the appreciative citizens along the parade route; we were touched by the extent of community efforts made in arranging the parade, which had so visibly honored us.

But the welcome was not yet completed, as following the parade we returned to the airport as guests at a luncheon in the International Room. The mayor welcomed us again and conveyed Oakland's pride in the hometown unit's accomplishments. Others reviewed the statistics of VF-871's Far East tour:

> Enemy positions were hit with 182 tons of bombs, 493,500 rounds of .50-caliber machine-gun ammunition, 167 tanks of napalm, and 493 rockets. We destroyed some 93 buildings, 14 rail cars, 9 railway and highway bridges, 32 vehicles, 15 gun positions, 10 coastal craft, and 14 supply dumps. A total of 141 enemy casualties were confirmed and credited to the squadron.

Sadly, our three pilot losses were also part of the statistics.

As our lives in mid-September 1951 were reverting to more peaceful endeavors, the war rumbled on with casualties mounting daily on both sides. The Essex, then on line with TF-77, had the duty of proving a new aircraft in combat, the twin-jet McDonnell F2H-2 Banshee. VF-172 of CAG-5 was the squadron assigned to measure the effectiveness of the new fighter-bomber, believed to be ideally suited for bridge and rail interdiction strikes. Additionally, the Banshees were expected to pro-

vide fighter escort protection for Air Force B-29s from the MiG-
15 fighter, while engaged in high-altitude raids against rail
yards in northeast Korea. And while we were safely at home,
pilots of VF-172 and other **Essex** squadrons, including future
astronaut Ensign Neil A. Armstrong of VF-51, were heavily engaged in missions over North Korea. Pilots and aircraft of the
Task Force were repeatedly launched into the dangerous environment over Korea. Casualties continued to climb while the
missions, machines, and tactics slowly evolved to cope with the
changing capabilities and strategies of the enemy.

   The testing of aircraft and pilots in these hazardous combat
conditions was part of the job. Often, however, the routine elements of daily flight operations presented the greatest danger.
On 16 September, almost simultaneously with our Oakland
celebration (one International Date Line calendar day later), a
major deck-landing accident involving a VF-172 Banshee occurred on the **Essex**. A damaged F2H-2, unable to drop its
hook, jumped the barriers and progressed down the deck forward of the island. The Banshee veered sharply to starboard
and rammed four unarmed and unrefueled aircraft. Although
the collision produced a huge fire, which lingered but was finally controlled, the **Essex** resumed flight operations the next day.
But, the landing accident had cost 7 lives, 27 injured, and 4 aircraft destroyed.

   The magnitude of the homecoming celebrations, both in San Diego for
the *Princeton* and in Oakland for Squadron VF-871, had been somewhat
overwhelming. During the many previous months we often had questioned
our role in the call-up program but had accepted and performed the tasks
assigned to us. During the ever-changing process, we had become accustomed to the necessarily authoritarian routine of Navy life. And though the
disciplined behavioral framework known as "the Navy way" was greatly
relaxed during our time at sea, we had gradually adapted to a structure
where things were done at a certain time, in a prescribed way. Upon our
return to San Diego, our lives were suddenly overwhelmed with hoopla

and commendation and then — as if out of the blue — separation. We were told that we had carried out our mission well, but suddenly found that we had no further mission and — for the moment — no structure to cling to. Change always produces some uneasiness, and even the happiness of being a civilian again was accompanied by some uncertainty.

Each of us would soon be facing life in the civilian world with familiar joy, questions, concerns, and problems. Many would routinely pick up suspended careers or educational endeavors. Other would inventory the skills gained during nearly 14 months of Navy life and attempt to apply them in civilian enterprises. As we separately prepared to go wherever our lives took us, we realized that we collectively had been very lucky, indeed. Our tour of duty had begun suddenly and, without notice, had ended the same way. And it really had been only of a short duration. We had performed tasks aboard the carrier that included predictable risks and all but three of us had emerged unscathed.

There was no question that we might have had it worse. We could have enlisted, or could have been drafted, into other armed services and could have found ourselves fighting on the ground as infantrymen in Korea, like some of my high school classmates. Despite all the griping, and the complexities of getting transferred to inactive status, or of obtaining hardship discharges, overall we had nothing to complain about. My mother recognized this and wrote, "I have said to mothers who have asked me about you that I would wish the same good fortune for their sons as I have prayed for my son." She placed great faith in prayer and believed, with our safe return, that her prayers had been answered. She also felt that I had fared well in the Navy and suggested "a good word for the Navy will go far with you."

With our destiny changed in the blink of an eye, and with the celebrations over, members of the squadron drifted away from the Oakland Airport, not far from NAS Oakland where our adventures had begun. In future days, this entire area of the airport would be referred to as North Field, part of a much larger Oakland International Airport.

We departed as a group of individuals rather than members of the closely knit unit we had grown to be. We expected to meet again in reunions, but we would never gather together again as an integrated functioning organization. Although still filled with the excitement of the occasion and with being free men, we left with a bit of sadness and a number of questions. Had we done the job we were expected to do? Did the organized Air

Reserve program prove effective in the Korean crisis? Was our training adequate for what we were called upon to do? Were our aircraft and equipment appropriate for the tasks we were expected to perform? And what had we proven that would enhance future naval air tactics and strategies? Only during later reflection and analysis would these and other questions be answered.

As civilians once again, we closed a significant period in each of our lives. Yet, despite the unquestionable finality of our active-duty tour, many still had a nagging feeling that this might not be the true end of our military experience. A squadron cruise book, published some months later, reflected the uncertainty some felt as we left our venerable Corsairs behind and drove away from the airport. The last page of the book closed with the admonition: "All through in 52 — home we be in 53 — back for more in 54." Only time and circumstance would determine whether we would, in fact, be "back for more."

Chapter 10

Tour Assessment Post-September 1951

*B*EFORE EVALUATING *our performance as a squadron, it is first appropriate to review the depth and quality of training. Often the effectiveness of training and resultant performance may be influenced, directly or indirectly, by the backgrounds of those being prepared. VF-871, upon recall, was comprised of members from every walk of life including students, salesmen, artists, teachers, coaches, lawyers, farmers, bankers, and policemen. Most of these everyday citizens came from the San Francisco-Oakland areas, though some were from San Luis Obispo and Sacramento. The orders to* report to active duty, pursuant to Bureau of Personnel Dispatch DTG 192334Z of 19 July 1950, had officially set in motion an accelerated program designed to blend these varied backgrounds into an integrated, unified fighting force. This was quite a challenge, especially as the unit would need augmentation by additional crew. However, a planned infusion of other recalled Reservists — with perhaps even more diverse backgrounds — from locations across the rest on the nation, was also underway.

After reporting to the Commander Air Force Pacific Fleet, San Diego, on 2 August 1950, it was clear that VF-871's development as a unit had a long way to go. Not only were we short the established complement of men, but we lacked the number and quality of aircraft to fly and maintain. It would be approximately five months before the squadron would receive all its aircraft. In addition, the lack of tools with which to maintain the planes initially presented practical delays as well as morale concerns, though the high-quality nucleus of maintenance personnel called up from Oakland helped overcome some of these early difficulties.

After we had settled in the limited office space available in Hangar 526 at North Island, and had attempted to obtain essential equipment, a primary emphasis on setting up operational and administrative procedures immediately followed. It was quickly evident that our unit was not prepared organizationally, and thus much time had been devoted from August to December 1950 to bringing VF-871 up to the standards required by COMAIRPAC.

Early development of the squadron's administrative organization and procedures had been geared to the requirements of the December annual COMAIRPAC inspection. Orders, notices, memoranda, and regulations had been written and files established. Essential squadron policies had been formulated, a training program had been developed, and, after much dedicated effort, we had successfully passed this first test. One fringe benefit of this preparatory process was that it had provided squadron members with a much keener understanding of Navy procedures.

Our performance in the annual inspection had reflected the intensity of effort put into getting ready. We came through with flying colors and were the first squadron to get a score above 90 for each department. The success of our efforts was illustrated further when the squadron's administrative department had received a score of 95, the highest mark of all Reserve squadrons inspected. We were also commended for our physical fitness program, public relations accomplishments, and for publishing a weekly squadron paper. Overall, the squadron was credited with a job "well done."

The inspection findings were beneficial to our morale as well as to our development as a functioning unit. It was thought, however, that our progress could have been accelerated if one vital publication, Technical Letter #8 — containing basic guidelines for organization and operations — had been introduced to us upon our arrival at the NAS. This comprehensive document would have been most useful when inter-squadron departments were being set up rather than coming several weeks later, as was the case. Much valuable squadron time might have been saved, which could have been used for necessary training. It is evident that our inability to secure anything but the most routine publications at that time had directly caused delays in readiness.

The impact of the documentation weaknesses upon our readiness led the Skipper, Lieutenant Commander Harrison, to submit corrective recommendations to COMAIRPAC for the future. He particularly recommended that closer liaison be maintained between the Naval Reserve Program, Commander Air Force Pacific Fleet, and Commander Air Force Atlantic Fleet. He reasoned that future Reserve squadrons ordered to active duty would be better prepared if they knew in advance the administrative and operational procedures required — such as in Technical Letter #8. The recommendations were accepted and later carried out. Subsequent squadrons were able to become organizationally functional more rapidly and get on with operational skill preparation more efficiently. The experience quickly pointed out that the existing Reserve readiness program had at least one identifiable significant shortcoming.

The emphasis in our preparation as a squadron had shifted to essential operational training from January to May 1951. On 8 January, all pilots were transferred to Saufley Field, Pensacola, Florida, for carrier qualifications aboard the *Monterey*. Each pilot was required to make eight carrier landings to be considered qualified. Although accidents had occurred during this process, all of our pilots passed. Training efforts had included the several weeks of rocket, gunnery, and bombing practice at NAAS El Centro, and during two of the three visits there all pilots qualified in aerial gunnery, strafing, dive bombing, rockets, and night flying.

A squadron historical report notes that the facilities offered at El Centro for our designated purposes were excellent as was the better and more frequent flying weather. The opportunity to use controlled targets, impact areas, strafing, etc., also made the time spent there much more valuable than had we passed an equivalent amount of time in San Diego. It was later discovered, however, that the standard banner that had been spread on the ground as a strafing target may have been somewhat limited. A post-combat report pointed out that "accurate strafing was an art that needs attention just as much as air-to-air gunnery." It stated further that "since operating in Korea we have found that low angle or almost flat angles or dives are very common and practice of such on all types of terrain in this phase would be invaluable."

The final elements of our operational training, during the month of April, had included the air group operations off San Diego aboard the *Essex*. Flights during which simulated strikes were conducted provided squadrons a much-needed opportunity to work with one another in the newly formed CAG-19X. This proved to be the first and only opportunity to train together as a unit, and it came at a crucial time.

The final step in squadron training had occurred on 7 May, with the departure of the advance party of seven officers and five enlisted men to observe operational procedures on the *Princeton*. That advance unit, consisting of four pilots, three ground officers, and five enlisted men, had deployed aboard the *Princeton* incrementally. Officers were flown aboard the afternoon of 13 May, and the enlisted personnel a few days later. For their advanced operations, unit members joined up with CAG-19's VF-193. On May 16, the first combat flights by members of Squadron VF-871 were flown against Communist forces in Korea. The advance group flew a total of 14 offensive sorties and one defensive sortie from 16 through 19 May. Our losses—two planes and one pilot—during this period were considered relatively heavy. On 19 May, the *Princeton* was relieved on station and returned to Yokosuka where the remaining members of our squadron reported, relieving VF-193. Ready or not, our training was over.

Squadron VF-871 was most fortunate that a number of the top-rated enlisted men recalled to active duty came from civil service jobs at local bases such as NAS Alameda. Many had held civilian jobs commensurate with ratings held in the Reserves. However, a number of the younger members of the crew were not so well prepared or technically competent. On-the-job training of lesser qualified men was given by the more experienced superiors, rather than in formal classes.

More training in the use of small firearms would also have been of value. During our tour, one Petty Officer reportedly discharged a .45-caliber pistol accidentally on two separate occasions while on watch.

Readiness of the pilots was generally recognized to be at a higher level than that of the enlisted men. All pilots had flown the Corsair before and demonstrated a thorough knowledge of fighter-bomber tactics. The training period was believed to be more than adequate in time, but perhaps not in scope. Combat experience later revealed areas of additional pilot training that would have been beneficial, including a napalm demonstration and at least one drop per pilot; actual full-load takeoff and proper ordnance-release sequence practice; one Tiny Tim rocket firing per pilot (the largest rocket used by the U.S. during the war, with 152 pounds of TNT); road reconnaissance training flights and doctrine; additional attack/fighter division tactical flights; additional contour navigational flights; shorter Naval Gun Fire Spot sessions available to all pilots; a short ordnance school for specific targets; camouflage target spotting; glide-bombing runs under 2,000 feet; and proper flak evasion and flight formation sessions. It was evident that the later real life experiences pinpointed more precisely what training had actually been needed.

Upon recall, however, the men were generally perceived to be in an excellent state of readiness. Pilot preparedness was not considered to be a serious concern and the skill level of rated mechanics was believed to be above average. It was obvious later, however, that an opportunity to send some younger enlisted men to various Navy schools would have been useful. Many could have benefited from technical schools in their "striker" rating specialties — those objectives they were "striking out" to achieve — rather than learning the hard way under the limited guidance of their skilled superiors. Additionally, the squadron was composed primarily of civilian-minded Reserves whose orientation was less rigid than the military standards of the peacetime Navy, and thus regulations and customs regarding how to render a proper salute or maintain standards of uniform dress were obviously not second nature. A number of non-rated enlisted men, including me, had not even gone through a standard Navy boot-camp. Despite such lack of indoctrination, during the deployment months VF-871 had no man at Captain's Mast — for disciplinary action — or on the Medical Restricted List — those who illness might be contagious or who were restricted from work — nor were there any justified complaints against any officer or enlisted man.

Because many of the men had never previously been aboard a ship, except for the short week on the *Essex*, additional time for training specific to shipboard — and flight deck — safety would have been desirable. Although no one in the squadron suffered injury due to this lack of preparedness, there were close calls. I had narrowly escaped injury on more than one occasion while on flight-deck catwalks. While I was once observing recovery operations aft of the island, I was resting my arms on the deck when a member of the ship's flight-deck crew suddenly warned me to move my arms. Unknowingly, I had been resting on a section of deck where a raised heavy barrier cable stanchion would shortly return to a retracted position after a recovered aircraft would be moved forward.

Another incident occurred late one day while I was observing port catapult Panther jet launches. Immediately following launch, a large piece of metal flew from the catapult into the gun tub outside the matériel office where I was standing. The flying debris barely missed my unprotected head.

My job and designated clothing permitted me access to the flight deck and adjoining areas, and thus I frequently crossed between aircraft with whirling propellers. One day, while aboard the *Essex*, a crew member from another unit had walked into a moving prop and was killed. Yet I had been provided no safety training relative to these, or a variety of other, hazards in or about the flight deck. The few days aboard the *Essex*, although valuable in terms of pilot flight operations preparation, were generally inadequate for other training. Only common sense and good luck served those of us whose duties took us onto or near the perilous deck.

Trips far below deck to retrieve necessary supplies also occasionally presented fearful moments, whenever I stood on, or walked along, edges of large open internal hatches between two — or sometimes three — deck levels. My only mishap aboard ship, however, was a fall caused by my own clumsiness, while climbing down a ladder.

When we first had reported to NAS San Diego, all tools were difficult to obtain and many productive hours were lost because of this inadequacy. Compounding the situation, most ground handling and servicing equipment was in poor condition and the replacements that were provided were also substandard. Further, the supply of needed parts and accessories at El Centro was insufficient. It was often necessary to borrow parts from grounded aircraft to keep others flying, while waiting for parts to be acquired from San Diego. It was recommended that this problem be remedied by instituting a closer liaison with auxiliary fields. Although most of these shortcomings were corrected in succeeding months, they frustrated our ability to expeditiously meet readiness objectives.

A conclusion was easily reached that much more could have been accomplished by setting up the squadron at NAS Oakland where, at least, we had aircraft to fly. Hangar and space to park even the few available aircraft was limited at North Island, San Diego. In fact, not much was accomplished during the first month there that couldn't have been done at Oakland. If we had temporarily remained at Oakland to get organized, things could have been set up concurrently at NAS San Diego to properly receive the squadron. So much for hindsight!

Upon reporting aboard the *Princeton*, most of the frustrating shore-based difficulties were no longer a problem. Many of our maintenance crewmen considered their transition to the *Princeton* an easy task. Before our arrival, virtually all routine maintenance problems with *Princeton* F4U-4s had either been anticipated or worked out under combat conditions. Although we expected a variety of problems relating primarily to the age and usage of the aircraft over the preceding months, the assigned aircraft were found to be in much better condition than expected, despite the wear and tear equivalent to one standard combat tour. All aircraft received were mechanically sound, but some signs of deterioration and corrosion were physically evident.

Efforts were immediately begun to solve a problem with tail-wheel bolts that had been caused by the large number of carrier landings. The Corsair tail-wheel bracket assembly was found to have been replaced six times in a period of 45 days before our arrival. All tail-wheel bolts were again inspected in accordance with COMAIRPAC F4U/FG Aircraft Bulletin #1. However, a lack of molybdenum powder and magnaflux facilities complicated necessary shipboard maintenance. Routine replacement was not immediately feasible either, as the problem assemblies were not normally carried in stock aboard carriers. Until a redesign fix could be effected, it was recommended that as an interim solution they should be routinely stocked aboard and replaced as required.

An aircraft ordnance deficiency involving wing racks and launchers was also discovered. When the planes were first turned over to us aboard ship, it was found that the wings were equipped with old Mark 5 rocket launchers. Adapters for conversion to newer Aero 14A combination rack and launchers had been brought aboard but were inadvertently transferred to another ship before they could be installed. The three inboard launchers on each wing were equipped with 100-pound bomb adapters, with the outboard position used for rockets. The combination of aircraft age and inherent weakness of the wing structure at the points of attachment of the outboard launcher posts was a concern. For these reasons, it was believed inadvisable to hang the relatively heavy 5-inch high-velocity aircraft rockets (HVAR) from this position. The solution was to remove the bombing adapters from the position next to the outboard on each wing and to hang the HVAR from these posts. The outboard positions were then used only for lighter, antisubmarine rockets. A variety of other makeshift solutions to lesser problems were applied until the bomb adapters could be replaced by the newer racks. Any number of problems may have contributed to Ed Reed accidentally dropping a hung bomb over South Korea one day. Recommendations were also made to modify boresight patterns for .50-caliber wing machine-guns to prevent muzzle blast-tube explosions which, in most cases, required a wing change.

The crew routinely strove to maintain excellent aircraft performance and high availability. Ground officers also did a thorough job in their assignments, to keep the burden off the pilots insofar as possible. Aircraft availability was attributed in part to inspection, after every flight, for damage and discrepancies not noticed by the pilot during flight. Regular inspection of all exposed parts was added to each plane captain's daily check sheet, in an effort to prevent further corrosion. Utilization of platinum-tipped spark plugs also contributed greatly to high availability. Ship and squadron personnel working together, sometimes all night, also promoted maximum aircraft availability.

An evaluation was made of charts used by VF-871 pilots in the Korean area. At the beginning of area operations, all pilots were issued three World Aeronautical Charts (WAC) and ten USAF Aeronautical Approach Charts (AAC). USAF Aeronautical Pilotage Charts (APC) were also issued, but these proved too small to show necessary detail. The USAF AACs were considered satisfactory for overall work in the theater, but pilots occasionally used large map scale — LMS 751 — maps for close air support and naval gunfire spotting. It was found that the areas included on most missions could be covered by a total of 12 USAF AACs. The pilots took these charts on all flights, plus a large readily accessible map showing all of Korea, made by combining three WACs. Large maps of Korea were often marked with areas blocked off to correspond with areas shown on each AAC. They were then numbered by hand consecutively on the master chart and on the corners of smaller charts. Additional work was done on the AACs by marking friendly airfields by King (emergency airfield) number, as well as Navy coded reference points.

Considerable individuality was displayed by pilots in selecting the method most suitable for folding and carrying these maps. Smaller maps were often taped together and folded into one large map to avoid juggling when targets occurred at map intersections. This also minimized the loss of charts in the bilge or out of the canopy. Several of the pilots found it advantageous to supplement the AAC with a shaped topographical relief map of the close support areas. These aided considerably in the identification of terrain and landmarks and provided a continuity of area for navigational purposes.

In general, it was felt that maps and charts used by the squadron in Korea were adequate for the ordinary purposes of navigation and target location. Few inaccuracies were found and no difficulties were experienced by the average pilot in general usage. Despite the innovative improvements made by the pilots, it was suggested that a few additional recommendations might be put forward for consideration:

- squadrons expecting to operate in the area should attempt to obtain a larger AAC, which could be folded into a compact size and eliminate map juggling
- pilots should be issued all charts prior to deployment and instructed in their use before reaching the area
- pilots should be advised that villages and towns in Korea bear two or more different names depending on charts used
- care should be taken to obtain AAC editions that color-code highways and railroads black, and rivers and streams blue
- and squadrons should be certain that all WACs procured are gridded and pilots lectured on the grid system.

Flying over hostile territory was challenging and dangerous in itself but locating and destroying targets required a whole new dimension of pilot concentration. It was clear that the life of a carrier pilot over Korea, during this period, was anything but simple.

An overall assessment of personnel performance during the entire tour of duty is hindered by lack of an official evaluation grading us one way or the other. Certainly a statement from our Commanding Officer, Lieutenant Commander Harrison, in his 1 September 1951 memorandum to "All Hands," reflected his views:

> The manner and spirit in which you have all shouldered your responsibilities, the marvelous team work you have developed and that keen spirit of competition has made a profound impression on all and brought credit and praise on you and your Squadron.

He concluded,

> My heartfelt thanks to all for making my job a very pleasant one and bringing me an association that I shall never forget.

It was clear that the Skipper was awarding us high marks.

A more comprehensive assessment would necessarily involve a review of both objective data and the subjective experience, to draw overall conclusions. A variety of readily available statistics relating to hours flown, fuel, ammunition and weapons consumed, and targets damaged and destroyed may, of course, be examined. Numbers, however, can be interpreted in many ways and, by themselves, would not be objectively reliable determinants. An expanded approach, therefore, should also include a review of mission accomplishments, pilot performance, and crew support of flight operations.

All of the stateside organizational training, and accompanying frustration, culminated in the 483 combat missions flown by VF-871 pilots during the period commencing in May and ending in August 1951. The majority of the total sorties, 243 offensive and 133 defensive, were flown from 2 through 30 June 1951, clearly the heaviest and perhaps the most significant period of squadron combat activity. The squadron flew an average of one to two flights daily, of varying numbers of planes, during all but three remaining days in that month. The VF-871 pilots destroyed or inflicted severe damage over a broad spectrum of enemy targets. Major targets destroyed included 21 storage-type buildings, 4 supply dumps, 11 railroad cars, 1 highway bridge, 2 railroad bridges, 1 railroad junction, and 13 highway and 8 railroad cuts. Major targets damaged included 1 highway bridge, 9 buildings, 1 railroad bypass, 1 railroad bridge, and 4 railroad cars. In addition, the squadron assisted in the destruction of 3 army field pieces, 3 warehouses, 34 buildings, 4 bridges, 8 ammo dumps, and 1 highway and 1 railroad cut. Significant among the latter group were 300 enemy troop losses.

Targets in the operational area were often not actually seen, and thus evaluation of all strike damage could not always be made. Accordingly, a complete damage assessment by an individual squadron was not always possible. Strike assessments where likely destruction or damage could not be confirmed from air or ground reports were usually recorded as "undetermined damage." Despite the increasing intensity of enemy air defenses, our squadron contributed to impressive TF-77 sortie rates and statistics of destruction and damage. The results confirmed not only pilot courage and skill but also the skill and dedication of maintenance and other support personnel. Many of these crew members worked long hours to keep squadron aircraft in the air day after day.

There was no question that the frequency and intensity of air operations were most significant during the June tour, though the days at sea during July and August 1951 were still filled with increasingly hazardous flights. Because of weather conditions, however, the flights seemingly were not at the same hectic daily pace. Pilots continued to produce successful mission results despite the growing effectiveness of enemy ground air defenses. Aircraft returning with battle damage evidenced the increasing accuracy of enemy defensive systems. This became clearly evident when considering that, despite fewer flying days, our losses increased. Three additional planes were downed and, more importantly, two more pilots lost. Later, the reported Fleet overall loss of 53 Navy and Marine tactical aircraft during the July-September 1951 quarter verified the effectiveness of enemy defenses. Despite unacceptably high squadron losses, our pilots continued to perform at or beyond expected levels.

After reflecting on the general performance of Squadron VF-871 personnel, it seems an overall assessment should also consider certain larger, broader issues that relate to the squadron's altered post-recall role. During the uncertain early days of training, with the rumor mill churning full blast, it was difficult to envision what the Navy ultimately intended to do with us. Two traditional five-squadron air groups had been called up from the Reserves and assigned simultaneously to North Island. After finally receiving our complement of aircraft and getting organized, our squadron had settled into the routines of the all Reserve group CAG-102. Meanwhile, beyond the range of most crew members, high-level strategic considerations impacting us were quietly underway. Our destiny would be shaped by policies of the political and military powers in Washington, D.C.

In early fall 1950, spurred on by the increasing tempo of the war, the U.S. Navy was planning to quickly increase the number of TF-77 *Essex*-class carriers to four. On 8 October, the *Essex*-class carrier USS *Leyte* (CV-32) with CAG-3 aboard, reported on line after steaming 18,500 miles from the Mediterranean. Although three *Midway*-class carriers had joined the Fleet in the previous six years, they would all remain for strategic policy reasons in the Atlantic. The arrival of the *Leyte* marked the first time since World War II that four *Essex*-class carriers had operated together.

War conditions significantly worsened later in the year, as the Chinese advanced down the Korean peninsula. Demands upon carrier flight crews sharply increased in support of the withdrawing Allied troops. As the war's intensity increased, so did the pace of TF-77 operations. Repeatedly, the few available Task Force air groups were required to make back-to-back deployments. CAG-2 returned to the U.S. from Korea with the *Boxer* on 11 November, and only 25 days later was redeployed for another six months aboard the *Valley Forge* and the *Philippine Sea*. It was evident that new crews needed to be trained and made available in order to keep experienced crews rested and sharp. If untrained crews were sent into combat, attrition rates were expected to be unacceptably high. And thus consideration of possible strategies began in order to alleviate the inordinate demands.

During the period of uncertainty, as to duration of the war and the evolving role of the aircraft carrier, little help was expected from Washington, D.C. Post-World War II disputes about the relative strengths and missions of the Navy and the relatively new Air Force still lingered. An unsympathetic administration and Congress had reduced naval aviation to below minimum levels. Congress had limited the total number of Navy carrier air groups to nine, a number clearly inadequate

when weighed against the demands for naval air support in the Korean War. And shortened air group turnarounds, if continued, would undoubtedly take a toll in pilot morale and efficiency. Recycling the same limited number of pilots through frequent deployments was a serious concern and a creative solution within existing political constraints needed to be quickly found.

It had been determined that the *Princeton*, while still on its first TF-77 tour, would be required to stay on line longer than usual. Its air group, CAG-19, had been scheduled for rotation in May, but no replacement was available for the extended period. Although the July 1950 call-up provided additional authorized squadrons, they were attached to air groups already scheduled for sea duty. Individual Reserve Squadrons could be integrated into Regular air groups when necessary, but the basic problem was that there simply were not enough air groups. Any solution to this deficiency would have to somehow circumvent congressional limitations.

The answer to the complex problem began to emerge from the Korean theater of operations. Korean combat experience had discovered that the usual five-squadron air group format was unwieldy. It was believed that paring one squadron from each air group would allow greater flexibility and would free up squadrons for reassignment. Although shifting squadrons from familiar command environments to newly organized commands was untested, the plan would allow two additional air groups to be quickly formed and deployed. Thus, the needed air groups, later to be called Air Task Groups, were produced not by adding more personnel but by simply adjusting the existing operational organization structure. This simple solution eased the burden on existing air groups by increasing the number available, and conformed with the limits imposed by Congress. And Carrier Air Group 19X, formed as a result of this concept, was the first to test its merits in combat.

Shortly following the *Princeton*'s return home, in late August 1951, Air Task Group One (ATG-1) deployed aboard the *Valley Forge* in October. ATG-1 was composed of VF-52 and VF-111 flying F9F-2 Panthers, VF-653 with F4U-4 Corsairs, and VF-194 flying AD-2 and AD-3 Skyraiders. The newly designated ATG squadrons, however, retained the tail code letter designations of their originating air groups. After returning on the *Princeton* in August, the former CAG-19X squadrons, despite having been the concept's pathfinders, had reformed officially as ATG-2. The four ATG squadrons were joined, as their CAG-19X predecessors had been, by five detachments from VC-3, VC-11, VC-35, VC-61, and HU-1 (Helicopter Detachment).

In the overall performance assessment of VF-871, an additional element had also been determined. The unit proved that Reserve squadrons could effectively perform on short notice, right alongside Regular Fleet squadrons, under difficult combat conditions. The squadron meshed smoothly with unfamiliar Reserve and Regular squadrons in the newly formed air group. The replacement group joined TF-77 during a difficult period of heightened enemy radar-guided antiaircraft effectiveness, and Squadron VF-871 proved to be an effective component of the prototype ATG during this intense period. No Reserve/Regular interface problems were noted. A post-operational squadron report stated, "the overall performance of the officers and men under the trying conditions of a war time schedule set an example of team work, know how, initiative and ingenuity."

During this time another lingering issue was also resolved—whether or not the unit really had needed to be recalled. Although the July 1950 nationwide recall had sought to bring the Navy up to wartime operational levels authorized by Congress, all activated squadrons had to be capable of performing. The call-up selection itself confirmed the Navy's confidence in VF-871's Reserve readiness under the leadership of Lieutenant Commander Harrison. The congressional air group limitations had mandated that the juggled squadrons selected for the prototype group provide solid performances if the innovative solution was to prove valid, and squadron pilots and maintenance and support personnel all confirmed that the faith in the unit's capabilities was justified. They also verified that their cohesive organization and skills were, in fact, urgently needed during that particular time in history. The unit contributed toward the successful validation of the ATG concept with a high-level performance. Their Reserve unit's mettle was also tested in the most difficult way—under fire. One may easily conclude that the later public accolades received were well deserved.

While the *Princeton*'s predominantly Reserve crew in late August 1950 was adjusting to the shock of Regular Navy life, they found themselves quickly enroute to an unexpectedly long first cruise at sea where they would remain for nine stressful months. The early demands of the war greatly impacted this crew of the first large carrier demothballed since World War II. And even though the *Princeton*'s readiness marks at this stage were marginal, circumstances had demanded that the ship be declared ready, for the urgent and immediate needs in Korea where the U.S. 8th Army had been driven back almost to the sea.

Between 1 December 1950 and 6 August 1951, the *Princeton* earned eight battle stars and was awarded the Korean Service Medal with two bronze stars, Naval Unit Commendation, National Defense Service Medal, United Nations Service Medal, Korean Presidential Unit Citation, and Navy Occupation Ribbon with Asia Clasp.

The esteem held by Navy brass for the *Princeton*'s exemplary performance was captured in letters later printed in the ship's cruise book. Admiral A. W. Radford, Commander-in-Chief Pacific Fleet, wrote:

> During your participation in the Korean operation the performance of your gallant crew—most of whom are naval reservists recalled from their civilian jobs—has been an inspiration to Navy men everywhere. In your air strikes against the enemy you have established an enviable record of which the entire Pacific Fleet is proud.

Vice Admiral T. L. Sprague, Commander Air Forces Pacific Fleet, added his congratulation to the officers and men of the *Princeton*:

> Your arrival in Korean waters coincided with the Chinese Communist drive across the Yalu and to your efforts goes much of the credit for our success in halting their advance and in pushing them back to Manchuria. In view of the fact that many of your crew were in civilian life a little over a year ago the *Princeton*'s splendid record for the past 9 months is even more significant. It will remain a lasting testimonial to the outstanding spirit of cooperation and the can-do attitude of all hands aboard.

Another admirer was Vice Admiral C. T. Joy, Commander, Naval

Forces Far East, who after each phase of operations reflected his high regard for the performance of ship and men in congratulatory and commending communiqués.

The importance of carrier-based air interdiction operations, relatively early in the war, was evident. The 29,000 total naval interdiction sorties flown over Korea in 1951 signified the importance of the imposing Fleet effort. Admiral Ofstie, later Acting Commander Naval Air Forces Far East (COMNAVFE), released cumulative enemy damage totals for the 12-month calendar period. The data revealed that combined naval air and surface attacks accounted for the destruction or damage of 2,379 bridges, 4,519 vehicles, 7,028 items of rail rolling stock, and 4,674 separate rail cuts. These one-year figures indicted that naval attacks severely damaged enemy capabilities in terms of vehicles, rail lines, bridges, and munitions. The enemy was severely hindered in efforts to get supplies through to the front lines.

The area over which COMNAVFE held interdiction responsibility roughly covered the eastern half of North Korea, from the existing battle line to the Manchurian border. More than half of the rail transport trackage in North Korea was included within this area, encompassing about 1,140 miles. Also within the area were nearly 1,000 bridges and causeways and 231 tunnels, which if placed end to end would cover 54 miles, and some 2,000 miles of highway complemented the rail network. The Navy's interdiction program produced breaks in rail lines, damage or destruction to bridges, and craters in roads — all vital to the movement of enemy war materials.

Wonsan, on the east coast, was an important railhead from which heavily loaded trains moved ammunition and supplies to North Korean troops. Attacks on railroad lines south of Wonsan had rendered them unreliable, and they could only be effectively repaired at night. Marshaling yards and mountain trackage were likewise left twisted and torn. Enemy transport was forced to use slower secondary means, such as trucks and oxcarts, over bomb-damaged roads. The interdiction efforts effectively gained time for UN forces, as the resupply of front-line enemy troop movements which, when combined with supply and equipment damage and destruction, ultimately stopped a long overdue enemy offensive.

The *Princeton*, and her two air group contingents, contributed significantly to this intense effort to reduce the supplies and equipment required by the enemy. The first contingent flew 5,960 sorties, while the second

(CAG-19X, the ATG forerunner) flew 3,787. Some of the combined 9,747 sorties were specialized, including air patrol, weather research, antisubmarine patrol and escort, armed recon, gunfire support, courier, target air patrol, jet recon, and photography. Although some were uneventful, none was considered routine. The ship's mission to destroy enemy communications, supplies, and combat troops was accomplished at a record-setting level. The results were measured in many ways including oxen, wagons, or men strafed; bridge spans dropped; and locomotives or rail cars blown up.

Lieutenant Commander Harrison of VF-871 got our attention immediately with what he had already accomplished as a naval aviator. At a young age during World War II, he had demonstrated his superior flying skills and was heavily decorated by the end of the war. Through Reserve participation, he had honed his innate skills to motivate and direct others, ultimately garnering a Reserve squadron command. The fact that he took the diverse, unhappy civilians within his unit and molded them into a cohesive fighting organization was a tribute to his leadership skills. His leadership was also evident in the air as he led young squadron pilots on many combat missions. And he demonstrated his human side as he dealt with the many unique personal issues that arose with empathy toward the wants and feelings of the men in our squadron. He could, however, be as firm and decisive with personnel matters as with tactical military issues.

His leadership skills spilled on down through the chain of command in the squadron to all levels. He was ably assisted through the 14-month active-duty period by his Executive Officer, Lieutenant, and later Lieutenant Commander, Thomas G. Cooper. Although formal ranks existed, there was a certain sense of human equality among all. Most were more concerned with getting the job done than with the fineries of bureaucratic military etiquette. The rigid officer/enlisted barriers that would normally exist between the ranks seemingly were lessened. People interacted as people and, usually, with kindness and respect.

Combat leadership of the *Princeton* and the various squadrons within the two contingents of CAG-19 was displayed on a daily basis by the air group Commanders. Among the 31 pilots lost in combat during the long cruise were two air group Skippers: Commander Richard C. Merrick, killed in action 17 May 1951, and Commander Charles R. Stapler, killed in action 10 June 1951. Commander Stapler replaced Merrick and had assumed command of the CAG-19X second contingent only a short time earlier. Both were excellent pilots and were killed leading *Princeton* pilots on assigned missions. Neither delegated other pilots to lead the tough missions, preferring, when the heat was on, to assume the responsibilities themselves. The deaths of these two "take charge" Commanders helped weld the determination of air group pilots. Another outstanding leader, Lieutenant Commander John J. Magda, of jet Squadron VF-191 and former leader of the Blue Angels stunt team, was also killed in action. Commander A. L. Maltby, Jr., of VA-55, ably assumed the mantle of leadership for the CAG-19X contingent until the conclusion of the deployment. Inspired by the example set by such men, *Princeton* fliers sought and achieved outstanding results.

Assessing the leadership skills of the *Princeton*'s Commander, Captain William Gallery, is not difficult. It is doubtful if anyone else could have accomplished the impossible so quickly in getting a recommissioned ship seaworthy. Some might argue that it could have been handled by many other trained, experienced Navy officers. However, when considering the magnitude of the tasks after the recommissioning, refitting, and underway training, this conclusion becomes less certain. Captain Bill provided the energy and know-how to get the *Princeton* going with a relatively green, mostly Reservist, crew; and he kept her going during nine long months of intensive combat operations. Although outranked by Rear Admiral Ofstie, who flew his flag on the ship, Captain Bill was unquestionably in charge of the vessel.

The Captain's firm hand at the helm was one reason for the success of the *Princeton*. Under his guidance, the ship speeded up tanker refueling, set records in transferring stores, invented improved ways to fill napalm tanks, and instituted various ordnance handling improvements. Five million gallons of fuel were brought aboard, 1,600 tons of napalm mixed, and 8,000 tons of ordnance handled—all without mishap.

Although he was not reluctant to ask the impossible at times, he was greatly admired and respected by the crew. He demonstrated his innovative tactical talents when he suggested that 12 aerial torpedoes, stowed aboard, be used to attack the Hwachon Dam. The dam had previously been attacked with bombs for months without effect and he believed the flood gates were perfect targets for torpedoes. A torpedo, however, was one of the most complex pieces of ordnance, and the air group had no training in the specialized art of dropping them. Despite these disincentives, *Princeton* pilots blew out five flood gates in the dam.

When Captain Gallery was routinely relieved and detached to a new duty assignment as Commanding Officer of NAS Whidbey Island, Washington, two weeks before the ship's return home, there was no question of the men's esteem for him. All agreed that his leadership had produced amazing results aboard the workhorse ship.

And assisting Captain Gallery in achieving the many remarkable *Princeton* accomplishments were his Executive Officers, Commander R. E. Coombs, Jr., from August 1950 to February 1951, and Commander T. A. Christopher, from February 1951 to return. Commander Coombs served throughout the record-breaking rush to refit and organize the ship and during the first winter of strikes of the Marine withdrawal. Commander Christopher saw the ship through the heaviest engagements of day and night operations. During this period, the *Princeton* set a then all-time high for tonnage dropped on enemy targets by a single carrier.

Leadership at all levels quietly played a significant role in *Princeton* and air group successes. The presence aboard of Rear Admiral Ofstie and Rear Admiral Henderson, who each served as COMCARDIV 5, helped TF-77 and the *Princeton* rise to new heights. Each had also periodically served as Commander of the entire Task Force, as the position rotated roughly every two weeks through the three carrier division Commanders.

The officers and men of the *Princeton,* regrettably, did not bring about an end to the war. It continued until the truce finally brought it to a close in 1953. However, they, along with other TF-77 crews, did much to slow the enemy during critical early junctures in the conflict. These actions enabled vital strategic UN countermeasures to be undertaken, which ultimately resulted in a stalemate. The experience of the men of the *Princeton* confirmed that with effective leadership a vast diversity of backgrounds and interests could be successfully blended. It also proved that Regulars and Reserves could work efficiently and effectively under adversity. Air strike statistics by November 1951 revealed that nearly 75 percent of all Navy strikes were flown by Reservists. Later, in mid-1952, over 50 percent of 1st Marine Air Wing pilots were found to be Reservists.

The uncertain nature of the Korean conflict had placed demands on Navy and Marine air units from the outset. The aircraft carrier was again recognized as the most important naval asset in what, initially, appeared to be a conventional war, and the availability of ready Reserves was critical to each air arm in order to augment limited Regular forces. But unlike the Navy's Air Reservists, Marines generally did not return to active duty within their squadron units but instead were distributed among Regular units as dictated by need.

Considering all relevant factors, the performance of VF-871 Reservists, albeit on a much smaller scale, clearly paralleled that of the outstanding *Princeton* crew. All these reluctant warriors carried out their unwanted roles in remarkable fashion, easily validating the homecoming accolades. Each "well done" was, indisputably, well deserved. The ready availability of their skilled resources, at a time of acute need, fulfilled the destiny and purpose of all "weekend warriors."

Epilogue

*T*HROUGH THE YEARS, *most personal remem-brances of the Korean War have faded. Americans focus on contemporary events rather than on a long-ago conflict that wasn't even officially de-clared a war. But it was a war, without question, to those involved in it. Today, the official status of that two-mile truce buffer we called the DMZ (demilitarized zone) remains as it was then — a truce.*

Subsequent U.S. military entanglements, coupled with the passage of time, have nudged Korea into its niche as America's forgotten 20th-century war. Despite 37 months of fighting, 157,554 total casualties, and 18 billion (1953) U.S. dollars spent, little interest remains. Neither the costs nor the significance of this first confrontation between the major powers of the nuclear age could keep the lessons of conflict before us. Although the U.S. and the Soviet Union never officially engaged on the battlefield, Korea became the first post-World War II test of wills between the world's two principal powers of the day. The war signified the first major step in the eventual polarization of the Communist and Capitalist worlds — each of which had nuclear capability. No winner or loser emerged at the conclusion, and the conflict may have created a platform for future "tests" between the powers. It is disappointing that the staggering three-year cost in human lives alone would not be significant enough to keep the "war" from being forgotten.

In attempting to find the reason for diminished interest in Korea, we must consider the era in which the war began and ended. Weary veterans of World War II, home for a relatively short time, were understandably concentrating on rebuilding their lives. It had been only five years since the end of that horrendous conflict and yet, without a lot of notice, many veterans and young Americans were being called into service to aid another country in need. Public anxieties might have been lessened somewhat because the area of conflict appeared regional, not global — Korea was, after all, only a small peninsula and many did not even know where it was located. And although thousands had re-entered active military service, those drafted mostly went into the Army, and in numbers that seemed not to be excessive. The Navy, Marines, and Air Force meanwhile quietly met their needs through volunteers and Reserves.

Despite a brief period of support at the outset for the Korean cause, the general public continued to focus on a better lifestyle and was largely apathetic. Life on the home front went on pretty much as usual; there was no shortage of goods, nor rationing, as in World War II, and most importantly, no national outrage. Except for those personally involved with Korea, American life was not noticeably different.

Early efforts were made to end the conflict during a period when many naively thought it was something less than a full-fledged war. Slightly over a year into the hostilities, truce talks began on 10 July 1951. Hopes for an early end, however, proved elusive and required two more long years. Public opposition at home gradually had become more vocal during this time, and by the U.S. presidential election campaign of 1952, Korea was an issue. The new president, Dwight D. Eisenhower, visited Korea in December to view the situation and seek a way to end it, as he had promised. But despite his personal intervention, peace talks did not resume until April of 1953, following the death of Soviet leader Josef Stalin. The Korean War finally came to an official end — with a truce rather than a peace treaty — at 2200 on 27 July.

Homecomings of servicemen and women were very different from those of the prior war. The *Princeton*'s early return was greeted with traditional expressions of public appreciation, but most returns later appeared quieter than those of World War II. Many homecoming soldiers found public dissatisfaction with what had gradually become an unpopular war; most were simply happy to be back. They quietly resumed their civilian lives in the prosperous '50s and set out to forget Korea.

Only much later, when Vietnam veterans began to receive public attention, did Korean vets even bother to organize. An association formed in 1985 was principally designed to raise funds for a memorial in Washington, D.C. Yet passage of time and social unrest surrounding the subsequent highly unpopular and lengthy Vietnam War combined to push the Korean War into a place of diminished importance.

But though the preeminence of the war may have faded over the years, tensions existing between the two Korean nations have continued. The limited war strategy effectively reduced the potential for escalation, but produced no solution and left only a stalemate. The Korean peninsula remains essentially as it was, split between the Communist North and the Capitalist South. In 1954, in Geneva, Switzerland, a conference attended by representatives of all countries that had fought in Korea, and Russia, attempted to address some of the outstanding issues. But the well-intentioned group failed to solve the questions of either unification or withdrawal of foreign troops, and, thus, the tension between the two hostile camps has continued.

Early in 1958, the UN command announced that atomic weapons had been provided to its forces largely because of increased numbers of Communist troops in North Korea. China later responded by proclaiming that all Chinese troops had been pulled out of the North. Dialogue continued over the years — but little progress resulted — and tension, suspicion, and mistrust persists. Each has accused the other of "more than 1 million" violations of the armistice agreement, and incidents of varying intensity continue to occur, almost always culminating in heated political rhetoric.

The long-sought dream of unification still seems a long way off, but remains the stated goal of both governments. Yet, should the two Koreas unexpectedly unite in the near future, the South would likely bear an enormous economic burden due to the shaky North Korean economy.

During the decades since the negotiated end of the fighting, sporadic attention in news accounts has been devoted to the area. Major flareups around the DMZ or episodes such as the seizure of the USS *Pueblo* have been widely reported, but quickly fade. However, a famous novel, *The Bridges at Toko-Ri*, was published in 1953 and later made into a movie. The story was based on a troublesome interdiction target of the *Princeton* during the first cruise. Six vital rail bridges, used by North Korea to move equipment south from Manchuria, had for some time been targeted by TF-77 for destruction. The target area had been informally dubbed "Carlson's Canyon" in honor of Lieutenant Commander Harold G. Carlson of VA-195 from the *Princeton*. All of the target bridges were destroyed by the *Princeton*'s CAG-19 aircraft on 2 April 1951, and abandoned by the enemy. These key bridges, across a deep canyon south of Kilchu, were used as background for James A. Michener's successful work, which helped keep a few remembrances alive. Were it not also for *M*A*S*H*, a motion picture and long-running television series, recollections of the war might have faded sooner, though the 1990 40th anniversary of the war briefly revived some national attention, with print accounts and television documentaries grimly reminding us of the 54,000 American lives that were lost.

In early 1993, Korea began to appear with greater frequency in news accounts. Coverage of Korean issues mainly conveyed a growing unease with the impermanent nature of the 1953 stalemate. In April of 1993, North Korea denied reports that it had made a deal with Iran to develop nuclear weapons. By early May, our State Department announced that representatives from the U.S. and North Korea had met in Beijing, China, to discuss the North's decision to abrogate the Nuclear Non-Proliferation Treaty, signed in 1985. Encouraging July news accounts proclaimed that the U.S. and North Korea had agreed upon several steps to ease international fears about the country's ability to make nuclear weapons. The reports also quietly noted that a dispute remained over a U.S. demand for inspections of two suspected sites of nuclear materials. Robert L. Gallucci, the Assistant Secretary of State heading the U.S. delegation, characterized the progress made as "a small but significant step" in eliminating the spread of nuclear weapons in Asia.

Early August 1993 news remained hopeful, detailing expanded discussions then underway to resolve a lingering emotional war issue — retrieval of remains of U.S. soldiers — that had been announced by representatives of North Korea and the U.S.-led United Nations Command. The scope of remaining prisoner issues was dramatically highlighted by the U.S. government in September, by revealing the existence of a report titled "The Transfer of U.S. Korean War POWs to the Soviet Union." The U.S. government, for the first time, confronted Moscow with evidence that hundreds of U.S. Korean War prisoners had been secretly moved to the Soviet Union, imprisoned, and never returned.

November 1993 news stories expressed growing concern for a diplomatic solution because of the impasse over nuclear facility inspection. Annoyed North Korean leaders denounced the Clinton administration for suggesting that the U.S. would retaliate if the Communist state invaded South Korea. The Korean Central News Agency noted:

> We cannot but take a serious note of the fact that the U.S. president made bellicose remarks against us at the present moment when the world recognizes that we have no intention to "invade the South" and the North and South have committed themselves to non-aggression.

Mid-December 1993 press commentaries suggested that the escalation in rhetoric could turn into a full-bore military crisis. But announcements late in the month, of North Korean concessions to allow international inspections of all seven facilities, seemingly defused this. At the end of 1993 accelerated plans for talks further strengthened hopes, despite a U.S. Central Intelligence Agency statement that North Korea was believed to have developed one or two nuclear weapons.

Although the Korean War — up to that point — had not been a major source of public discussion, vestiges of the conflict were suddenly receiving repeated attention. January 1994 dawned with indications that Korean issues would demand significant U.S. attention, and few days passed without some mention of Korea either in print or television reports. Newspapers often contained articles on Korean issues ranging from the 8,100 unaccounted American servicemen to nuclear inspection. In mid-January, a new study ordered by the Pentagon revealed that about 50 missing servicemen had been taken secretly to the Soviet Union and never returned.

Later that month, Japan's Toen Trading Co. acknowledged it had sold 40 submarines to North Korea. In early February, North Korea accused the U.S. of trying to start another war. The harsh rhetoric of the previous year resumed with a statement that if a conflict breaks out, the U.S. " will suffer a more tragic and grave defeat than in the past Korean War, in which it was humbled and bruised all over."

News accounts from March of 1994 indicated that North Korea was developing two new ballistic missiles, one possibly capable of reaching the U.S. Territory of Guam. The International Atomic Energy Agency, a UN agency, complained that North Korea had denied inspectors access to a reprocessing plant they wanted to check for signs of nuclear material being retained for weapons use. The CIA director stated that North Korea was developing two new ballistic missiles with ranges long enough to present risks — not just to Guam — but to all of Southeast Asia and the Pacific. The failure of efforts to denuclearize the Korean peninsula prompted U.S. officials to suggest economic sanctions if inspections were not completed. The Clinton administration took a step to bolster South Korean security by announcing shipment of a battalion of Patriot missile interceptors and plans for resumption of joint U.S.-South Korean military exercises.

Tensions along the 151-mile border — the world's most heavily armed — escalated further with the North accusing the South of provoking war. The North Korean news agency proclaimed that the Patriot missile and joint military exercise plans were "provocative steps . . . and a declaration of war." On Wednesday, 23 March, South Korea put 650,000 forces on alert. Similar alerts by both sides were not uncommon, but this action took on special significance in view of North Korea's increasing belligerence.

In October 1994, the Clinton administration worked out a fragile agreement providing for North Korea to halt its nuclear program. In early December, however, the accord was criticized by several members of the Senate Subcommittee on East Asia, who believed that the U.S. had made concessions that might encourage other nations to engage in nuclear blackmail. The agreement was further threatened when on 17 December an off-

course U.S. Army helicopter strayed into North Korea and was shot down. One of the two Chief Warrant Officer pilots was killed and the other captured. The U.S. denied that the helicopter was on a spy mission and, although the body of co-pilot David Hilemon had been returned, stressed that continued captivity of the pilot would make implementation of the agreement difficult. Fortunately, pilot Bobby Hall walked unharmed to freedom in the truce village of Panmunjon on 30 December. His release ended a 13-day crisis that threatened to jeopardize the agreement, and sharply damaged earlier improved relations with North Korea.

North Korea's potential to be a world nuclear weapons merchant has become a growing international concern. Formation of a strong international coalition through the UN, perhaps similar to that forged in 1950, might forestall such an eventuality. However, if all diplomatic efforts fail and confrontation results, containment should be sought immediately to prevent spread of the conflict beyond the peninsula. It is hoped that skillful international diplomacy can prevent another armed conflict. If not, maximum support of the 37,000 U.S. troops stationed in South Korea is essential to bring the dispute to a permanent — not stalemated — resolution. It is debatable whether the American public would be willing to contribute more young lives to such a proven imperfect solution.

Although tension during 1994 continued to build progressively to crisis proportions, confrontation was averted by agreements negotiated during the summer and fall halting suspected North Korean nuclear weapon development. Fortunately, no crisis approaching this magnitude occurred in 1995; however, there was also little meaningful progress toward a lasting political solution for the divided peninsula. On the home front, however, the nation finally paid tribute to the 1.5 million Americans who fought in the Korean War by dedicating a memorial in Washington, D.C., on 27 July 1995, the 42nd anniversary of the armistice.

However, the uneasy relationship flared anew in early April 1996, when armed soldiers of North Korea moved into Panmunjon, the Demilitarized Zone village. The North issued a statement indicating it no longer recognized the DMZ provisions of the 43-year-old armistice agreement and announced it would "give up its duty" of jointly controlling the 2.5-mile-wide zone. North Korea boldly moved armed troops into the buffer zone on three consecutive days and described its actions as defensive. U.S. officials termed the violations serious but noted that similar incursions had been made in the past. Both U.S. and South Korean forces were placed in a "higher state of surveillance," which largely affected military intelligence and other units assigned to watch for any North Korean buildup along the DMZ. The "Watch Condition, Level 2" alert was the highest in 15 years for the South Korean military, though no major southern troop movements or mobilizations were involved and most of the 37,000 American military in South Korea were unaffected. The declaration was viewed as the latest step in a series of moves by the North designed to force the U.S. to negotiate a peace treaty by proving the armistice ineffective.

On April 16, President Bill Clinton and South Korea President Young Sam proposed peace talks between North and South Korea "without preconditions," with both the U.S. and China as direct participants. This was a departure from a long-standing U.S. position that the North and South negotiate a permanent peace agreement directly without outside participation. But three days later, China rejected the new initiative, suggesting that the two Korean governments work out their differences before involving outside powers.

Tensions escalated sharply on May 17 when seven North Koreans crossed the DMZ into South Korea near Yonchon and began firing weapons into the air. They were chased by South Korean troops, who fired warning shots. This was the first violation of the armistice since the DMZ incursions in early April. The incident sparked concerns that tensions could erupt with devastating consequences. The U.S. administration characterized the fracas as a "minor incident" but noted that a bloody war could be triggered by accident along the border, the most heavily militarized strip of land in the world. The following day, the South warned that it would "resolutely respond" if the North continued provocations along their border; however, it did not indicate exactly what that action might be.

Another dramatic incident took place six days later when a North Korean pilot flew his MiG-19 across the border, triggering some South Korean alarm systems. The pilot, apparently on a routine training flight from an air base near the North's capital, Pyongyang, broke formation and turned south. When confronted by South Korean jets, he waggled his wings and lowered the landing gear to signal his intention to surrender. The defecting pilot, Captain Lee Chul Soo, later stated, "I couldn't live under the North's system any longer." His was the first defection by a North Korean pilot in 13 years. The incursion caused air-raid warning alarms to wail in Inchon and surrounding areas west of Seoul as the jet turned south. Millions of South Koreans rushed for cover in underground shelters during the five-minute alert. In the capital, Seoul, however, an automatic switch had been turned off and manual operators failed to sound the alarm. Four civil defense officials were later arrested for failing to sound air-raid sirens in the capital. The Seoul government also reported that just hours before the jet had entered the South's air space, five North Korean gunboats had intruded into South Korean coastal waters. The North denied the allegation and instead accused the South of entering its waters. At the end of the month, a North Korean scientist and a writer for the state-run Central Radio Station also sought political asylum in South Korea. Rising tensions were likely aggravated by the North's severe food shortages and other hardships, plus an economy in shambles with little hope for improvement. The UN viewed the economic crisis in North Korea as one that threatened to degenerate into famine. This grim projection dampened hopes for a political solution for the troubled peninsula.

A formal peace treaty has never been signed and the two sides remain technically at war. The beat goes on.

In 1996, many of the issues that contributed to the start of the war in 1950 still remain, but with the major nuclear element added. Old concerns pale in significance to these ominous weapons. Like it or not, Korea and its smoldering conflict has not gone away and remains a threat to peace. This "forgotten war" could suddenly rise to the forefront of American consciousness. As the nation warily wonders if history may repeat itself, one must question were we really ready then, and are we ready now?

It is evident that the U.S. was not prepared in 1950 to engage in a protracted conflict, whether on the ground or in the air. Only limited ground troops were readily available in Japan and the expectation of the new Air Force being the central conveyor of air operations quickly proved infeasible. A traditional ground war had been precluded by terrain, weather, and tactics of the numerically superior enemy. The early loss of nearby ground staging bases had created a sudden need for mobile carrier airfields which, in the early going, were in short supply. These factors, plus the imposition of political rules governing the conduct of the war, had combined to make readiness preparation difficult.

And the Korean War quickly altered traditional concepts regarding the use of carrier aviation. No longer was the primary objective to destroy enemy fleets, or attack island strongholds. The carrier was needed to provide floating airfields close to hostile shores, for long periods of time, and to provide air cover and interdiction support.

The air war over Korea marked the beginning of a new jet age, with tactical air power, utilizing smaller, faster planes that prevented North Korean and Chinese forces from overwhelming South Korea. And although heavy bombers were used, the smaller aircraft proved essential to close air support and interdiction efforts.

From the outset, the conflict was intentionally limited to restrict a spread into a larger, more expansive, "real" war. But this new limiting concept produced major frustrations for our military strategists. Geographic restrictions, allowing the enemy sanctuary in Manchuria, generated major concerns. Interdiction efforts were especially hindered, as principal enemy sources of production and supply could not be attacked. Not surprisingly, our Commanders, while complaining about the politically imposed boundaries, often failed to acknowledge our own *de facto* sanctuaries in Japan and Okinawa.

Vessels, units, and men drifted into whatever was destined for them in the post-war period. As with other wars, once the shooting stops it is easy to lose track of those who had fought in it, though historical accounts contain references to the *Princeton*'s service following Korea, and to a lesser degree to some of the units cited.

The *Princeton* had the distinction of being the first demothballed carrier to meet the new challenges of the Korean War and following completion of that first deployment, the ship remained an active component of Task Force-77 carrier rotation until war's end. The ship later completed two additional deployments. In 1953, on the last day of the war, the *Princeton*, under the command of Captain O. C. Gregg, was one of four carriers operating off the east coast of Korea. Shortly before the truce, the *Princeton*'s CAG-15 pilots had set a single-day record for the most sorties from an *Essex*-class carrier and produced the Navy's first and only night ace of the war. The fifth and final enemy kill, by Lieutenant Guy Bordelon of VF-152, was accomplished over North Korea on 17 July, just ten days before the ceasefire.

Following the end of hostilities, the *Princeton* was converted for antisubmarine warfare. As CVS-37, the *Princeton* left San Diego on 2 November 1954 to become the first vessel of its type to operate in the Western Pacific. This pioneering antisubmarine tour, carrying twice the might formerly used by the smaller escort carriers, was completed on 31 May 1955. The *Princeton* continued to serve actively as a support carrier and by 1959 had completed her seventh Far Eastern tour since Korea. Before her return home, as the last of the Pacific Fleet's axial — or straight-deck — carriers, she belatedly received her commissioning plaque at the Yokosuka Naval Base. Although the ship had been commissioned on 18 November 1945 at the Philadelphia Naval Shipyard, she apparently went to sea without the plaque, the nautical counterpart of a building's cornerstone. Years later, the bronze was discovered by a Marine jet fighter pilot at NAS Atsugi, Japan, in a file cabinet. There was no explanation as to how it had traveled from Philadelphia to remain concealed, for an undetermined time, in an obscure file drawer in Japan.

Occasionally, during 1957 and 1958, the Navy made carrier decks available for use by Marine helicopters in amphibious training exercises. A permanent need was recognized in October 1958 and thus in January 1959 the *Boxer* (CVS-21) was formally transferred to the Atlantic Fleet and redesignated LPH-4. In March the same year, the *Princeton* was also transferred to this new amphibious assault ship activity and redesignated as LPH-5, for service in the Pacific. The axial decks of the two *Essex*-class carriers were considered ideal floating platforms for Marine helicopter assault operations. Both of the carriers had been scheduled for mothballing until selected for this new Fleet assignment.

In late 1960, Jane Taylor, the *Princeton*'s first post-recommissioning homecoming queen, was honored again. She became the guest of the officers and men of what was then the Pacific Fleet's largest helicopter assault ship and was presented a check for $1,000 by Captain C. M. Brower, on behalf of the *Princeton*, for the United Cerebral Palsy Foundation of San Diego. The Foundation had by that time, in 1960, received contributions from the *Princeton* in Jane's name totaling over $32,000. In honor of the ship's continued support, the Foundation named its daycare facility the Princeton Center. Despite changes in personnel and designation during the intervening nine years, the collective "heart" of the *Princeton* crew had not diminished.

The "Sweet Pea," no longer an attack carrier, subsequently saw service off the coast of Vietnam in the 1960s as LPH-5. In November 1964, she was recognized for her efforts to help Vietnamese flood victims. The ship had delivered 1,300 tons of food and clothing to Quang Ngai, South Vietnam, to aid victims of typhoons Iris and Joan, which had claimed more than 7,000 lives and had left 700,000 homeless. South Vietnamese officials and Army General William C. Westmoreland visited the *Princeton* to personally thank Captain Paul J. Knapp and the ship's bakers for producing over 8,000 loaves of bread for the needy. Marine Helicopter Squadron 162 provided delivery service from the ship.

In early 1969, the *Princeton* also provided support services to the nation's ambitious space program. On the morning of 26 May 1969, the Apollo 10 spacecraft returned from 31 orbits of the moon and splashed down in the Pacific Ocean. The spacecraft landed four miles from the *Princeton*, the primary recovery ship, which was waiting about 400 miles east of American Samoa. Apollo 10 astronaut crew members Gene Cernan, Tom Stafford, and John Young were recovered from the Command Module by *Princeton* helicopters and flown to the ship. The flight had gone so well that two hours after they had landed they were dining in the ship's wardroom.

The *Princeton* had served long and well, but with the arrival of newer, larger carriers, her tenure came to an end on 30 January 1970, with her decommissioning. But LPH-5's newsworthiness was not over, however, as the 7 September 1973 issue of the Portland (Oregon) *Register* newspaper contained a story with the headline "Carrier Princeton Hulk Sinks." The article chronicled the demise of the fighting lady as she began sinking in the Willamette River while being dismantled. The venerable carrier had been sold for scrap metal in June 1971 to Zidell Exploration of San Francisco, California. This final sad event marked a disappointing end to a distinguished career as an attack, antisubmarine, and amphibious assault aircraft carrier, designations CV-37 (1945-1952), CVA-37 (1952-1954), CVS-37 (1954-1959), and LPH-5 (1959-1971). The *Princeton*'s three tours of duty during the Korean War had highlighted her record of top-flight service.

In 1951, following Squadron VF-871's return aboard the *Princeton* and the surprise separation of Reserve enlisted men, the squadron remained active as a unit but underwent a period of reorganization. Most of the original Oakland pilots and ground officers, retained until completion of two years active duty, were reassigned to various Navy shore bases. Lieutenant Commander Bill Harrison remained on active duty for a short time, assisting with the squadron's transition from CAG-19 to ATG-2, and, later, helped develop the procedures utilized in the *Princeton*'s recovery of the Apollo 10 crew. After retirement, he worked in the West Coast aerospace industry until making his home in Hawaii. Lieutenant John Underwood also served in a number of pilot and command assignments until retirement. Before call-up, he was a college roommate of Gerald Jacobsen and had encouraged him to join the Reserves and VF-871. John was alleged, on occasion, to have sneaked enlisted man Jake into the NAS Oakland BOQ and Officers Club on duty weekends. Underwood resides in Arlington, Virginia.

Pilot Lieutenant (JG) George Watts retired with a total of 28 years of Navy service. He was later employed by a county sheriff's department in California, where he now resides.

Lieutenant Ed Reed served as a pilot and instructor at NAS Glenview, Illinois, for the balance of his tour. After his service, he returned to work at the Chevrolet Motor Division of General Motors in Oakland. He advanced within the automotive industry and later served as Western U.S. Manager for a large truck body company. He is retired and makes his home in San Leandro, California.

Lieutenant Don Frazier, not recalled with VF-871, deployed again with the squadron for a second Korean tour lasting eight months. Following release, he remained in the Reserves and was later recalled for an additional period. He combined his Reserve activities with 34 years as a commercial pilot. He is now retired from both and lives in Florida.

A number of men resumed or started college, including Jim Blyler, who graduated from the University of California, Berkeley, majoring in industrial relations, while working full time at the Standard Oil Company refinery in Richmond, California. He settled in the nearby city of Pinole, where he served for a time as a member of the City Council, and later retired from a public administration career with the city of Oakland. Ensign Gerald (Jake) Jacobsen, who after commissioning received notification that he had passed his Petty Officer 3rd Class exams, completed his term of service as a naval officer. Following his release in July 1952, he returned to California State University, San Luis Obispo, and graduated with a degree in engineering. His career in refrigeration engineering was conducted not far from his home in Lakeside, California.

Lieutenant (JG) Dan Miller also returned to college at the University of California, Berkeley, and graduated with an engineering degree. In conjunction with his twin brother Donald, he formed successful engineering and other enterprises near his California home.

George (Frank) Musso received his degree via mail from San Francisco State while on active duty and was quickly able to get a head start on his career. He retired from a city management career as a planner and city administrator in California.

Ed Watson, who ceremoniously conferred the A.B. degree upon fellow yeoman Musso, retired from a long career as a consultant with the State of California Department of Employment, and resides in Pinole, California.

My two high school classmates, Vince Anzilotti and Jim Haughian, also had Oakland roots, though neither were members of VF-871, nor did they serve aboard the *Princeton*. Serving with me as "white hats," their naval careers took a different turn than mine. Prompted perhaps by the Korean War's impact upon local Air Reserve units, they joined the Naval Air Cadet program shortly after my recall. Following acceptance and issuance of orders, they entered the program in January 1951. After progressing through preflight and flight training, each was commissioned in June 1952, as an Ensign USNR, with naval aviator designation. Their individual assignments took them into different specialties and duty assignments. Jim was selected to fly multi-engined aircraft and assigned to patrol squadron duty. He served initially on the East Coast, and later spent the bulk of his four-year assignment in the West Indies, flying out of Trinidad. Following his release to inactive duty in late 1954, he resumed his college education at U.C. Berkeley, where he earned a Master's degree in engineering. His long career with the famous Lawrence Berkeley Laboratory concluded with retirement in 1993. He makes his home not too far from the location of the former NAS Oakland.

Vince began his first assignment in the Bay Area with VF-94, then homeported at NAS Alameda. He deployed with the squadron to join TF-77 where he piloted F4U-4 Corsairs over Korea aboard the *Philippine Sea* (CV-47). After his release from active duty, he earned a degree in

International Economics at U.C. Berkeley. Continuing his affiliation with the Air Reserves at NAS Oakland, he served with various fighter and antisubmarine squadrons. In 1961, he was recalled to active duty for a 12-month period during the Berlin crisis. Following this release, he resumed his active participation in the Reserve program and subsequently held a number of major commands, until his retirement in 1988. Rear Admiral Anzilotti's last assignment was as Commander, Naval Reserve Readiness Command Region Twenty. The command, headquartered at Naval Station Treasure Island, San Francisco, was composed of 13 Naval Reserve Centers, with over 5,000 drilling Reservists. Admiral Anzilotti resides in California and has retired from his civilian career with Gaylord Container Corporation.

In November 1951, Lieutenant Commander F. C. Hearrell assumed command of VF-871 when ATG-2 was officially formed. Commander James G. Daniels, III, assumed command of ATG-2 at San Diego on 30 November 1951. The squadron's second Korea deployment was aboard the *Essex* (CV-9), which had earlier served as CAG-19X's shakedown as well as the *Princeton's* relief ship. The *Essex* and ATG-2 departed San Diego on 16 June 1952, bound for the Western Pacific. During the period from 18 July 1952 to 11 January 1953, the air group launched 7,606 sorties with 5,719 classed as combat. Five pilots including one prisoner of war and 15 aircraft were lost. After 204 days, ATG-2 and the *Essex* returned home to San Diego on 6 February 1953.

VF-871, a charter member of the successful new air group concept, was destined to close out its unit history as a Reserve and Corsair squadron. On 18 February 1953, VF-871 was assigned to NAS Miramar and redesignated as VF-123. The squadron then shifted to jet air craft and flew F9F Panthers. The active-duty chapter of the squadron, originally formed as a Reserve unit at NAS Oakland, had officially closed. The unit, and the many men who proudly performed under its designation in two Korean deployments, had served with distinction.

Although the armistice was signed in July 1953, ATG-2 again boarded the *Essex* and was deployed to guard the peace. The air group made subsequent deployments aboard the *Philippine Sea* (CVA-47) and the *Hancock* (CVA-19) in 1955 and 1957, respectively. The ATG air groups, which had solved an early critical Navy problem, grew in number over the years — but officially did not exist, even on Navy location and allowance summaries. The conditions that had caused their formation were no longer present, and ATG-2 was disbanded 1 April 1958. Naval aviation was by then adequately funded and had moved into the era of supercarriers.

The ultimate fate of NAS Oakland, where this account of Naval Air Reserves in the Korean War began, is also worthy of mention. The Air Station was established on a section of Oakland Airport in 1926, when Reserve programs were reorganized in an attempt to place Reserve aviation forces on a permanent basis. Definite complements of officers and enlisted men were established for the "Fleet Reserve Aviation Division and Squadrons," the new terminology for Reserve components. The number of Reserve stations was increased nationally to include Detroit, Minneapolis, Long Beach, and Oakland. This buildup was intended to provide more weekend training for inactive duty aviators, rather than for the primary training of recruits. NAS Oakland, during the many succeeding years, provided training and skill maintenance of air Reservists. Organized units, such as VF-871 and VF-874, as well as individual Reservists, were called to active duty from the Air Station at various times to meet needs of the Navy.

In March 1961, a decision was made to relocate NAS Oakland Air Reserve units to nearby NAS Alameda. More than 80 airplanes were flown by weekend warriors to their new home. Naval Air Reserve Training Unit (NARTU) Alameda then retained a position as an important component of the Naval Air Reserve Command, comprised of 13 Air Stations and 6 NARTUs. During June of 1961, the NAS Oakland station, along with four other naval air facilities around the country, was formally disestablished. The small Oakland Airport facility came to an end after 35 years, and the airport's North Field was designated for general aviation use.

When I was recalled to duty, I felt shock and dismay at being suddenly compelled to join a strange military unit with which I had no prior affiliation. My disappointment was increased, when it became clear that my friends, Jim Haughian and Vince Anzilotti, would not be joining me on this unwanted adventure. But once the difficult mental and emotional adjustments of leaving Marie, family, home, and friends were made, the enveloping structure of Navy life took over. The goodbyes experienced when our troopship, the USNS *Weigel*, pulled away from the pier in San Diego, were painful then and remain so today, but these difficult moments, and the life at sea that followed, accelerated my maturity and my understanding of the realities of war.

Although much of my experience was exciting, I was not motivated to pursue either a military or an aviation career. Mostly, I gained an appreciation for the ability of diverse groups of people to organize and to effectively carry out an objective. Early squadron debate regarding the validity of our call-up, in the absence of either a national emergency or a declared war, led me to reflect on the purpose and structure of government. And indirectly this caused me to explore courses in political science and to become involved with regional and local government. I was able, later on, to participate in local and regional public administration and policy formation.

The brief experience also sparked what has continued to be a lifelong fascination with military aircraft. My interests in naval aviation actually began as a teenager during World War II, in discussions with a civilian staff member of the Saint Mary's College Naval Preflight School in Moraga, California. Those talks centered on the athletic programs of prospective pilots, but the broader discussion of the cadet program may have had a subtle influence on my decision to enlist in the Naval Air Reserve. Although I never piloted Navy planes (other than a brief hands-on session sitting in the co-pilot seat of a SNB for about an hour in flight), I did my share of fueling them on weekends and obtaining parts to keep them flying. My only aviation connection later in life was as a member of a county airport land-use commission. I am pleased to have served with the brave pilots and supporting crew members in carrying out our unplanned roles in the first UN "police action." It is most regrettable that three of our squadron and so many other Americans had to die in a futile attempt to reconcile differences that remain a threat to world peace today.

The continuing talks with the North Koreans have produced results from optimistic predictions to impending confrontation. U.S. goals have shifted from establishing that the North does not possess a bomb, to one designed to prevent acquisition of more.

A major concern has been who would ultimately manage North Korea's military, or deal with the nuclear program? Only time will determine if the support base of Kim Jong Il, the late

*Kim Il Sung's successor and son, is solid enough to ensure his
rule.*

*The end of the Korean War in a draw was the result of the
enemy finally realizing he could not win. Additionally, it was
equally clear that the will of the UN forces would not be worn
down to the point of abandoning South Korea. Arguments have
been made that an easing of the sanctuary restrictions might
have expedited the armistice. Nevertheless, it is evident that the
limitations introduced in the Korean War marked the beginning
of an era in which military force could no longer operate unre-
strained. The unwritten understanding of the U.S. and Soviets
not to introduce nuclear weapons into the conflict was a major
constraint overshadowing all others. Such a limitation might be
difficult today in view of our suspicion that North Korea has
nuclear capabilities, and the revelations that South Korea, as
recently as 1991, had worked on plans to develop similar
weapons. The potential for a nuclear arms race continues to
threaten peace on the divided peninsula.*

*In addition, North Korean concentration of 1.2 million
troops close to the border suggest willingness to engage in
another conventional land war, and U.S. global strategies of the
'90s could dictate heavy involvement of naval aviation. If history repeats itself the application of the earlier containment
strategies should be weighed carefully. Reimposition of the
politically imposed geographic limitations of the '50s, protect-
ing enemy production and supply at the source, seem inadvisable. The Korean War demonstrated the futility of such a strategy and may have ultimately prolonged the conflict at a cost of
additional lives. Diplomacy must prevent the use of nuclear
weapons.*

*A primary military and political consideration would be
whether U.S. military forces should again be committed to such
struggles. Former Secretary of State Henry A. Kissinger, with
regard to the Vietnam War, contended that should we decide to
commit forces we must also set out with the will to prevail. He
urged that we not set out to fight a war for stalemate but for victory. Those who fought in Korea coped with political ground
rules that resulted in stalemate — a deadlock that cost more*

than 54,000 American lives. These ground rules may also have set a "no win" tone for Vietnam, at an even greater cost. The Kissinger thesis should be seriously considered before entering into future military entanglements.

Reservists during the Korean War have demonstrated that when the nation called, they responded superbly. At a critical point in the evolution of international relations these "weekend warriors" did more than simply show up for duty; they effectively augmented the nation's trained professionals — the Regulars.

Neither those who fought or died nor the lessons learned from this painful national experience should be forgotten. Closing this bloody chapter of international strife without acknowledging the significance of their sacrifices would be unjust.

Bibliography

T HE FOLLOWING IS a selected listing of published books, magazine articles, and various Navy publications that were consulted in the course of preparing this account.

Doll, Thomas E. *USN/USMC Over Korea*. Carrollton, TX: Squadron/Signal Publications, Inc., 1988.

Epstein, Moray. *All About Hawaii — Thrum's Hawaiian Annual*, 76th Edition. Honolulu, HI: The Honolulu Star-Bulletin, Ltd., 1951.

Hallion, Richard P. *The Naval Air War in Korea*. Baltimore, MD: The Nautical and Aviation Publishing Company of America, Inc., 1986.

Holliday, Kate. "I Lived With 3000 Men," *V.F.W.* (Veterans of Foreign Wars) *Magazine* (Aug. 1952): 14-15, 28-29.

Hoyt, Edwin P. *On to the Yalu*. New York: Jove Books, published by arrangement with Stein and Day, Publishers, 1984.

MacArthur, Douglas. *Reminiscences*. New York: Crest Books, published by arrangement with McGraw-Hill Book Company, 1964.

Michener, James A. *The Bridges at Toko-Ri*. New York: Bantam Books, published by arrangement with Random House, Inc., 1953.

Sellers, Con. *Brothers in Battle*. New York: Pocket Books, 1989.

Shane III, Patrick Custis. "The 13 Wild Weeks of the USS *Princeton*," *The Saturday Evening Post* (Mar. 14, 1953): 28-29, 74-76, 80.

Sullivan, Jim. *F4U Corsair in Action*. Carrollton, TX: Squadron/Signal Publications, Inc., 1977.

Tillman, Barrett. "Air Task Group Two: Ready When Needed," *The Hook* (Summer 1989): 43, 52, 54-59.

United States Navy. *871 Scoop*. San Diego, CA: Periodic newsletter published by VF-871, 1950-1951.

United States Navy. *Fighter Squadron Eight Seven One Bulletin*. Weekly bulletin published by VF-871 aboard the USS *Princeton, 1951*.

United States Navy. *History of Fighter Squadron Eight-Seven-One*. Historical report prepared by VF-871, 1951.

United States Navy. *Morning Press News*. Daily newsletter published by the USS *Princeton*, 1951.

United States Navy. *Naval Aviation News* (Jan. 1949): 24-25; (Oct. 1950): 1-3, 25-31; (Dec. 1950): 25-27; (Mar. 1951): 1-5, 34; (Apr. 1951): 29; (July 1951): 19; (Mar. 1952): 14, 25; (Feb. 1955): 1, 10; (Apr. 1955): 18, 27; (Aug. 1955): 10; (Feb. 1956): 15; (Apr. 1957): 39; (May 1957): 29; (Feb. 1959): 2; (Mar. 1959): 15; (June 1959): 7; (Oct. 1960): 25; (June 1961): 30; (Oct. 1961): 3, 30; (Nov. 1961): 11; (Feb. 1962): 9.

United States Navy. *The Naval Reservist*. Washington, D.C.: Bureau of Naval Personnel, Navy Department, 1951.

United States Navy. *The North Islander*. San Diego, CA: Weekly newspaper published by NAS San Diego, 1950-1951.

United States Navy. *Slipstream*. Periodic bulletin published by the USS *Princeton*, 1951.

United States Navy. USS *Princeton CV-37*. Cruise book published by the USS *Princeton*, 1951.

United States Navy. *Voyage of the Conquistadores* [*sic*]. Cruise book published by Fighter Squadron Eight Seven One, 1951.

United States Navy. ***Weigel** Word*. Daily newspaper published aboard the USNS *General William Weigel*, 1951.

USS *Princeton* Assn. *USS **Princeton** Newsletter*. San Diego, CA: Periodic newsletter published by USS *Princeton* Assn., 1994.

Whitesitt, Sheila, and Dick Moore. *USS **Princeton** 1945-1969 — A Brief History*. Abilene, KS: Tree Stump Press, 1986.

World Book. Encyclopedia, vols. 2 and 11. Chicago, IL: Field Enterprises Educational Corporation, 1968.

Index

by Lori L. Daniel